Exploring China Along the Grand Canal

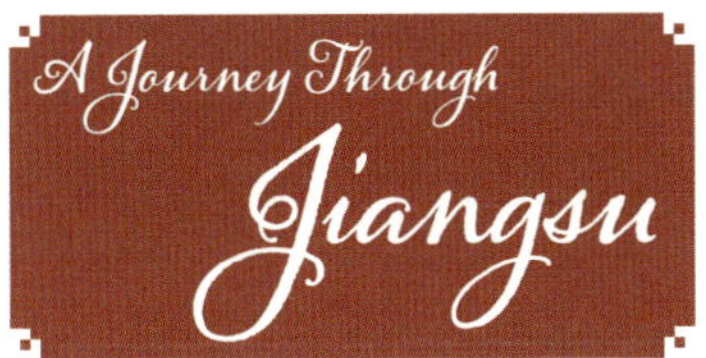

www.royalcollins.com

Exploring China Along the Grand Canal

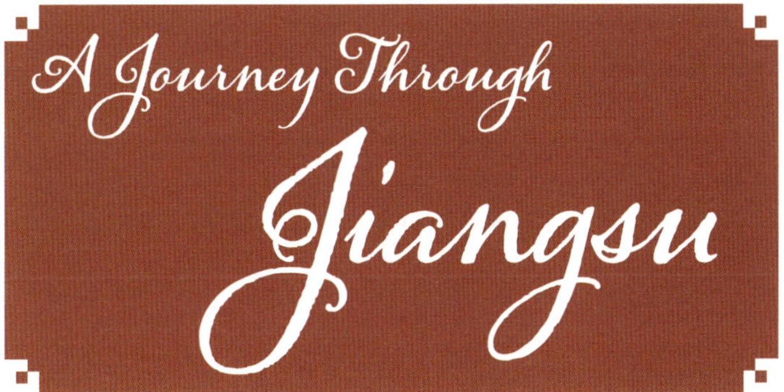

Compiled by Yangzhou Municipal People's Government

Chief editor: He Yun'ao

Editor: Zhang Bing

Translators: Zhang Hairong, Zhu Ying, Li Xianhong, Huang Qidong, Daniel Jingyuan Ni, and Vivian Qinwen Yan

Exploring China Along the Grand Canal: A Journey Through Jiangsu

Compiled by Yangzhou Municipal People's Government
Chief editor: He Yun'ao
Editor: Zhang Bing
Translators: Zhang Hairong, Zhu Ying, Li Xianhong, Huang Qidong, Daniel Jingyuan Ni, and Vivian Qinwen Yan

First published in 2025 by Royal Collins Publishing Group Inc.
Groupe Publication Royal Collins Inc.
550-555 boul. René-Lévesque O Montréal (Québec) H2Z1B1 Canada

10 9 8 7 6 5 4 3 2 1

ISBN: 978-1-4878-1325-3

To find out more about our publications, please visit www.royalcollins.com.

Preface

"Qi Huan carved a river new, / Its endless waters ever flow. / His mighty deeds bless all below, / Though heaven and earth will fade in woe." These two majestic lines of poetry by Li Bai, a poet of the Tang Dynasty (618–907), aptly describe the historical significance of the Beijing-Hangzhou Grand Canal, the treasure of Chinese civilization and the World Cultural Heritage. The mainstream of the Grand Canal flows through the cities and provinces of Beijing, Tianjin, Hebei, Shandong, Jiangsu, and Zhejiang, connecting the five major river systems of the Hai River, Yellow River, Huai River, Yangtze River, and Qiantang River. The excavation of the Grand Canal was a highly imaginative and determined endeavor, a remarkable achievement of the Chinese people in adapting to their geographical environment, utilizing the natural landscape, and continuously exploring, innovating, and creating. Spanning over 2,500 years of history and extending more than 1,700 kilometers, it is the world's earliest, longest, and largest canal system. Even to this day, the Grand Canal continues to function as a vital waterway for shipping, water conservancy, ecological protection, and economic communication between the north and south. It is a living and flowing human heritage, and an important symbol of Chinese civilization.

General Secretary Xi Jinping has pointed out: "The Grand Canal is a precious heritage left to us by our ancestors. It is a flowing culture that we must comprehensively protect, inherit, and utilize well." Since the 18th National Congress of the CPC, General Secretary Xi Jinping has placed great importance on the protection and inheritance of China's historical and cultural heritage. He has required in-depth exploration of the historical and cultural resources centered on the Grand Canal, integrating the protection of the Grand Canal's cultural heritage with the enhancement of the ecological environment, the preservation and restoration of historic cities and towns along the canal, the integration of cultural tourism, and the transformation and upgrading of canal transportation. The Grand Canal vividly embodies the continuity, innovation, unity, inclusiveness, and peaceful nature of Chinese civilization, and carries on the long history and culture of the Chinese nation, providing rich cultural nourishment for the economic and social development on both sides of the canal. We should endow the Grand Canal with new spiritual connotations and contemporary values, giving the ancient Grand Canal a "new look" and creating a brilliant calling card that showcases the image of China, promotes Chinese civilization, and demonstrates our cultural confidence.

Let us explore China along the Grand Canal. We will take the first step in Jiangsu Province. With the Yangtze River as the horizontal axis and the canal as the vertical axis, we will trace the historical trajectory and feel the rhythmic beauty of Jiangsu's water culture along the canal. As the cradle that nurtured the Grand Canal, Jiangsu has the longest history of being nourished by the canal, and thus it is the province with the longest river course, the most cities along the canal, the richest canal heritage, and the most World Cultural Heritage sites. Through long historical accumulation, the specific geographical and human environment have given birth to a brilliant pearl of Chinese culture—the Jiangsu section of the Grand Canal cultural belt. Poetic and prosperous, the Grand Canal flows through Jiangsu. From the northern Jiangsu with the style and charm of Chu and Han, to the southern Jiangsu with gentle Wu dialect, the Jiangsu section of the Grand Canal is about 690 kilometers long. The cities along the canal have "thrived and prospered because of the canal." These cities have integrated the distinctive local products, cuisines, customs, and historical and cultural landscapes, forming the colorful Jiangsu Canal culture. The bustling scenes of ships coming and going on the historical canal have been framed as thick historical paintings. The rise and fall witnessed by the "twenty-four bridges," and the sorrows evoked by the "maple trees by the river and fishing lights" are forever etched in people's hearts.

Telling the stories of the Grand Canal well and building the Jiangsu section of the Grand Canal cultural belt into the most prosperous, splendid, and beautiful "Jiangsu calling card" of the Chinese Grand Canal are the fervent hope of the Provincial Party Committee and the Provincial Government of Jiangsu Province in recent years for the construction of the Grand Canal cultural belt. To this end, we need to strengthen our cultural confidence and cultural awareness and promote the high-quality development of the Jiangsu Grand Canal cultural belt. We must comprehensively protect, inherit, and utilize the Grand Canal culture, making this "flowing culture" shine even brighter. Only by truly walking along the Grand Canal can we deeply understand why the Grand Canal is "flowing culture." It is not only a cultural belt, but also an ecological belt, an economic belt, and an urbanization belt. In a sense, the Grand Canal exists in two forms, the geographical form and the cultural form. These cultural symbols exist in the written records, pictures, and images that document the Grand Canal, as well as in the daily lives of the people along the canal in terms of their clothing, food, housing, and transportation ... All these will eventually become precious historical documents for people to study.

Therefore, we have selected thirteen cities in Jiangsu Province that have been nourished by the Grand Canal, and organized the book into thirteen chapters. Revolving around the historical and cultural landscapes, local customs and practices, as well as food cultures, we have written this book to introduce the basic features of the Jiangsu section of the Grand Canal culture, hoping to allow readers to understand the flowing history and enduring sentiments of the Grand Canal. The content of this book is written in a straightforward and concise manner, and with abundant illustrations. The design of this book is exquisite. However, due to limited space, it is inevitable that some aspects may have been overlooked. We sincerely welcome readers' feedback and corrections.

Yangzhou City, as the origin city of the Grand Canal, has grown together with the Grand Canal, and the Grand Canal culture has long been integrated into its very essence. In the process of topic planning and content writing of this book, we have received valuable help and support from Yangzhou Municipal People's Government and World Historic and Cultural Canal Cities Cooperation Organization. We extend our sincere gratitude for their contributions.

HE YUN'AO

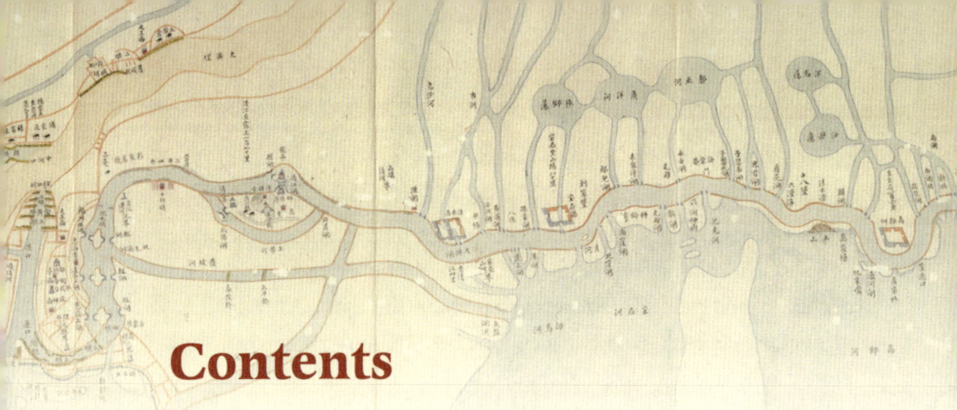

Contents

棲霞
加善寺
燕石矶
江寧府
至金山一百三十里

Nanjing:
The Capital of Ten Dynasties

The Cultural Essence of Mooring by the Qinhuai River at Night

A Million Households in Jinling, Imperial Capital of Six Dynasties

The Oldest Canal in the World

Compared to the ancient excavation of the Han Ditch in the Yangzhou region, Nanjing's Xu River was excavated 20 years earlier (506 BC). It is located in the Gaochun District of present-day Nanjing, also known as the Xuxi River. The similarity between the two rivers lies in the fact that their initial excavation was driven by military needs. The excavation of the Han Ditch was due to King Fuchai of Wu's desire to attack the State of Qi, while the excavation of the Xu River was attributed to his father, King Helü of Wu State's intention to attack the State of Chu.

Attire and the Southward Migration

The phrase "attire and the southward migration" originally referred to the mass exodus of aristocratic families from the Central Plains during the chaos at the end of the Western Jin Dynasty (265–317). This migration of Central Plains civilization or its government spanned over 100 years. In 316, with the fall of the Western Jin Dynasty, the Sima family, along with numerous gentry, were forced to relocate with their families to Jiankang (present-day Nanjing) to establish a new capital, an era known as the Eastern Jin Dynasty (317–420).

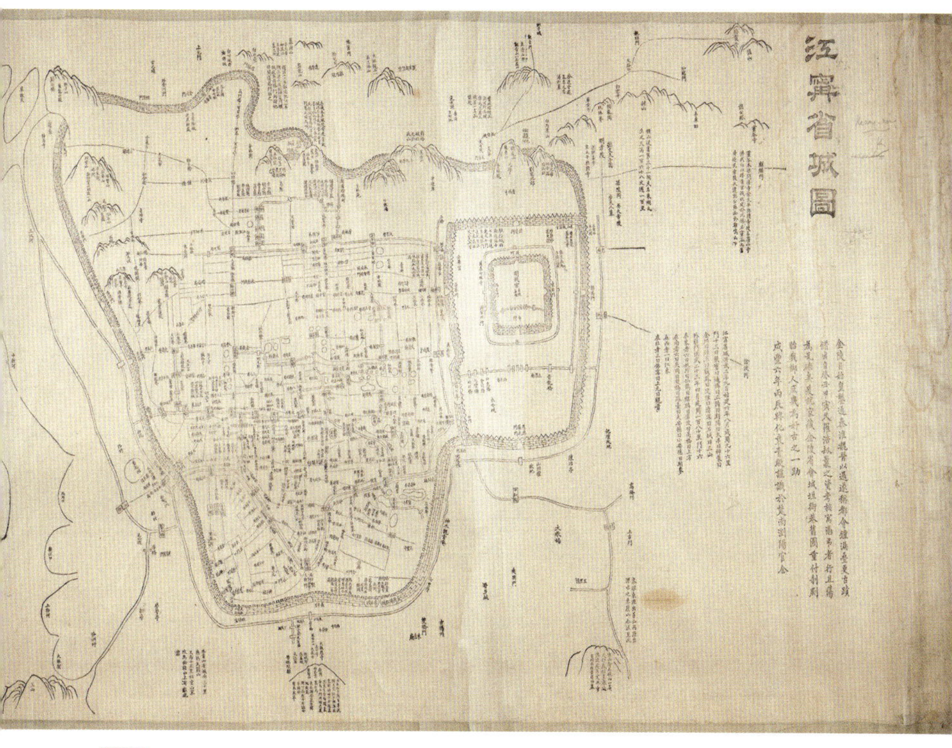

Map of Jiangning City

The map, drawn by Yuan Qingshou during the sixth year of Xianfeng's reign (1856) in the Qing Dynasty (1616–1911), provides a detailed depiction of the city walls and a textual explanation of the background and historical development of Nanjing. At the time of creating the map, Yuan Qingshou served as the magistrate of Liuyang in Hunan Province. The city walls are depicted with great precision, while other elements, such as government offices, military camps, neighborhoods, bridges, temples, and other religious buildings, are labeled with text. The map also includes detailed explanations and backgrounds about various scenic spots, historical sites, and ancient battlefields.

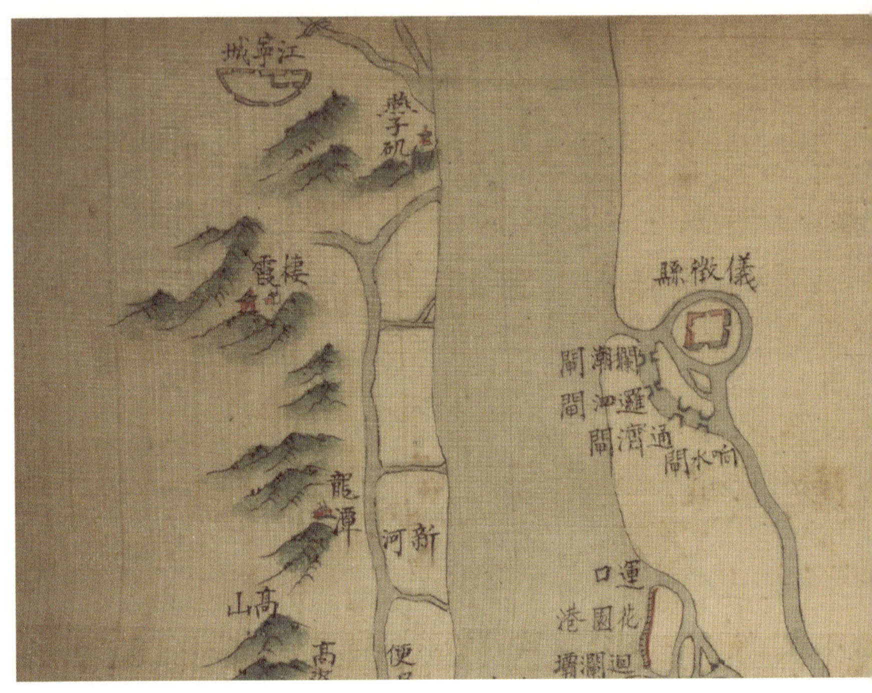

Complete Map of the Yellow River, Grand Canal, Lakes, and Rivers (partial)

The term attire specifically denotes clothing and headgear. In ancient times, only individuals of the scholar-official class and above were permitted to wear ceremonial headgear, and thus attire came to symbolize the clothing of the elite. Wen Tianxiang once wrote, "Do not say the mountains and rivers are not my homeland, / At the sight of attire and headgear I see my hometown." This reflects the symbolic connection between attire and one's cultural identity. Over time, attire also became a metonym for the gentry and scholar-officials, extending further to represent civilization, etiquette, and cultural customs.

The Birthplace of the Grand Canal

Some say that the Six Dynasties (222–589, a collective term for six Han-ruled dynasties) that established their capitals in Nanjing were "short-lived dynasties" and simply unable to be compared to ancient capitals like Xi'an and Luoyang. Despite their short existence, Nanjing, during the nearly 300 years when it was known as Jiankang, was the bona fide center of canal transport. Originally, the Jiangnan region (south of the Yangtze River) was still practicing primitive slash-and-burn agriculture. Then the introduction of advanced farming techniques from the North facilitated the transformation of agricultural methods and economic development in Jiangnan. The grain output increased significantly and was transported via the developed waterway network to Nanjing for distribution, supplying the needs of royalty and nobility. In Nanjing, there are nearly ten lakes, including Xuanwu Lake, Mochou Lake, and Shijiu Lake, and over 120 rivers and canals of various sizes, such as the Qinhuai River and Yanzhi River, forming a sophisticated canal transport system itself. Lu Haiming, the president of the Nanjing Urban Culture Research Association and an expert in history and culture, believes that after over 300 years of development by the Six Dynasties, the economy of Jiangnan rose abruptly, making this region another granary of China. The economic development of Jiangnan can

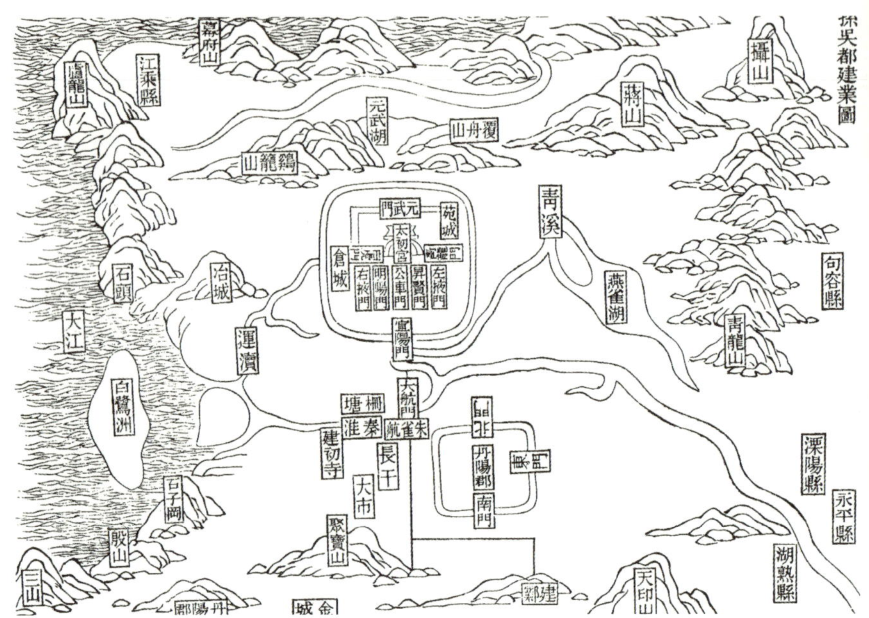

Map of Sun Wu's Capital at Jianye (from *Illustrated Examination of the Ancient and Modern Nanjing*)

be a direct inducement for the excavation of the Grand Canal during the Sui Dynasty (581–618). In other words, the Six Dynasties centered around Jiankang (known as Jianye during the Three Kingdoms period) played a decisive role in the economic development of Jiangnan, making Nanjing the birthplace of the Grand Canal.[1] Despite the "short-lived" dynasties, the Six Dynasties period in Nanjing truly impacted the development of Chinese civilization for over a thousand years thereafter. In this respect, as an ancient capital, Nanjing is by no means inferior to Xi'an or Luoyang.

The Yanzhi River

The Yanzhi River in Nanjing was an inner river excavated for canal transport on the orders of Zhu Yuanzhang after he established his capital in Nanjing. The excavation of this river was extremely challenging, requiring work on the Yanzhi Rock Hill which stretches for about 5 kilometers and reaches heights of up to 30 meters. According to the *Lishui County Annals*, the method adopted in the work made use of the principle of thermal expansion and contraction: use iron chisels to carve notches in the rock, fill the cracks with hemp, pour tung oil on the hemp, and set on fire. When the rock was heated red-hot, pour cold water over it, causing the rock to naturally crack. Finally, the stone blocks were pried apart and carried out. Due to this excavation method, the rocks on the hill took on a purplish-red color after being scorched by fire, similar to the rouge (*yanzhi*, 胭脂 in Chinese) used by women, the Yanzhi River hence its name.

1 "Nanjing Is the Birthplace and Participant of the Grand Canal," *Nanjing Daily*, December 11, 2020, B1 ed.

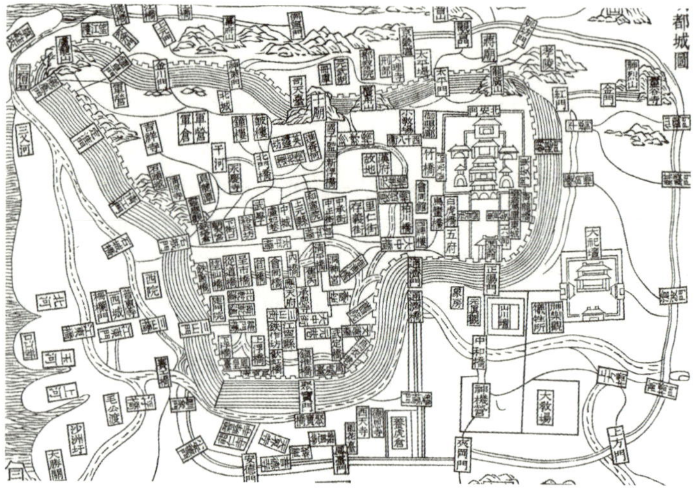

Map of the Ming Capital (from *Illustrated Examination of the Ancient and Modern Nanjing*)

Zheng He's Voyages to the Western Seas

To accomplish Zheng He's monumental voyages to the Western Seas, it was essential to build ships, even seafaring ships and treasure ships. Where did the timber come from? It is said that the timber was cast into the Yangtze River and drifted downstream for thousands of *li* (1 *li* = 500 m) in order to supply the Jiangnan region and the southeastern provinces.[2] Zheng He's seven voyages to the Western Seas created a huge demand for timber in the southeastern coastal areas. In addition, due to the depletion of timber along the rivers, the price of wood soared dramatically. Eventually, even Emperor Xuande had no choice but to cease these grand maritime endeavors. During the Qing Dynasty, the government still attempted to control the price of wood but ultimately failed.

[2] Refer to *Seeing Prosperity Again: The Story of Suzhou* and *The World Made by Trade: Society, Culture, and the World Economy Since 1400.*

Image of the treasure ships portrayed in the *Tianfei Sutra*

The Opium War

In 1840, the Opium War erupted. The British forces advanced northward along China's coastline, entering the Yangtze River from its mouth and capturing Zhenjiang. The First Opium War, which lasted two years, ended with the Qing government seeking peace with the British forces and being forced to sign the unequal Treaty of Nanjing. One of the British invaders' goals was to cut off China's major artery—the Grand Canal. Although not located along the Grand Canal, Nanjing served as the center of grain transport for the southeastern coastline. The building at No. 126 Zhanyuan Garden Road was originally part of the mansion of Xu Da, a founding general of the Ming Dynasty (1368–1644). During the mid to late Qing Dynasty, this building served as the office of the Jiang'an Grain Supervision Bureau, playing a crucial role in managing the grain transport affairs of the Jiangnan Province. "The grain supplied to the capital was loaded onto ships in Nanjing and transported to Beijing via the Grand Canal."[3] Once this grain route was cut off, the Forbidden City instantly lost its supply. This plan had been considered by the British Foreign Secretary a year before the outbreak

[3] Julia Lovell, *The Opium War*, trans. Liu Yuebing (New Star Press, 2020), p. 139.

British original of the Treaty of Nanjing

of the Opium War. After the signing of the Treaty of Nanjing, the British troops "immediately withdrew from Nanjing, and the transport along the Beijing-Hangzhou Grand Canal returned to normal."[4]

Jiangning Weaving Administration

During the Ming and Qing dynasties, especially in the Qing Dynasty, there were three major weaving administrations in the Jiangnan region—Jiangning (also known as Nanjing) Weaving Administration, Suzhou Weaving Administration, and Hangzhou Weaving Administration. Thereinto, Jiangning Weaving Administration became the most well-known one due to its reference in the classic Chinese novel *Dream of the Red Chamber.* In the novel, the Jia, Shi, Wang, and Xue families wielded significant power in the southeast, a depiction that was true for Jiangning Weaving Administration as well. At that time, within the city limits of Jiangning, there were more than 30,000 weaving looms and about 50,000 male and female workers. Residents relying on silk weaving numbered over 200,000, and the annual production value reached 12 million taels of silver. The imperial court's brocades, silks, the officials' court attire (including the badge of rank worn on the chest), and even the emperor's dragon robes were supplied to Beijing via the Grand Canal by the Jiangning Weaving Administration. Furthermore, when Cao Xueqin's grandfather, Cao Yin, held an official position in the Jiangning Weaving Administration, he also served in the role of Salt Commissioner for the North and South Huai River Region, responsible for collecting salt taxes and supervising the salt monopoly.

---

[4] "Nanjing Is the Birthplace and Participant of the Grand Canal," *Nanjing Daily*, December 11, 2020, B1 ed.

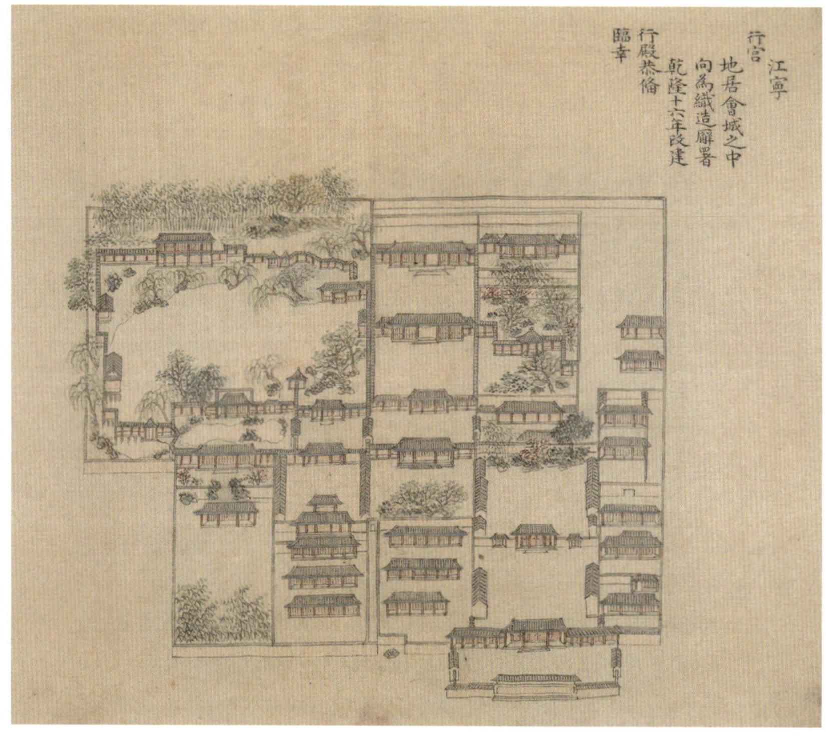

Map of Qianlong Emperor's Southern Tour and Stops **(The painting depicts the Jiangning Imperial Lodge during Emperor Qianlong's southern tour.)**

This painting is one of the 23 paintings in the album *Map of Qianlong Emperor's Southern Tour and Stops*, drawn by Qian Weicheng of the Qing Dynasty between the 30th and 45th year of Qianlong's reign (1765–1780). Each painting is annotated in the upper left or upper right corner with the time of Emperor Qianlong's southern tours, the surrounding scenery, and the content of the painting.

Qian Weicheng (1720–1772), courtesy name You'an, also known as Zongpan, with the pseudonyms Ren'an, Chashan, and another alias, Jiaxuan, was titled Wenmin posthumously. He was a native of Wujin (present-day Changzhou), Jiangsu during the Qing Dynasty. He became the top scorer in the imperial examination in 1745, during the tenth year of the Qianlong reign, and eventually rose to the position of Deputy Minister in the Ministry of Punishments. He was skilled in painting and calligraphy. He is the author of *Chashan Collection*. His biography is included in the *Draft History of Qing*.

The Dynastic Glory and the Timeless Qinhuai

Capital of Ten Dynasties: The Origin of the Name

The term "capital of ten dynasties" refers to Nanjing's historic significance as the capital of several dynasties throughout Chinese history. Nanjing, with different names in various periods, has served as a major political and cultural center in a long history. During the Zhou Dynasty (1046–256 BC), it was part of Wu; by the end of the Spring and Autumn Period (770–476 BC), it became part of Yue; approximately 140 years after the fall of Yue, it came under the control of Chu; and 110 years after Chu, it was taken over by the Qin Dynasty (221–206 BC). A fortune teller in the Qin Dynasty once predicted that "five hundred years later, Jinling [present-day Nanjing] will have the aura of an emperor" (Zhang Dunyi, *Compilation of Records on the Six Dynasties · Preface*).

During the 16th year of the Jian'an (211) of the Eastern Han Dynasty (25–220), Sun Quan established his capital in Nanjing, renaming it "Jianye," marking Nanjing's first status as a royal capital. Subsequently, the Eastern Jin and the four Southern Dynasties (Song, Qi, Liang, and Chen) (420–589) established their capitals here as well, creating a city pattern that was both beautiful and practical. The term "ancient capital of six dynasties" originated from this period. The "capital of ten dynasties" includes not only the capital of these Six Dynasties, but also that of the Southern Tang (937–975), Ming, the Taiping Heavenly Kingdom, and the Republic of China. "Jiangnan is a beautiful place, / Jinling is the state of emperors. / Winding with green waters, / Towering with red buildings" (Xie Tiao, "Entering the Court Song"). Days of splendid buildings and painted rafters have turned to smoke and ash, leaving only relics that prompt modern people to reminisce about the past grandeur.

"Four hundred eighty temples of the Southern Dynasties, / How many remain lost in mist and rain." The line from Du Mu's "Spring in the South" reflects the period of turmoil during the Southern and Northern Dynasties (420–581) when Confucianism declined, and both rulers and common people were in urgent need of a form of ideological control and spiritual solace, respectively. The introduction of Buddhism to the Central Plains met this need. Consequently, the era witnessed extensive construction of cave temples and monasteries. In the Northern Dynasties (386–581), the *Record of Buddhist Monasteries in Luoyang* alone described more than 70 Buddhist temples; while across the river, the Southern Dynasties did not lag behind. According to Liu Shiqi's *Historical Investigation of Temples in the Southern Dynasties · Preface* written in the Qing Dynasty, "There were 2,846 temples in the Liang Dynasty with over 700 in the capital alone," which refers to Nanjing. Temples like Jiming Temple and Qixia Temple today, founded during the Six Dynasties period, still stand. This period also saw the excavation and improvement of the Pogang and Shangrong waterways in the southeast of the city, connecting Jiankang City with the Taihu Lake basin and solidifying Jiankang's status as a true "canal transport center."

Jiming Temple

Jiming Temple was originally built in the first year of Yongkang (300) during the Western Jin Dynasty. Emperor Wu of the Southern Liang

Dynasty (502–557) built the Tongtai Temple on the site of Jiming Dike and "donated his wealth to pray for Buddhist blessings" at this temple. He chose to be a monk four times, which contributed to the temple's prosperity. According to the *Compilation of Records on the Six Dynasties · Tongtai Temple*, "Tongtai Temple was built within the city walls, where funds were borrowed to construct a seven-story grand Buddha pavilion," showcasing the Southern Liang Dynasty's lavish dedication to Buddhism. In 1387, Zhu Yuanzhang, the founder of the Ming Dynasty, inscribed the name "Jiming Temple." Today, Jiming Temple stands majestically atop Chicken Cage Hill, adjacent to Xuanwu Lake. Every spring, the cherry blossoms along the temple's path bloom abundantly, making it one of Nanjing's recent "internet-famous check-in spots." The constant stream of visitors admiring the scenic views inside and outside the temple adds new vitality to this millennium-old ancient monastery.

Ten Miles of Qinhuai River: A Convergence of History from the Six Dynasties to the Qing

If you were to ask modern Nanjing people where to go to see the Qinhuai River, most would give an answer seemingly unrelated to the "river," the Confucius Temple. Today, this area is officially known as "Confucius Temple–Qinhuai Scenic Belt," a short street that includes many historical and cultural sites, such as the Great Hall of the Confucius Temple, Qinhuai River segment, Wuyi Lane, Jiangnan Imperial Examination Hall, and Zhanyuan Garden.

The Confucius Temple was initially constructed in the third year of the Xiankang era (337) during the Eastern Jin Dynasty, following Wang Dao's advice that "governing the country relies on nurturing talents," leading to the establishment of the Imperial Academy on the south bank of the Qinhuai River. In front of the Confucius Temple, there is a screen wall, Lingxing Gate, and east-west archways, with a

semi-circular pool in front of Lingxing Gate, known as the "Pan Pond." Its main building is the Great Hall, rebuilt based on its appearance in the eighth year of the Tongzhi era (1869) during the Qing Dynasty, complete with an outer terrace used for music and dance during the Spring and Autumn sacrifices, surrounded by stone rails on three sides and bronze torches at the corners burning tung oil. The sacrifices often took place at midnight (from 11 p.m. to 1 a.m.), illuminating the area as if it were daytime.

Wuyi Lane is also one of the remains of Jinling, the capital of the Six Dynasties. At the end of the Western Jin Dynasty, the turmoil in the north initiated the political process of the literati migrating to the south. The Langya Wang clan from the north and the Xie clan from the Chen commandery moved to Jinling and settled in Wuyi Lane.

The Jiangnan Imperial Examination Hall was founded in the fourth year of the Qiandao era (1168) of the Southern Song Dynasty (1127–1279) and expanded through successive dynasties, reaching its peak during the Ming and Qing dynasties. Today, on the site of the Jiangnan Imperial Examination Hall, Nanjing has established the China Imperial Examination Museum, preserving some of the ancient relics like the Mingyuan Building.

"Ten miles of Qinhuai River evoke spring dreams, / The smoke and moon of the Six Dynasties gather in Jinling." Behind Nanjing lies the smoky moonlight over Qinhuai River and the dreams of the Six Dynasties, as well as the tales about the tide hitting the empty city and the

***Landscape Painting of Xiao Temple* by Li Cheng of the Northern Song Dynasty**

The Supplement to the History of the Tang Dynasty by Li Zhao of the Tang Dynasty records that "Emperor Wu of the Liang Dynasty built the temple, and ordered Xiao Ziyun to write the character '*xiao*' [萧] in large regular script, and to this day the character '*xiao*' still remains." Later generations thus refer to the Buddhist temple as the Xiao Temple.

Confucius Temple area in the shadow of lights (photographed by Pan Ruizhi)

phoenix's departure from the platform in solitude. The long history and rich cultural atmosphere make Nanjing one of the "four great ancient capitals."

Nanjing Brocade: An Intangible Cultural Heritage

Nanjing brocade, or cloud brocade, is an outstanding representative of China's exquisite traditional culture, originating in the Southern

Dynasties and flourishing during the Ming and Qing dynasties, with a history of over 1,600 years. The words in its name, "cloud" and "brocade," speak to its elegance and refinement, luxurious and detailed craftsmanship, and its appearance as dazzling as clouds at sunset, which earns it the reputation of "an inch of brocade, an inch of gold." "The Jiangnan region is splendid, where the looms steal the skills of the gods, peacocks adorn flowers on the brocade brilliant as clouds, and ice silkworms spit phoenix mist on thin silk, creating new patterns of little dragon clusters" (Wu Weiye, "Looking at the South of the Yangtze River · Original Intention · Part Eleven"). Nanjing brocade uses carefully selected materials with up to 18 different colors, employing the "color gradient" technique to enhance the main flower design, resulting in its richness and elegance, sturdy texture, and beautiful thick patterns with vivid and dignified colors. It also favors the use of gold thread to create a magnificent golden splendor.

In ancient times, "brocade" represented the highest level of textile craftsmanship. The hand-weaving technique of Nanjing brocade, especially with the wooden loom flower decoration, is the foremost among brocade weaving techniques, encapsulating the essence of Chinese silk weaving skills and representing the pinnacle of Chinese silk craftsmanship. Nanjing brocade, together with Chengdu's Shu brocade, Suzhou's Song brocade, and Guangxi's Zhuang brocade, is known as the "four famous brocades of China."

Salted Duck

Salted duck is a famous delicacy in Nanjing, representing one of the signature dishes of Jinling cuisine. With a long-standing history, generations of practice have allowed the accumulation of rich experience in its preparation. Nanjing salted duck is known for its tender taste and delightful savory flavor, not overly dry or fatty. The salted duck made around the Mid-Autumn Festival when the osmanthus flowers are in full bloom boasts an even more unique taste and appearance. It is also known as "osmanthus duck" and is greatly cherished by the masses.

Duck Blood and Vermicelli Soup

This dish is renowned for its delicious taste, with soft and glutinous vermicelli, smooth duck blood, and crunchy duck intestines in it, creating a delightful texture that appeals to tastes from both the north and south and gaining fame nationwide.

Osmanthus Sugar Taro Shoots

The smooth and refreshing bite of the polished taro shoots, tender and sweet, comes in a sauce that has a bright, enticing reddish-brown color. Topped with sweet osmanthus, the rich aroma lingers on the diner's lips and teeth.

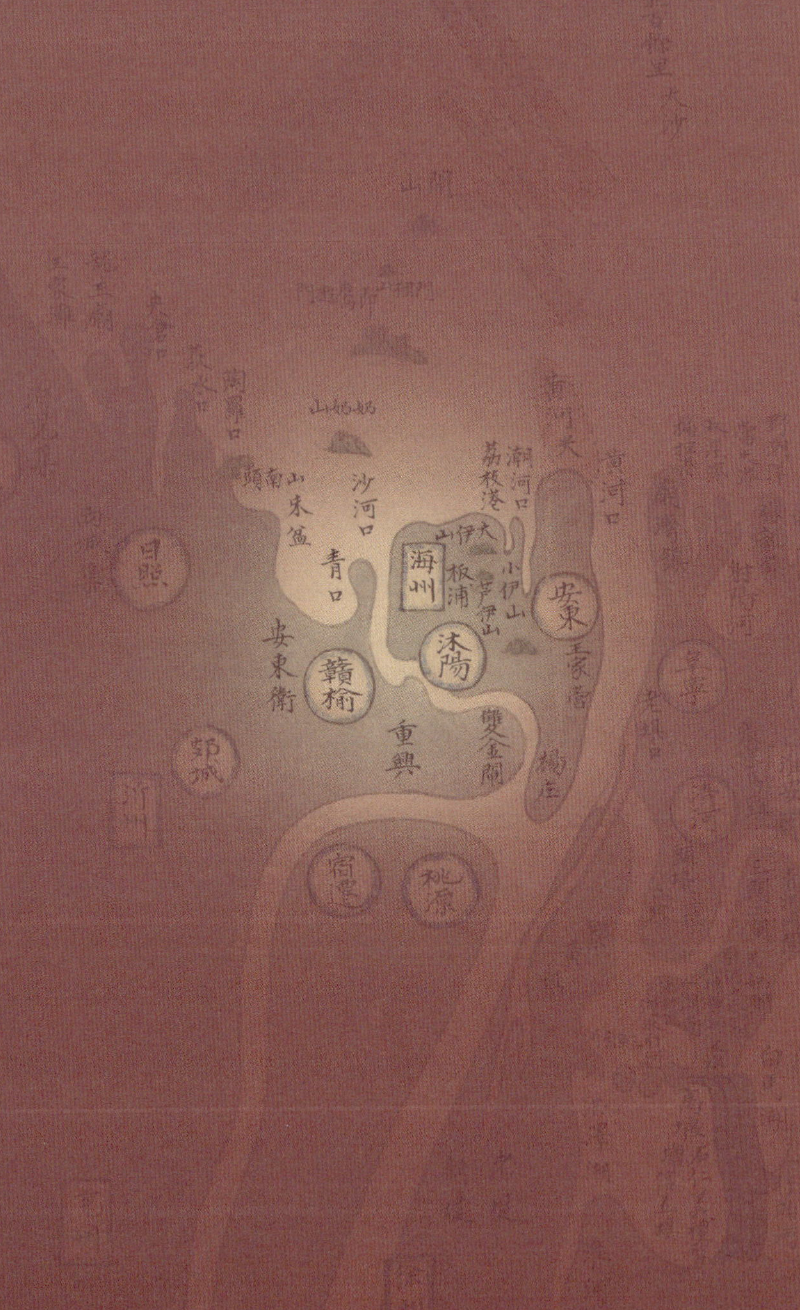

海州
沭陽
贛榆
安東
安東衛
青口
沙河口
重興
雙金閘
楊庄
王家营
板浦
大伊山
小伊山
潮河口
黃河口
宿遷
桃源
日照

Lianyungang: The Famous District of the East China Sea

The Eastern Bridgehead of the Belt and Road Initiative

Perhaps It Could be Called the "Port of Fortune"

Haizhou

Lianyungang, known as Haizhou in ancient times, was established during the seventh year of Wuding (549) in the Eastern Wei Dynasty of the Northern Dynasties. Considering the regional advantage of "controlling the Qi and Lu territories to the north and shielding the Jianghuai region to the south," Haizhou was created to govern six prefectures and nineteen counties. From then on, Haizhou became the political, economic, cultural center, and military stronghold of the northern Jiangsu and southern Shandong coastal areas.

Silla People

During the Tang Dynasty, the construction of the official canal in Haizhou connected the canal with the seaport, turning Haizhou's seaport into a bustling commercial harbor, a dock for the collection and distribution of goods from the north and south, and a naval port for resupplying military provisions. After that, this place also became an important port for China's external exchanges and communications. Many Silla immigrants (i.e., immigrants from the Korean Peninsula)

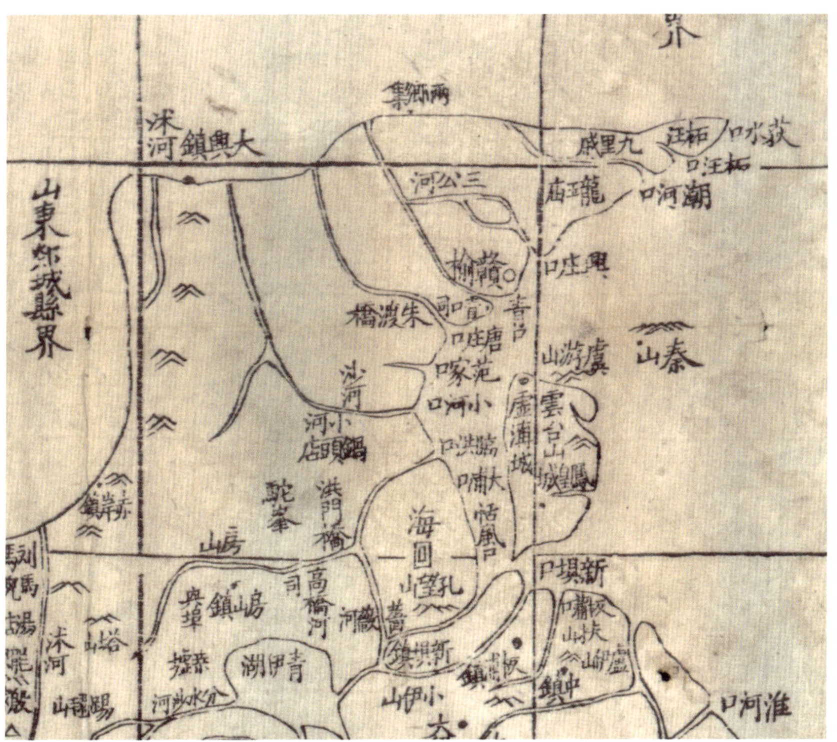

Complete Map of Jiangsu (section of Lianyungang)

Complete Map of Jiangsu was completed in the third year of Tongzhi's reign (1864) of the Qing Dynasty. It depicts the administrative divisions of Jiangsu Province, including eight prefectures, three departments, three directly governed states, three states, and sixty-two counties, as well as the distribution of rivers, lakes, and islands along the coast within its territory. This map is part of the *Complete Geographical Map of the Imperial Provinces*, a series based on the national administrative region maps drawn since the Kangxi period, referring to the *Qing Dynasty Unified Map* compiled under the supervision of Hu Linyi (1812–1861).

Image of Choe Chiwon

Choe Chiwon (857–?), also known by his courtesy name Guyun and pen name Haiyun, posthumously honored as Wenchang, was a famous scholar of sinology studies during the Silla period of the Korean Peninsula and a highly significant figure in the history of Korean literature. In the ninth year of the Xiantong era (868) in the Tang Dynasty, Choe Chiwon traveled from Silla to the Tang Empire by merchant ship. At that time, the Tang Dynasty's imperial examinations were open to foreigners. After six years of study in Chang'an (present-day Xi'an), Choe passed the civil service examination. In 876, he was appointed as the magistrate of Lishui (present-day Lishui in Nanjing). In 884, with the approval of Emperor Xizong of the Tang Dynasty, Choe departed from Yangzhou, sailed up the Grand Canal, went out to sea from Haizhou, and returned to Silla. Today, there is a Choe Chiwon Memorial Hall in Yangzhou.

came here for trade and exchanges, and some even established villages to reside in.[1]

The Salt River

The Salt River, historically known as the Official River or River Crossing Salt Fields, is located in the northeastern part of Jiangsu Province. It was dug in the fourth year of the Chuigong[2] era (688), "stretching 138 *li* long and 8 *zhang* [1 *zhang* ≈ 3.33 m] wide. It connects the Salt River of the Qinghe River in the upper reaches with Banpu in the lower reaches, serving as a route for transporting salt from the north of Huai River."[3] During the Song Dynasty (960–1279), to enhance the sea salt export from Lianzhou, Haizhou, and other areas, waters from Lianshui were also merged into this water system, hence it was also named the Tonglian River.[4] In the early Qing Dynasty, due to its distance from the coast, Huainan gradually experienced a decline in salt concentration, and the Xinpu (now in Haizhou District, Lianyungang City) area gradually became a distribution center of the salt industry in the north of Huai River.[5] The Banpu, Zhongzheng, and Linxing salt fields in Lianyungang gradually flourished, leading to prosperous salt transportation. In the twenty-sixth year of Kangxi's reign (1687), the river was dredged again for transporting salt from the north of the Huai River internally. Due to frequent salt transportation, the Official

---

1 Qu Jinliang, ed., *Comprehensive History of Chinese Maritime Culture: Wei, Jin, Northern and Southern Dynasties*, Sui and Tang volume (China Ocean University Press, 2013), p. 420.

2 Chuigong: This was the era name of Emperor Ruizong of Tang (Li Dan), but in reality, Empress Wu Zetian held power, so it is generally considered as an era name of Wu Zetian.

3 Compiled by the Place Names Committee of Guannan County, *Gazetteer of Place Names in Guannan County, Jiangsu Province* (1983), p. 161.

4 Zhang Qiang, *Research on China's Canals and Grain Transport: Yuan, Ming, and Qing Volume* (World Publishing Corporation, 2021), p. 419.

5 Compiled by the *Overview of China Geography* Editorial Group, *Overview of China Geography* (Orient Publishing Center, 1996), p. 496.

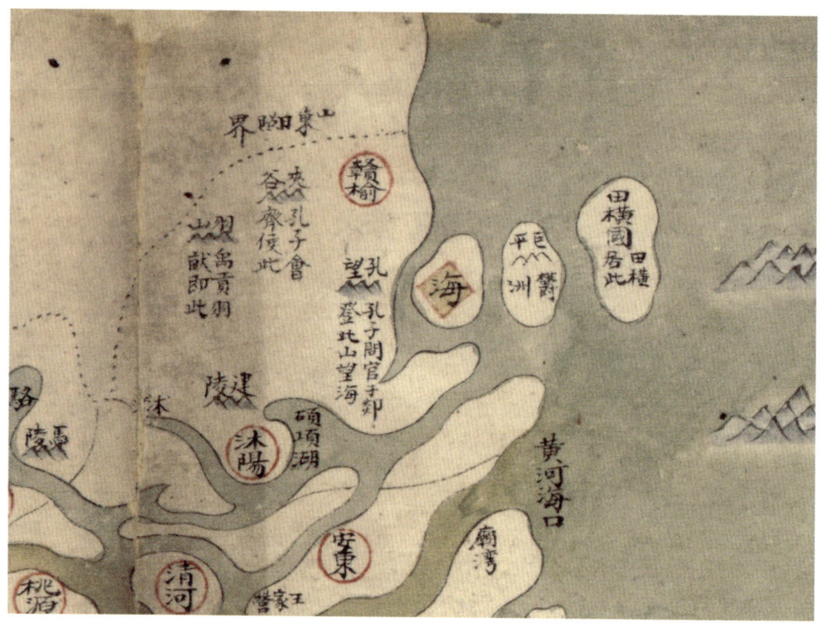

Map of the Qing Dynasty's Provincial Divisions (section of Jiangsu)

Map of the Qing Dynasty's Provincial Divisions was created around the 19th to 25th year of Qianlong's reign (1754–1760). The atlas is titled *Map of the Qing Dynasty's Provincial Divisions*, likely named according to its content, with supplementary notes on the cover, later stamped with "Made by Heshunzhai." The atlas consists of a general map and individual maps for Shengjing, Zhili, and other eighteen provinces, nineteen scrolls in total. The names of the maps are not annotated. In the map above, the location marked with a square labeled "海" (*hai*, sea) refers to the Haizhou of time (present-day Lianyungang).

River was renamed as the Salt River. At that time, "official boats and merchant ships filled the river, with masts and sails densely spread." Today, the Salt River, with a length of 175 kilometers originates from the Huaiyin Water Control Hub in Huai'an City, flowing northeast, passing through the Liutang River, Official River, Xinyi River, Wutu River, Chezhou River, and Guboshanhou River to Haizhou District, Lianyungang City, merging into the Linhong River.

Salt and Lianyungang

The name "Salt River" derives from the close relationship between salt and Lianyungang. In ancient times when private salt production was not permitted, Lianyungang served as one of the bases for salt production in the north of the Huai River. The systems for salt production and distribution were highly developed there. Lianyungang, together with Huai'an, Yancheng, and other places, formed a network of canal salt culture. Salt became one of the major bulk materials transported on the canal, bringing substantial fiscal revenue to the state.

Maritime Transportation

After the Sui and Tang dynasties, the decline of each dynasty was accompanied by the deterioration of the Grand Canal transportation system. Each new ruling dynasty would always make efforts to restore and improve the canal system for efficient transportation. However, the situation was different during the Yuan Dynasty (1206–1368). In the first year of the Zhiyuan era (1264), which was the fourth year after Kublai Khan proclaimed himself emperor, he dispatched Guo Shoujing[6] to dredge the ancient channels within the Western Xia

[6] Guo Shoujing (1231–1316) from the Yuan Dynasty, courtesy name Ruosi, was a native of Xingtai in Shunde (now part of Hebei). He was a renowned astronomer, mathematician, and hydraulic engineer of the Yuan Dynasty.

Maritime routes in the Yuan Dynasty

The dashed lines on the right side of the diagram represent the three maritime routes used during the Yuan Dynasty.

territory.[7] During Guo Shoujing's tenure, he repeatedly submitted memorials suggesting the construction of a canal for transportation to Beijing, but Kublai Khan showed little interest and took no concrete action. It was not until the 28th year of the Zhiyuan era (1291) that Guo Shoujing was appointed as the supervisor of the water affairs and tasked with repairing and improving the canal from Dadu (present-day Beijing) to Tongzhou (present-day Nantong). The canal was completed in one year, known as the Tonghui River today. However, for nearly 30 years, the canal system connecting the Jiangnan region with Beijing was insufficient for inland transportation. Therefore, the emperors of the Yuan Dynasty resorted to maritime transportation for grain shipments, and Lianyungang served as one of the transit

---

7 "Biography of Guo Shoujing" in the *History of the Yuan Dynasty*: "In the second year, he was appointed Deputy Commissar of the Directorate of Waterways. Guo Shoujing said, 'A boat can travel from Zhongxing along the river to Dongsheng in four days and nights, making it possible to transport grain. There are many ancient canals such as Chabo and Wulang Hai, which should be repaired.'"

stations.[8] In the 30th year of the Zhiyuan era (1293), Guo Shoujing completed the construction of the canal, but during the entire Yuan Dynasty, maritime transportation became the primary means of grain transportation between Jiangnan region and Beijing.

Spillway Dam

As the name suggests, a spillway dam allows water exceeding its capacity to "spill and flow out" on its own. The spillway dams on the Salt River were primarily constructed of stone, with the crest of the dam five feet above the riverbed and one foot lower than the farmlands on the west bank of the Salt River. Such construction meets the requirement for ships carrying heavy loads to navigate in the water four feet deep, as the stone spillway dams could store water up to five feet deep, which sufficiently meets the needs for navigation. When the water level exceeds the top of the spillway dam, it automatically flows out.

In the 11th year of Qianlong's reign (1746), Wei Zhezhi, drawing on the experience of Tang Shaoen, the prefect of Shaoxing during the Ming Dynasty, who built sluices and erected water level markers at the estuary of the rivers, submitted a proposal to Yin Jishan, the Governor-General of the regions of Jiangnan and Jiangxi. He suggested building a spillway dam next to each of the existing grass dams at the entrances of six rivers on the east bank of the Salt River, namely the Wuzhang River, Xiangchong River, Yize River, Liuli River, Dongmen River, and Niudun River. Additionally, he proposed erecting water level steles and opening the spillway dams when the water exceeded the level markers, so as to benefit both agriculture and water transport. In the late Qing Dynasty, the spillway dams were often neglected and silted up, leading

[8] "Treatise on Food and Goods I" in the *History of the Yuan Dynasty*: "Initially, the maritime route started from Liujiagang in Pingjiang into the sea, passing through Xihai Prefecture, Donghai County in Haining Prefecture, Mizhou, and Jiaozhou, spanning a total of 13,350 *li*."

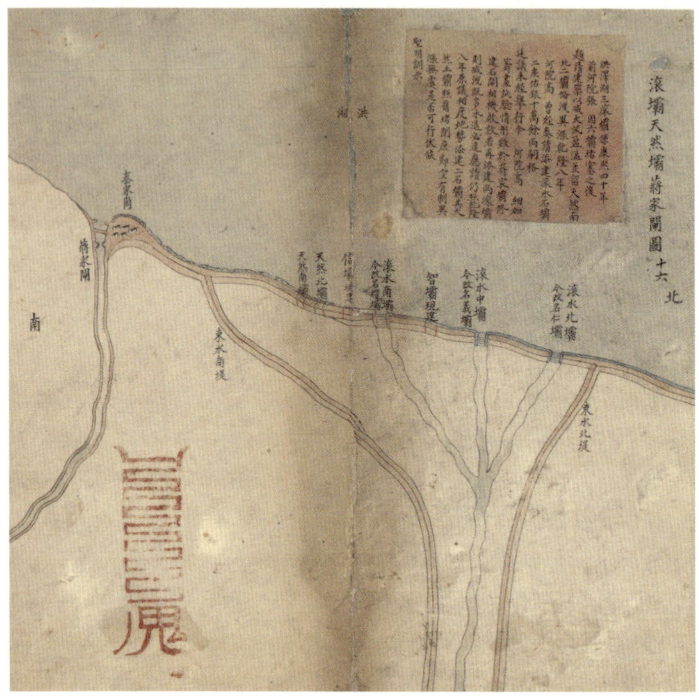

Map of the Dams and Barrages in the Lower Reaches of the Yellow River · Diagram of the Spillway Dams, Natural Dams, and Jiang Family Gate, No. 16

Map of the Dams and Barrages in the Lower Reaches of the Yellow River primarily depicts the various gates, dams, and embankments along the southern flow of the Yellow River in Jiangsu Province. The album was created during the Qianlong era of the Qing Dynasty. The album is named on the basis of the titles of the 20 maps and diagrams included; its original title has been lost, and the name of the author is unknown.

to continuous protests and even lawsuits from the local people against the government, which reflects the gradual decline in the governing capacity of the Qing government.

Waterways in New Era: A Fresh Starting Point

Huaguo Mountain, a Blessed Place; Water Curtain Cave, a Heavenly Abode

During the Tang and Song dynasties, South Yuntai Mountain was called Cangwu Mountain, and North Yuntai Mountain was known as Donghai Mountain. It was not until the Ming Dynasty that they collectively came to be referred to as Yuntai Mountain. Today, Cangwu Mountain is known as Huaguo Mountain which is even more familiar to households. It is the real-life inspiration for the fictional Huaguo Mountain in the classic novel *Journey to the West*. Huaguo Mountain integrates rocks, sea views, historical sites, and mythology. Its main peak, the Jade Maiden Peak, rises 624.4 meters above sea level, making it the highest peak in Jiangsu Province. The Water Curtain Cave of Huaguo Mountain is located over a mile east of Sanyuan Palace. Gu Qian, a local of Haizhou in the Ming Dynasty, listed "thirty-six views of Yuntai Mountain." Thereinto, the fourth view, "Divine Spring's Generous Moisture," describes the scenery of the Water Curtain Cave. His description notes, "The stone spring inside the cave is very shallow, yet it never dries up in winter. Its water is sweet and refreshing, and the cave is said to be the place where immortals used to cultivate the way." The "stone spring" mentioned refers to a "spiritual spring," a source of water directly hewn from the mountain, and folklore suggests that this spring connects to the Dragon Palace in the East China Sea. Facing the heavenly realm of the Water Curtain Cave, Gu Qian composed the "Thirty-Six Views of Yuntai Mountain": "The earthly veins connect to the vast sea, / The heavenly source to the Milky Way. / We gaze upon the place where the waters gush forth, / As mist and rain hide the emptiness above."

In 1977, Li Hongfu, a staff member of the Lianyungang Museum, wrote the first monograph on Huaguo Mountain—*Yuntai Mountain, Wu Cheng'en and Journey to the West*—arguing that Yuntai Mountain in Lianyungang is the prototype for the Huaguo Mountain in *Journey to the West*. He also presented materials found in Haizhou called *Remnants of Mr. Sheyang*, verifying that Wu Cheng'en indeed visited the ancient Haizhou area. With his efforts, the identification of Yuntai Mountain in Lianyungang as the real-life inspiration for Huaguo Mountain in *Journey to the West* gained academic support and widespread recognition.

What "Clouds" Does Lianyun Connect?

Between mountains and sea, where the sky meets the ocean, Lianyungang was anciently known as "Haizhou." In 1933, with the completion of the terminal port of the Longhai Railway, the port was named "Lianyungang" (literally "clouds-connected port") because it faces the Lian Island and backs against the Yuntai Mountain. As early as the end of the Longshan Culture period, human activities had already been present in the Yuntai Mountain area, with the emergence of the ancient city of Tenghualuo. *The Book of the Southern Qi Dynasty · Annals of States* from the Southern Dynasties by Xiao Zixian records, "Yuzhou

Huang Shenjin, *Twenty-Four Views of Yuntai · No. 2 · Sand Dyke Connection*

lies in the midst of the sea, spanning hundreds of miles around, with white deer emerging from the island, the land benefiting from fields, fish, and salt." Su Shi, a poet from the Song Dynasty, wrote in "Using the Rhyme Scheme of Prefect Chen's Reflections," "Layers of verdant Cangwu rise from the vast sea, / The ethereal Penglai touches the realm of immortality." The ancient Yuntai Mountain amid the sea was embraced with an aura of mysticism, just like the legendary Penglai. Following the Tancheng earthquake in the seventh year of the Kangxi era (1668), the sea gradually receded eastward, and the strait between Banpu, Qushan, and Yuntai Mountain gradually silted up into land. At the beginning of the Qianlong era, Huang Shenjin painted *Twenty-Four Views of Yuntai*, in which the second view, *Sand Dyke Connection*, refers to the land route to Yuntai Mountain that formed after the strait silted up. Today, Yuntai Mountain is renowned for its extraordinary mountains and unparalleled seas, with winding hills and flowing green waters. Within the mountain lie the Longevity Valley, Maple Bay, Penghu Wonderland, Yuntai Stone Forest, Wudao Hermitage, and other sights, all praised for their wondrous waters, as well as ancient and serene beauty.

The "Hub" of Buddhist Chants

Yuntai Mountain historically hosted numerous temples, among which Faqi Temple was the most flourishing, hailed as the "foremost jungle of Huaihai." In the Three Kingdoms period (220–280), the eminent monk Kang Senghui from the Kingdom of Kangju in the Western Regions first arrived in Jianye during the Chiwu period of Wu's. The ruler of Eastern Wu, Sun Quan, built a pagoda and established the Jianchu Temple for him, marking the beginning of Buddhist temples in the southern region of the Yangtze River. Later, Kang Senghui went to Faqi Temple in Sucheng to preach and passed away there. The name Faqi Temple is derived from the meaning "the origin of the dharma." Originally, Faqi

Temple housed the Jiufeng Pagoda, serving as the gravesite for monks from the Western Regions. The temple reached its zenith during the Ming and Qing dynasties. Gu Qian wrote in his *Thirty-Six Views of Yuntai Mountain—Mountain Temple at Dawn*: "Faqi Temple, located in the mountains of Sucheng and established during the Han Dynasty [206 BC–AD 220], was a thriving monastic community. The sound of morning bells and evening drums, pure and far-reaching, made it a place of serene cultivation." The Japanese monk Ennin once came here, and people from Silla regarded Sucheng, where Faqi Temple was located, as their second homeland.

Faqi Temple was destroyed by a Japanese aircraft bombing in 1938. In 1963, local people built a reservoir on its original site, leaving no trace of its past. Today's Faqi Temple was reconstructed in 2006. Although Faqi Temple has vanished into the rivers of long history, Lianyungang still preserves some of its relics, as if to retain the faint echoes of Buddhism through time and to support research into the eastward dissemination of Buddhism and the onset of the Maritime Silk Road. Such relics include the Liuxian Spring, traditionally believed to be "where the Han monk drank and left behind a spring," with the words "Liuxian Spring" carved into the cliffside; and Zhenya Bridge, located at Hukou Ridge, built by Zhenya, the abbot of Faqi Temple during the Republic of China era, to facilitate the pilgrimage of the faithful, with both the bridge and the inscriptions preserved. Together, Faqi Temple and the Kongwang Mountain Buddhist diff carvings in Haizhou attest to another route by which Buddhism entered via the Maritime Silk Road. With Faqi Temple serving as a hub, the dharma was once again carried across the seas to Japan, the Republic of Korea, and so on. The historical significance of Faqi Temple has contributed to Lianyungang's status as the eastern bridgehead of the Belt and Road Initiative, encouraging its people to embrace openness and advance in cooperation.

Intangible Cultural Heritage: The Five Major Haizhou Palace Tunes

The five major Haizhou palace tunes refer to an ancient form of folk music performance that is prevalent in Lianyungang and its surrounding areas. It primarily consists of five types of tunes, "Soft and Flat," "Stacked Falling," "Oriole Tune," "Southern Tune," and "Waves and Billows." These art forms represent the achievements of the *qupai* (曲牌, tune name) traditional folk song cluster and constitute a precious heritage of popular songs from the Ming and Qing dynasties in China.

The five major Haizhou palace tunes are divided into two categories according to the content of the *qupai*: major tunes and minor tunes. The melodies of the major tunes are generally soft and delicate, with a slow rhythm, elegant and splendid lyrics, and fewer words but more tunes, primarily expressing emotions. Performers often feel as if each phrase is followed by three sighs when singing. In contrast, the characteristics of the minor tunes are diametrically opposite to those of the major tunes. They are structured in a four-phrase form of rising, continuing, turning, and concluding and are good at narrating stories, with a more distinct and brisk rhythm, more words but fewer tunes.

During the Ming and Qing dynasties, with the flourishing of the salt industry of the North and South Huai River Region and the salt transportation along the Grand Canal moving from south to north, on the one hand, the geographical connectivity promoted the blending of the arts, allowing the five major Haizhou palace tunes to widely absorb folk tunes from the Jianghuai region and gradually mature; on the other hand, some local salt merchants and literati paid high attention to the five major Haizhou palace tunes, elevating it to a new height and gradually shaping its present form.

Exploding Squid Blossom

Exploding squid blossom is a dish made by processing a squid's skin, which is even in thickness, with a wheat head-shaped way of cutting and then deep frying it in oil heated to 30%–40% of its maximum temperature. The final product showcases fine knife work, presenting a white and beautiful appearance, with a crispy, tender, and refreshing taste.

Ganyu Steamed Gazami Crab

The waters of Lianyungang are abundant with gazami crabs, with spring being the breeding season each year. During this period, gazami crabs are particularly plump and meaty, making it the best time to enjoy them. People often choose the special gazami crabs from Haitou Town in the Ganyu District of Lianyungang, favoring the natural deliciousness of the ingredients. Steamed gazami crabs are the most popular way to prepare them.

Fish Maw with Crab Roe

Fish maw with crab roe uses fish maw, one of the eight delicacies from the sea, paired with the abundant sea crabs from Lianyungang. After stir-frying, the finished dish of fish maw with crab roe features a bright yellow color, a rich sauce, and a texture that is smooth, tender, and fresh, leaving a lingering fragrance on the lips and teeth.

雲龍山
戶部台
石狗湖
藕堤
石工
徐州
茶亭
土山
陡山口

Xuzhou: The Crossroad of Five Provinces

The Golden Waterway of Inclusiveness and Integration

Pengcheng of Old: Xuzhou's Legacy Among the Nine Provinces

Passing as It Does

During the late Spring and Autumn Period, the turbulent waters of Lüliang in the Si River rushed like arrows, waves charging like stampedes. Confucius, accompanied by his disciples, made a special trip to observe the Lüliang floodwaters, from which he was inspired to utter the timeless expression, "Passing as it does, day and night without cease." Lüliang is located 50 *li* southeast of Xuzhou City, at the foot of Lüliang Mountain, named so due to its positioning south of the ancient city of Lü and the presence of a stone bridge in the waters. The Lüliang was divided into upper and lower sections, stretching over more than 7 *li*. In the Yuan Dynasty, Zhao Mengfu described the challenge of navigating ships through Lüliang: "When boats reached this point, hundreds of poles and men strained at the ropes, sweat dripping to the ground. They advanced by mere inches, the difficulty akin to ascending to heaven. People aboard would often cry out, seeking divine assistance."[1] Even before the Han Dynasty, the Lüliang and Baibu rapids were known as treacherous spots in

---

1 Zhao Mengfu from the Yuan Dynasty, *Inscription on the Stele of the Commander of the Spirits*.

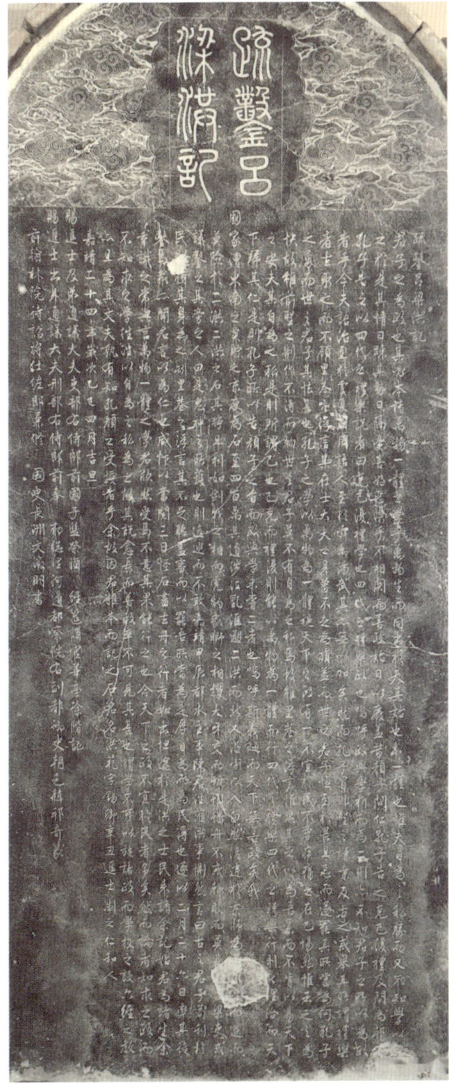

The stele of *Record of the Dredging of the Lüliang Flood*, chronicled by Xu Jie, calligraphed by Wen Zhengming, and inscribed by Han Bangqi

the Si River, with historical records mentioning that "since the Han and Tang dynasties, grain transport has avoided these areas." In the second year of Jianyan (1128) during the Southern Song Dynasty, the Yellow River seized the course of the Si River into the Huai River, and by the fifth year of Mingchang (1194) in the Jin Dynasty (1115–1234), "the northward flow ceased, with the entire river entering the Huai," making the current even more rapid and dangerous than before. The Grand Canal runs approximately 1,800 kilometers in length, with Xuzhou City boasting about 181 kilometers of this route. It is the urban area with the longest segment of the Grand Canal running through eight provinces and cities. Furthermore, Xuzhou is situated at the intersection of the Bian, Si, and Yellow Rivers and the Grand Canal, boasting highly developed transportation. Such convenient waterway conditions have brought prosperity to Xuzhou, leaving behind a wealth of cultural relics and stories about famous personalities. In 1604, to ensure the smooth flow of canal traffic, the court ordered the diversion of two rapids in the Yellow River section near Xuzhou—the Baibu and Lüliang rapids. Water was diverted from Lijiakou, ten *li* east of Xia Town (today part of Weishan County, Shandong Province) through Hanzhuang, merging with the Jia and Yi Rivers, to the direct entrance of the Yellow River in Pizhou, thus creating the Jia Canal. The Lüliang, once lamented by Confucius as "passing as it does," gradually silted up, submerged in the old course of the Yellow River.

Crossroad of Five Provinces

The term "crossroad of five provinces" was a summary of Xuzhou's geographic location by people in the Qing Dynasty. The so-called five provinces refer to Zhili (present-day Beijing), Shandong, Henan, Jiangnan (present-day Jiangsu and Anhui), and Zhejiang, which were administrative regions during the Qing Dynasty. Located at the mid-section of the Grand Canal from Beijing to Hangzhou, Xuzhou's geographical position was of paramount importance, making it a strategic military battleground. Many famous historical battles took place in Xuzhou. In fact, according to research by historian Shi Nianhai, aside from the canal, there were also eight significant land routes radiating from Xuzhou as a central point:

1. West through Suiyang to Luoyang, reaching Chang'an and other places
2. Northwest through Shanyang, reaching Dingtao
3. Heading north from the County of Fan and Xue, passing through the state of Lu, and arriving at various areas in Jinan
4. Through Northeast Donghai, reaching Langya
5. Through Huaiyin along the Han Ditch, southbound to Guangling, crossing the river to reach Kuaiji
6. Southbound through Linhuai, Yinling, and Dongcheng, crossing the river from Danyang, reaching counties in Eastern Yangtze
7. Westbound to Huaiyang, the state of Chen
8. Southwest across the Huai River to reach Jiujiang, Shouchun

Utilizing the Yellow River for Transport

The canal in Xuzhou is closely related to the Yellow River. As early as the fifth year of Shaoxi (1194) in the Southern Song Dynasty, the Yellow River changed its course at the Yangwu breach, encroaching on the Bian and Si Rivers, flowing through Xuzhou into the Huai River. After Jia Lu's management in the Yuan Dynasty, the Yellow River flowed solely through Xuzhou, and the section of the Grand Canal in Xuzhou entirely relied on the "utilization of the Yellow River for transport," thus making Xuzhou a crucial location for grain transport.

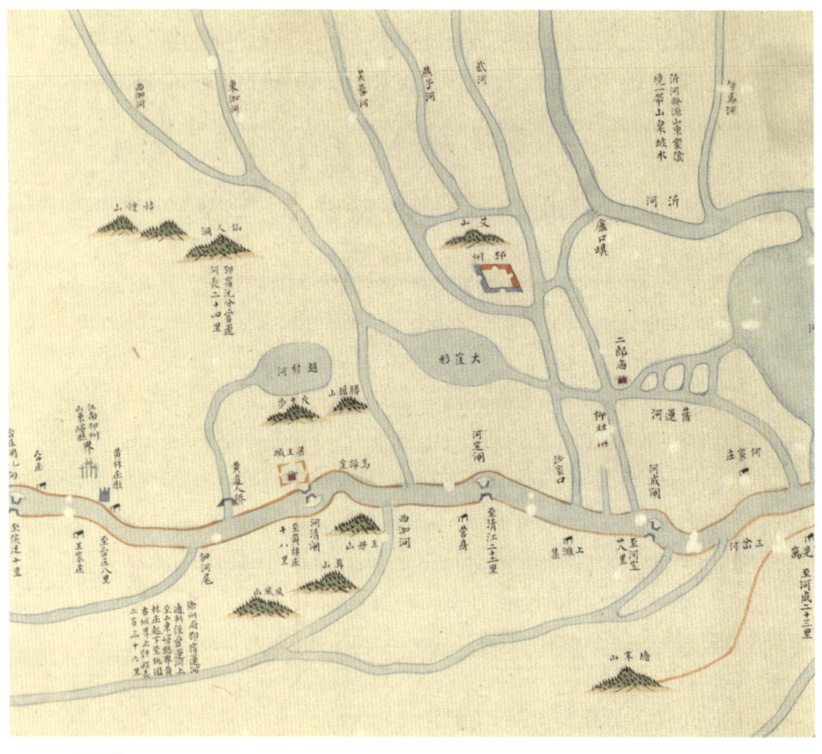

Complete Map of the Canal from Jiangsu to Beijing **(partial)**

The map roughly outlines the flow of the Jia River, which has two sources. The east Jia River flows down from the mountainous area at the border of Cangshan County (present-day Lanling County, Shandong Province) and Fei County, while the west Jia River originates from the northeast of Zaozhuang City. After merging at Sanhe Village, the rivers flow southward until they converge into the Yellow River in Pizhou.

Yaowan Ancient Town

Yaowan Ancient Town is located at the convergence of the Grand Canal from Beijing to Hangzhou and Luoma Lake, the fourth largest freshwater lake in Jiangsu. During the Ming and Qing dynasties, it became one of the main docks of the Grand Canal, and the verse, "By day, a thousand masts pass by, / By night, boats anchor for ten miles," describes the bustling scene of Yaowan Ancient Town at that time. Its unique geographical position at the confluence of river and lake resulted in the abundant production of a unique black mud. Making use of the local resources, the people created black pottery, crafting life utensils, such as pottery jars, pots, and basins. Spreading over an area of more than 20 *li*, the pottery kilns in the town are the reason why this place is known as Yaowan Ancient Town.[2]

Xuzhou Tax Station

At the end of the 15th century, Korean official Choi Bu mentioned in his work *Pyohaerok*: "To the north of the Yangtze River, places like Yangzhou, Huai'an, as well as north of the Huai River, such as Xuzhou, Jining, Linqing, are prosperous and flourishing, no different from south of the Yangtze River." In the early Ming Dynasty, the number of merchant ships passing through the canal at the Xuzhou section was substantial, making the tax revenue from these ships an important source of finance. The government set up tax stations at these gathering

---

2 The Pizhou gazetteer documents the prosperity of Yaowan during its peak: "Yaowan, located at the border of Pizhou and Su County, serves as a significant hub. In the past, boats for transporting grain would dock here, with sails densely covering the skyline. The streets were bustling with commerce, a variety of goods were abundant, and travelers coming and going, either by boat or carriage, would find lodging here. The town was wealthier than both counties (filled with affluent merchants carrying gold and jade). (Women by the market would play the zither and walk gently on tiptoes), reminiscent of the styles of Yangzhou and Zhenjiang." During the late Qing period, Yaowan had 18 provincial guild halls and over 600 businesses, including banks and pawnshops, earning it the nickname "little Shanghai of northern Jiangsu."

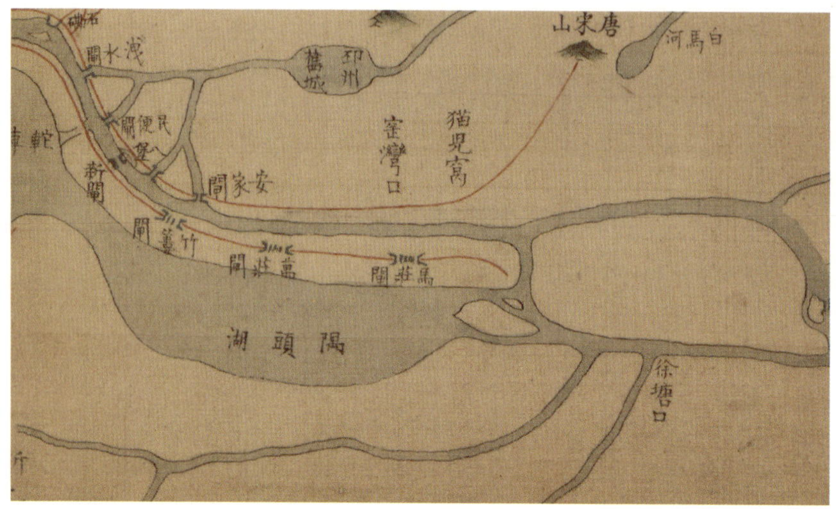

Complete Map of the Yellow River, Grand Canal, Lakes, and Rivers (partial)

Map of the Dams and Barrages in the Lower Reaches of the Yellow River · The River Below Dams of Gaobao, No. 12 (partial)

points for merchants, "thus there were tax stations at counties, such as Huoxian, Jining, Xuzhou, Huai'an, Yangzhou, Shangxin River, Hushu, Jiujiang, Jinshazhou, Linqing, and Beixin, where the levy was adjusted according to the size of the ships, known as 'ship tax,' without taxing their goods. Only Linqing and Beixin also collected goods tax, with each assigning a censor and a principal officer from the Ministry of Revenue to supervise collection" (*History of the Ming Dynasty*, vol. 81). The Xuzhou Tax Station was managed by the Xuzhou subdivision of the Ministry of Revenue, tasked with collecting taxes on the circulation of goods. Additionally, there was also the Lüliang Floodwaters Department, the subdivision of the Ministry of Works, responsible for collecting the ship tax; "from Nanjing to Tongzhou, passing through Huai'an, Jining, Xuzhou, and Linqing, every ship with one hundred materials, the tax was one hundred strings" (*History of the Ming Dynasty*, vol. 81). The establishment of the Xuzhou Canal Tax Station shows the large number of merchant ships and the prosperity of the commodity economy in Xuzhou during the early Ming Dynasty.

The "Crossroad of Five Provinces" Archway

Xuzhou, owing to its exceptional geographical location traversed by both water and land routes, has been dubbed the "crossroad of five provinces." Those today wishing to catch a glimpse of the historical crossroad within the city of Xuzhou can venture to the outside of the northern gate, Wuning Gate, and the former southern bank of the Yellow River to find an archway. Built in the 23rd year of the era of Emperor Jiaqing (1818), it was erected by Li Shixu, the River Transport Governor and a noted official of river management during the Qing Dynasty, to celebrate the accomplishments in controlling the Yellow River. On the north side of the archway is a plaque written by Li Shixu with the words "*Dahe Qian Heng*" (大河前横, The Great River Lies Before), indicating the Yellow River flowing at its base. In the ninth year of Guangxu's reign (1883), Zhao Chunping, the prefect of Xuzhou, inscribed the words "Crossroad of Five Provinces" on the south side of the plaque during the reconstruction of the Yellow River archway, thus giving it its appearance seen today.

In reality, the Grand Canal does not flow around the archway. However, due to the natural course of the Bian River from the west and the Si River from the north converging at the northeast corner of Xuzhou City, the canal transportation in Xuzhou has a long history. The early canals in Xuzhou were primarily used for military purposes, including the transportation of military supplies, and the development of Xuzhou also had a strong military emphasis. During the Yuan Dynasty, the Beijing-Hangzhou Grand Canal was fully connected, linking the Hai River, Yellow River, Huai River, Yangtze River, and Qiantang River, making up five major water systems with Xuzhou

Old photo of "Crossroad of Five Provinces" archway

belonging to the section of "Jizhou River." At this time, northward, Xuzhou could utilize the Si River to reach Jining; southward, Xuzhou could transport goods by use of the Yellow River. People could float down the stream to the Yangtze River. A poem says, "In days of old, the Yellow River and Si River, / Merged as one stream, flowing past the city walls free" (Chen Lian, "Lüliang Floodwaters"), illustrating the significant status of Xuzhou's water transport network.

Guests from All Directions Staying in Pengcheng

The Sifang Guild Hall of Yaowan Ancient Town

Yaowan Ancient Town was founded during the Tang Dynasty and became a gathering place for merchants from all directions. The town thrived due to the canal, described as "moored boats everywhere, masts standing tall, bustling streets, and abundant goods" (Dou Hongnian, *Supplement to the Pizhou Records*). To find a sense of home among strangers in a foreign land and escape from the solitude, merchants from different places built distinctive guild halls in Yaowan, creating a unique landscape and witnessing the inclusivity of this ancient town in northern Jiangsu toward guests from all directions.

Among all the guild halls in Yaowan, the Shanxi Guild Hall takes precedence. The reputation of Shanxi merchants spread far and wide during the Ming and Qing dynasties. People from Shanxi, leaving their hometown, chose to settle here seeing the Guandi Temple and the ancient locust trees in Yaowan. It is said that under the ancient locust tree lie Guan Yu's horse trough and sharpening stone from the late Han Dynasty. People from Shanxi prayed for the blessings from Guan Yu, who also came from Shanxi. Thus, seven Shanxi families pooled funds to build the guild hall next to the temple. After expansions over generations, the guild hall now houses the Confucius Hall, Hall of Yue Fei, and the Bell and Drum Tower. The guild hall not only provided protection for Shanxi people but also ensured the safety of merchants' assets from other places. Its surrounding night markets and entertainment venues made it famous at the time.

In the early years of the Kangxi period of the Qing Dynasty, merchants from Suzhou, Zhenjiang, and Yangzhou came to Yaowan and established the "Suzhou-Zhenjiang-Yangzhou Guild Hall." The guild hall, with its four courtyards and black-tiled, blue brick structure,

Shanxi Guild Hall

boasts distinctive features of southern China. Initially, it operated grain and salt industries, and by the early Republic of China period, it dealt in grains and local specialties exported to Europe and the Americas, established match companies, and Xiangji Anglo-American Cigarette and Kerosene Company, wholesaling and retailing foreign goods. Moreover, the guild hall was devoted to culture, education, and charitable activities, producing many renowned figures.

Jiangxi merchants were known for their business acumen dating back over 900 years. With substantial financial and material support, merchants from Jiangxi established their signature architecture across the country—the Wanshou Palace. In the 37th year of the Kangxi period (1698), seven Jiangxi merchants jointly constructed the Jiangxi Guild Hall, also known as the Wanshou Palace of Yaowan Ancient Town. The Jiangxi Guild Hall mainly dealt in Chinese medicinal herbs and traditional Chinese medicine, with major pharmacies in the town operated by its traders. They imported herbs from outside areas, selling them retail or wholesale, or processing them into traditional Chinese medicines while being charitable, leading to the saying "the poor get medicine and the rich payback."

As time passed, apart from the nine shopfronts of the Jiangxi Guild Hall's pharmacy that are relatively well-preserved, the rest of the ancient buildings have disappeared.

Other guild halls in Yaowan Ancient Town include the Fujian Guild Hall, Shandong Guild Hall, and Anhui Guild Hall. In addition, there are historical buildings, such as the Wu Family Mansion, Yaowan Post Office of the Qing Dynasty, and the major pawnshops of the east and west.

Intangible Cultural Heritage: Xuzhou Scented Sachets

Scented sachets, commonly referred to as "scented cloth bags," have a long-standing tradition in China. They are a product of the ancient

Han agrarian culture, symbolized by men plowing while women weaving, and are a traditional Han Chinese folk craft. The long poem from the Music Bureau of the Han Dynasty, "Peacock Flying Southeast," mentions "a crimson canopy drapes the bed, with scented sachets hanging overhead," indicating the presence of scented sachets in Xuzhou since that time. Developed up to this day, Xuzhou scented sachets are now known throughout the world.

The craft of making scented sachets is quite unique and is especially renowned for its exquisite embroidery. They feature a variety of patterns that are lively and vivid, characterized by novelty, beauty, authenticity, and a solid and simple shape. The sachets are brightly colored and finely crafted, and their three-dimensional shapes are lifelike. They often convey auspicious blessings and folk tales, interspersed with bold and exaggerated floral patterns at times. Besides being convenient to wear and attractive in appearance, scented sachets also hold medicinal value, which is one of the reasons why they have been favored from ancient times to the present day. The craftsmen often select dozens of types of traditional Chinese medicinal materials that emit natural fragrances and have health-boosting and evil-warding properties, which are specially processed and filled into the sachets. The scented sachets produced in Xuzhou incorporate local characteristics and are generally lively, simple, robust, and rustic, with great decorative appeal. The detailed and delicate embroidery work in certain parts of the sachet is exquisitely lifelike, achieving a wonderful combination of form and spirit.

Sha Soup

Sha (饣它) soup is said to have a history of over 4,000 years. "饣它" is pronounced similarly to "啥" (*sha*, what) in Chinese but does not have an exact character representation. Authentic *sha* soup requires five main ingredients and over a dozen auxiliary ingredients. When a customer places an order, the chef first cracks an egg into the bowl, then ladles soup over it, resulting in golden strands of egg floating on the surface. The soup is soft, moist, and rich in flavor, offering a delicious and mellow taste.

Bazirou

Bazirou (把子肉, pork meat) is related to the folk custom of "*bai bazi*" (拜把子, becoming sworn brothers), involving various auxiliary ingredients that are bundled together and seasoned appropriately. The finished *bazirou* features layers of fat and lean meat with soft, glutinous skin. It is rich in taste but not greasy, offering a mellow and refined flavor.

Misandao

Misandao (蜜三刀, literally "honey-three-cut") is one of Xuzhou's local special pastry items, known for its shiny, non-sticky texture, sweet and soft taste, and strong sesame aroma. The "*mi*" refers to malt syrup, which is made from grains like barley through fermentation and saccharification. Hence, this snack is also known as "malt food."

柳園頭
碎石工
房家涵
馬陵山
草工
宿迁閘
撐堤
十字河
宿迁縣
真武庙
護城堤

Suqian:
The Hometown of the Overlord

The Rivers and Mountains in Early Spring Are Most Enchanting

A Strategic Passage Between the Two Capitals

Suyu County

During the early Tang Dynasty, Suqian was known as Suyu County. In the twenty-third year of the Kaiyuan period (735) in the Tang Dynasty, due to flooding, the state administration moved southward, and the county administration moved northward. The state was Si State, and its administration moved southward to Linhuai County, while the county, Suyu County, moved its administration northward to the birthplace of Xiang Yu—the ancient city of Xiaxiang. Later, to avoid the taboo of the name of Emperor Daizong of Tang, Li Yu,[1] it was renamed Suqian, which denotes "the relocation of Suyu County."[2] Today, within the Sucheng District, there are two ancient city sites named "Xiaxiang City" and "Suyu City."

---

1 In ancient times, to uphold the dignity of the hierarchical system, when speaking or writing, people would refrain from directly stating or writing the names of monarchs or respected elders as a sign of respect. "*Yu*" (预) of Suyu (宿预) County is homophonous with "*yu*" (豫) of Li Yu (李豫), thus necessitating the avoidance.—Trans.

2 This statement refers to *A Brief Study on the Relocation of Ancient Suqian City Sites*, in *Liu Yunhe Academic Collection* (Xiling Yinshe Publishing House, 2007).

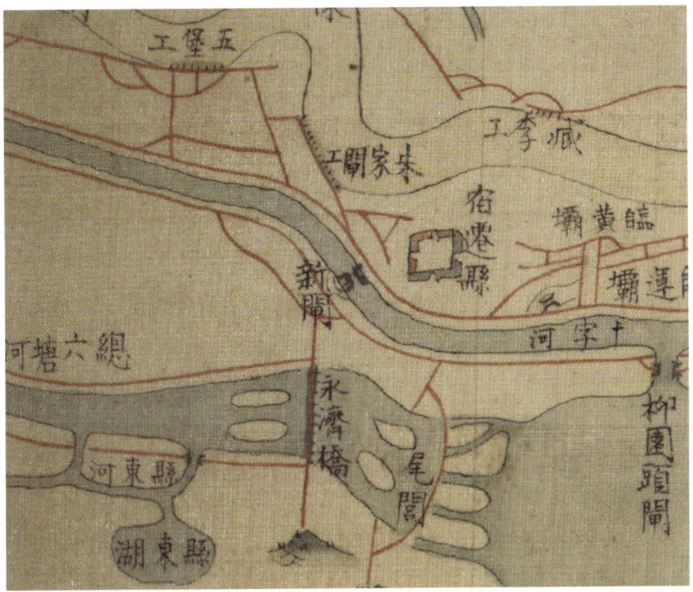

Complete Map of the Yellow River, Grand Canal, Lakes, and Rivers (partial)

The Endpoint of the Tongji Canal

"Looking north to Qi and Lu, connecting south to Jianghuai, situated centrally between two waters, it controls the throat of two capitals." This is an accurate depiction of the geographical location of Suqian City. In the first year of the Daye era (605) of the Sui Dynasty, Emperor Yang of Sui ordered the gathering of over a million laborers from Henan and Huaibei to dig the Tongji Canal. Because the terrain of today's Sihong County in Suqian was low-lying, further excavation was carried out in the third year of Daye (607), rerouting the canal through Linhuai County to flow into the Huai River.[3] Only with this alteration did the

3 Zhang Qiang, *Research on China's Canals and Grain Transport: Sui and Tang Volume* (World Publishing Corporation, 2021), p. 89.

Tongji Canal truly become navigable. The poet Pi Rixiu from the Tang Dynasty praised it with a poem: "People say the Sui perished because of this river, / Yet a thousand miles still depend on its flow. / If not for the water palace and the dragon boats, / Yu's merits would not seem greater than his own." During the Southern Song Dynasty, when the court moved south, maintenance of the Tongji Canal gradually decreased, and the canal's bed silted up, causing the water to cease flowing. Today, only the old Bian River in Sihong of Suqian (over 30 kilometers) still maintains the original appearance of the Tongji Canal.

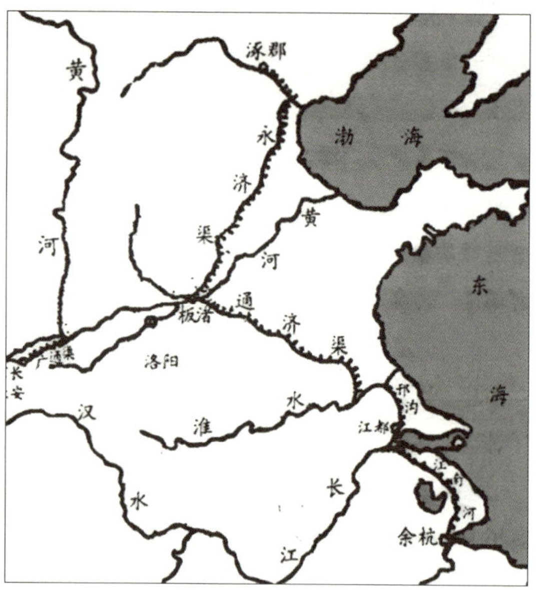

The Tongji Canal and the Yongji Canal of the Sui Dynasty

The Abandoned Yellow River

Jiangsu is the only province in the country that has two great rivers, several great lakes, and the sea. One of the great rivers naturally refers to the Yangtze River, the great lakes refer to bodies of water, such as the Taihu Lake and Hongze Lake, and the sea is self-explanatory given Jiangsu's coastal location, while the other great river refers to the Yellow River. From the Southern Song Dynasty to the Xianfeng period of the Qing Dynasty, the Yellow River flowed through Jiangsu into the sea for 661 years. In the fifth year of the Xianfeng period (1855), the Yellow River changed its course, returning to the channel to the north of Mount Tai. In the centuries prior to that, the Yellow River crossed through the territory of Suqian.

Zaohe Town

"The land fronts the great river and backs onto the transport canal, with raging torrents and rapids gathering from far and near, known as the most perilous."[4] This is the description of Zaohe in the imperial inscription by Emperor Qianlong at the Anlan Dragon King Temple in Zaohe Town. Zaohe, with its abundant waterways including the Middle Canal, Yan River, the ancient Yellow River, Luoma Lake, and Huangdun Lake, converging here, is an important location for flood control, water conservancy, and facilitating grain transport. In the middle and late Ming Dynasty, dangerous sections of the Yellow River such as Xuzhou and Lüliang were extremely perilous, dubbed as the "Gate of Hell" by the boatmen. Consequently, in the thirty-second year of Ming Wanli (1604), the then Chief Minister of River Transportation, Li Hualong, petitioned the court to dredge and open the Zhi River (present-day Yan River) to the west of Zaohe Town (present-day Wangying Village),

---

4 Compiled by the Editorial Committee of *Water Conservancy Records of Sucheng District, Suqian City*, *Water Conservancy Records of Sucheng District, Suqian City* (China University of Mining and Technology Press, 2016), p. 227.

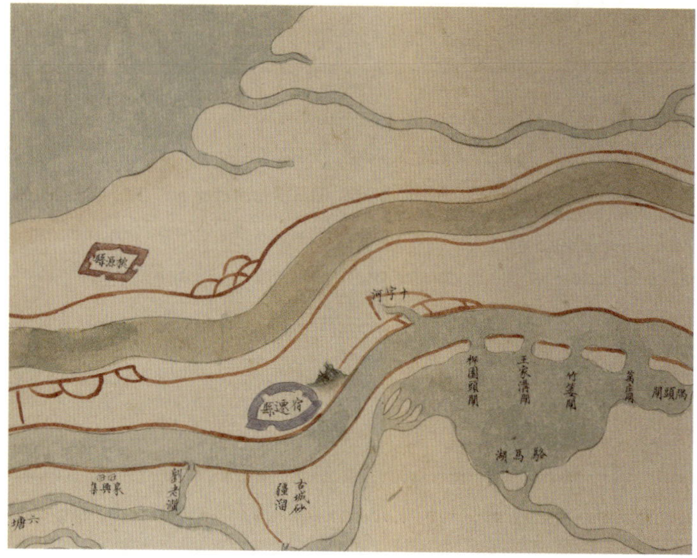

Complete Map of Canal Transport Routes (partial)

Below the title of *Complete Map of Canal Transport Routes*, there is a signature: "Respectfully painted by Duan Bikui in the mid-spring of the Jiashen year during the Guangxu reign." There is no biography available for Duan Bikui in the history of the Qing Dynasty, and his birth year is unknown. It is only known that he served as the guard in Xiangyang in the fifteenth year of the Guangxu period (1889), and he passed away due to illness in the twenty-second year of the Guangxu period (1896). The yellow section of the river drawn above the Suqian County in the map is the old course of the Yellow River that crossed through the territory of Suqian.

connecting to the Jia River in Pizhou to the north, historically known as the Jia Canal. The opening of the Zhi River not only bypassed the perilous sections of the Yellow River from Zaohe to Xuzhou but also shortened the distance of grain transportation. It also spared the boatmen from having to brave the "Gate of Hell."

Luoma Lake

When Emperor Qianlong of the Qing Dynasty was 41 years old, the Empress Dowager happened to be 69 years old. Consequently, Qianlong accompanied his mother on her first southern tour. They traveled down the Grand Canal, across the Yellow River, to Suzhou and Hangzhou. On their return journey, they offered sacrifices at the Tomb of Emperor Taizu of Ming in Nanjing, then at Mount Tai's temple in Taizhou, before finally returning to Beijing. During this southern tour, when arriving in Suqian, Qianlong's first task was to inspect Luoma Lake. After learning the details, he composed a poem titled "Luoma Lake": "Facilitating transport through heaven's design, safeguarding the earth's paths from flood and flow. / Strategically storing and releasing, carefully balancing excess and need below. / Islets and sandbanks charm the riverside towns, while ducks and gulls on spring waters glide. / From six ponds reaching eastward to the sea, the people's welfare stays close to my mind." This poem succinctly explains the hydraulic function of Luoma Lake: storing water in times of drought and releasing water in times of abundance. It also emphasizes the need for "strategically storing and releasing, carefully balancing excess and need below," calling for meticulous surveying and control of the water level in the lake to prevent drought or flooding.[5]

---

5 Compiled by Suqian Local Chronicles Compilation Committee Office, *Suqian Anecdote* (Jiangsu People's Publishing House, 2016), pp. 32–33.

***Map of Qianlong Emperor's Southern Tour*, vol. 4 (partial), colored on silk**

Map of Qianlong Emperor's Southern Tour, led and painted by the Qing Dynasty artist Xu Yang, depicts the scenario of Emperor Qianlong's first southern tour in the sixteenth year of his reign (1751). The series comprises twelve volumes, with the fourth volume illustrating the emperor inspecting the critical engineering works at the confluence of the Yellow River, the Huai River, the Grand Canal, and the Hongze Lake on that day and the next. The illustrations reveal the surging waterways of the Jianghuai region's canal systems and the solid embankments over 200 years ago. *Map of Qianlong Emperor's Southern Tour* exists in two versions: silk and paper. The silk version has been scattered and is now housed in different museums around the world. The paper version was preserved intact in the Beijing Palace Museum and was transferred to the National Museum of China in 1959, where it is now treasured.

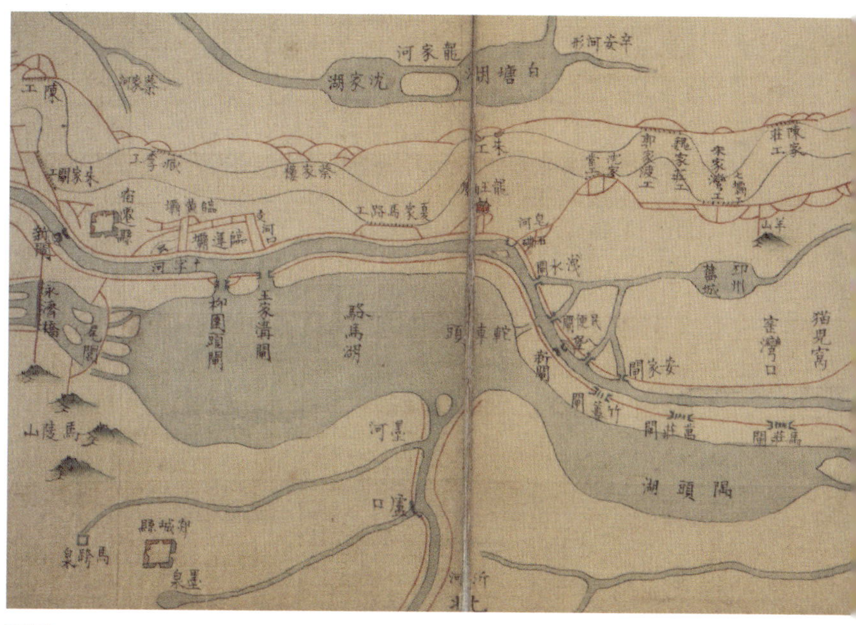

Complete Map of the Yellow River, Grand Canal, Lakes, and Rivers (partial)

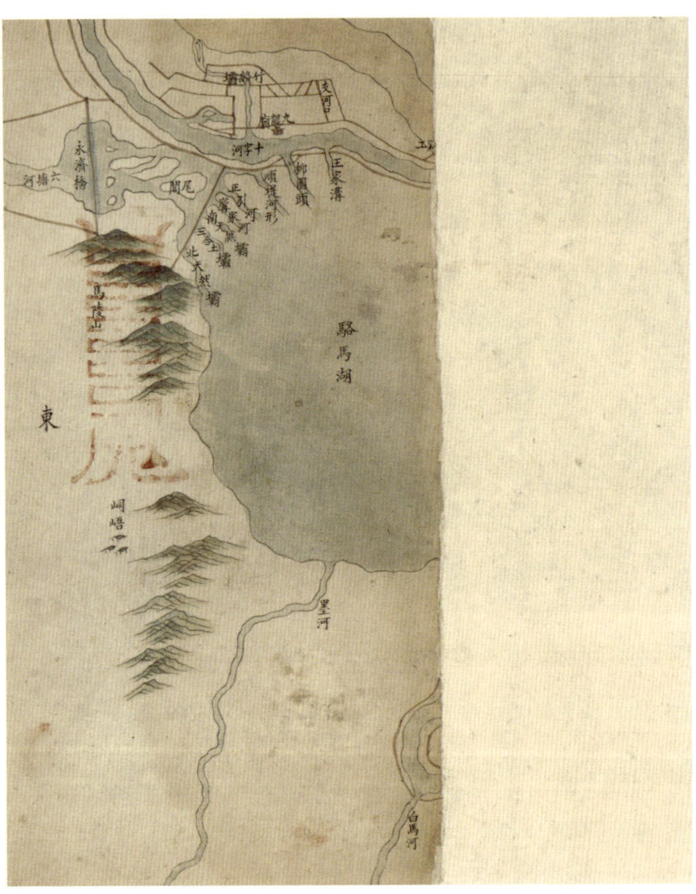

Map of the Dams and Barrages in the Lower Reaches of the Yellow River · Luoma Lake (fragment) (partial)

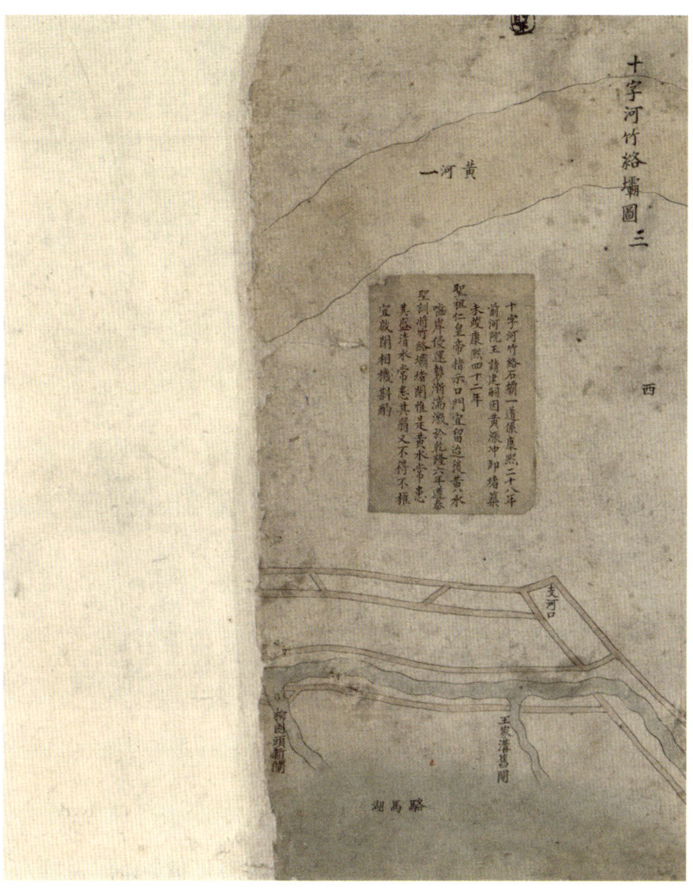

Map of the Dams and Barrages in the Lower Reaches of the Yellow River · Cross River Bamboo Weir, No. 3 (fragment) (partial)

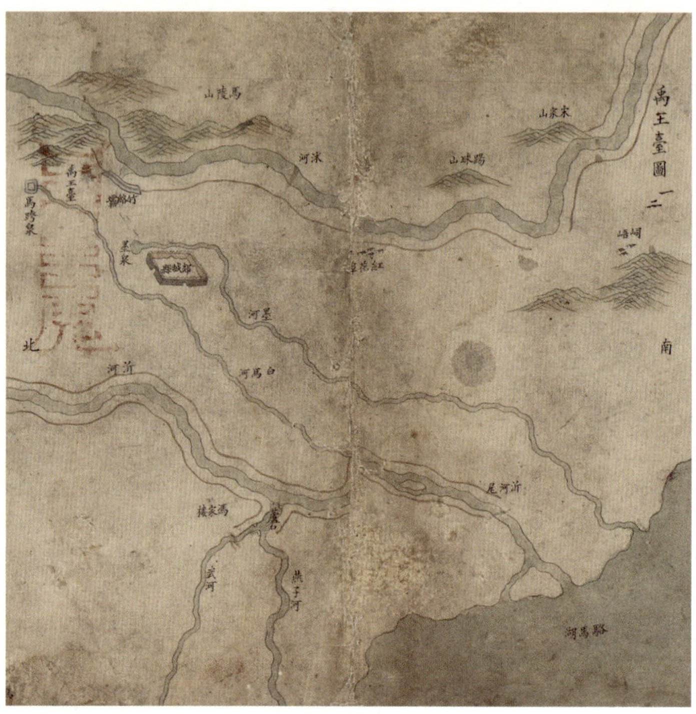

Map of the Dams and Barrages in the Lower Reaches of the Yellow River · King Yu's Terrace, No. 1 and 2 (partial)

However, Luoma Lake was not always there. Historical records indicate that "Luoma Lake was originally a clay field," and it was not mentioned until after the Wanli era of the Ming Dynasty, meaning it was originally a depression that gradually accumulated into a lake during the course of the Yellow River flowing southward into the Si River and Huai River. As the Yellow River's waterway became increasingly silted and overflowed, Luoma Lake gradually expanded, forming a lake with dimensions of "sixty *li* in length and a circumference of one hundred and fifty *li*."[6] Today, Luoma Lake has become the fourth largest freshwater lake in Jiangsu Province and plays a very important role in the water system of the Grand Canal.

Separation of the Yellow River and the Grand Canal

Since the Yellow River changed its course during the Southern Song Dynasty, Suqian once became the main channel of the Yellow River, leading to frequent water disasters. In the 25th year of Kangxi's reign (1686) of the Qing Dynasty, Jin Fu, who was then the Director-General of River Channels, "dug a canal from Luoma Lake, passing through Suqian, Taoyuan to the outlet at Zhongjiazhuang in Qinghe, named the Middle River. Grain boats heading north would enter the Middle River, reaching Zhangzhuang Port directly, to avoid the hazardous stretch of the Yellow River spanning 180 *li*." Afterward, the Yellow River and the Grand Canal were completely separated, with the canal's waterway remaining unchanged for 200 years. This project also marked the total artificial control of the entire Grand Canal.[7]

---

6 Zhang Qiang, *Research on China's Canals and Grain Transport: Yuan, Ming, and Qing Dynasties Volume* (World Publishing Corporation, 2021), pp. 306–307.

7 Hu Mengfei, *An Introduction to China's Canal Cultural Heritage* (The Yellow River Water Conservancy Press, 2020), p. 32.

Why Did Qianlong Make Five Stays Here?

Dragon King Temple: The Lodging Place of Qianlong

The Dragon King Temple palace complex was initially built during the Shunzhi period of the Qing Dynasty and rebuilt in the 23rd year of Kangxi's reign (1684), originally named "Imperial Anlan Dragon King Temple." It was later expanded by successive emperors, forming the present three-courtyard, nine-entrance enclosed Qing Dynasty official building complex. Emperor Qianlong traveled to the south six times, for five of which he stayed at the Dragon King Temple palace and built pavilions and erected steles. Hence, the complex was colloquially known as "Qianlong's Temporary Palace." The southern part of the palace is the ancient theater, followed by the plaza, mountain gate, Imperial Stele Pavilion, Yi Hall, Dragon King Hall, Dayu Hall, etc., in the northward direction. Among them, the Imperial Stele Pavilion, which is 11 meters high with flying eaves and arches, has a unique design and is commonly referred to as the "Imperial Umbrella Pavilion." The Dragon King Temple palace complex is the most prestigious and largest among the numerous temporary palaces of Qianlong across the country.

The Dragon King Temple palace is located in Zaohe Town, a small water transport town that flourished due to the canal. During the Kangxi reign of the Qing Dynasty, Jin Fu dug the Zao River and the Middle Canal, making the area around the Zao River mouth a hub for river channel project management and grain transportation, and gradually thriving. In the 24th year of Kangxi (1685), Jin Fu petitioned to relocate the patrol inspector's office originally situated in Liumazhuang, along with the Canal Registrar, Zao River Flood Defense Commander, and other official institutions to the Zao River settlement, responsible for the repair and defense of the northern bank of the Yellow River, highlighting the importance of the Zao River mouth. Suqian, as "the key location for protecting and facilitating transportation and delivering supplies, the first bay of the thousand-mile canal," and the only city in the country that has three main navigation channels from different historical periods of the Tongji Canal of the Sui and Tang dynasties, the old course of the Yellow River from the Song to the Qing dynasties, and the Middle Canal of the Qing Dynasty, its prosperity over thousands of years is closely related to the Grand Canal. As for Qianlong's southern tour, the complete ceremonial boat fleet also started from Suqian, sailing south along the Grand Canal, making this place a must-stay for Qianlong's southern inspection tours. During the Xianfeng reign of the Qing Dynasty, the Yellow River changed its course away from Suqian, and the millennium-long canal grain transportation was then shifted to sea transportation. Zaohe Town, once a strategic canal node, gradually declined. Apart from the Dragon King Temple palace, Zaohe Town also has the Chen Family Courtyard, Confucian Temple ruins, Imperial Horse Road, and Imperial Dock ruins.

Yanghe Town: The Premier Liquor Town of the Grand Canal

Yanghe, also known as Baiyang River, was originally the name of a river that connected with Bailu Lake in the former Suqian County. Due to its low-lying terrain, Yanghe was referred to as a flood corridor,

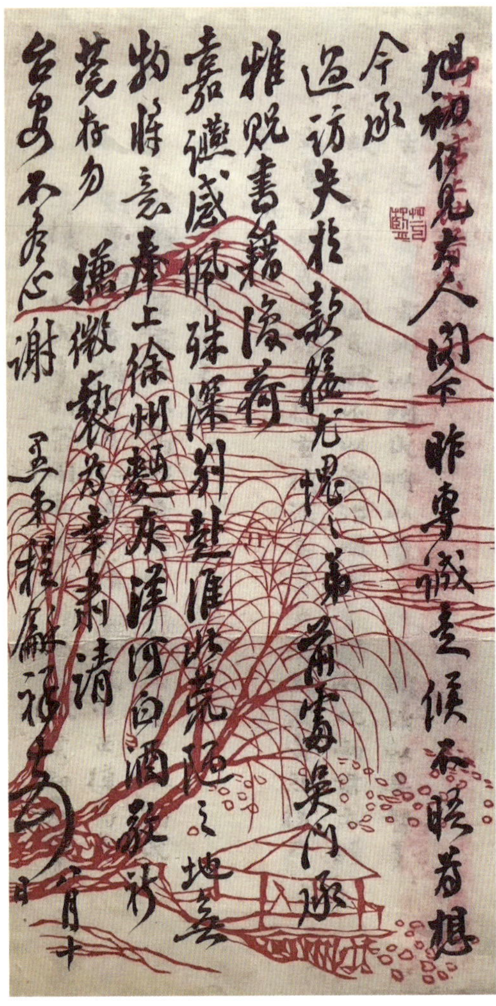

During the Daoguang period of the Qing Dynasty, the correspondence between Cheng Hexiang, the Salt Transport Commissioner, and Mao Changxi, the Minister of Personnel, mentioned using the liquor produced in Yanghe Town as a distinguished gift.

where billowing white waves reached the skies during the flood season, looking as vast as the ocean, hence the name. Later, during the Shunzhi era of the Qing Dynasty, the Baiyang River was silted up due to a breach in the Yellow River.

During the Sui Dynasty, Yanghe Town began to "draw from the northern techniques of Baiduo and Sangluo, adopting the southern methods of Qu'e and Ruoxia," utilizing "*shugu*" (秫谷, a variety of glutinous rice) for brewing liquor. By the Tang Dynasty, the Yangzhou area had a huge demand for liquor, and the liquor produced in Yanghe Town flowed southward along the canal, achieving the grand scene that "guests reciprocate poetic inspirations as river sails depart, and boats carry the fragrance of liquor up the canal." The liquor industry of Yanghe Town reached its zenith during the Ming and Qing dynasties. During the Ming Dynasty, the poet Zou Ji, saw the taverns lining up on both sides and the aroma of liquor filling the air, and wrote the lines "Baiyang River under the spring water is clear, / Baiyang River is full of buying guests" ("Ode to Baiyang River"). Emperor Qianlong of the Qing Dynasty also tasted the liquor from Yanghe Town during his stay in Suqian and highly praised it. Yanghe Town has a long history of liquor production, with the liquor industry as its economic pillar, inheriting the thousand-year-old culture of brewing.

Intangible Cultural Heritage—Hongze Lake Fish Drum

"Hongze Lake fish drum" is an art form of storytelling and dancing performed during olden times by "*shenhan*" (神汉, a shamanic figure or a kind of entertainer) for fishermen's paper-burning rituals to fulfill vows or pray at altars. It originated in the Tang Dynasty and stemmed from Mudun Island in Bancheng Town of Sihong County and the surrounding area of Hongze Lake. The dance is often performed on the lake surface, connecting two large boats to serve as the stage, where various divine effigies are suspended on the backdrop decorated with multi-colored paper-cut patterns. The performance follows strict procedures: the artists wear bright costumes, hold a one-sided sheepskin drum shaped like a banana leaf fan in their left hand, and use a thin bamboo rod in their right hand to strike the drum. They step in tune with the drum rhythm, the body swaying with the motion of the boat, imitating the vessel's journey through the water. The whole performance comprises music, dance, and narrative singing, with lyrics featuring intricate meters and diverse, charming rhymes. Performances are commonly seen when lake-area fishermen celebrate a bountiful harvest, pray, continue family lineages, or wish for longevity and blessings.

"Hongze Lake fish drum" carries the primitive memories of the fishermen's life and production in the lake area, blending the unique regional folk art and belief customs, serving as a direct reflection of the fishermen's aesthetic taste. With its rich regional characteristics, it holds significant reference value for studies in folklore, dialects, society, and history.

Plump Chicken

Plump chicken is one of the famous specialties of Siyang in Suqian. It is often served as the "first course" at banquets prepared for weddings and funerals in rural households. The top layer is as white as jade, and the bottom layer is red like agate, accompanied by seasonings such as ginger and green onions, creating a harmonious display of green, red, and white colors. When the plump chicken is served, the aroma is enticing. Tasting it reveals a texture that is neither too fatty nor greasy, but smooth and refreshing to the palate.

Wheel Cake

The wheel cake, prolific in Yanghe Town, gets its name from its appearance, which resembles a wheel. It has a golden-brown crust that is fragrant, crisp, and crumbly. The filling is sweet and rich in flavor.

Double-Skinned Carp

Double-skinned carp is a traditional specialty dish from Sihong County in Suqian City. The carp is crispy on the outside and tender on the inside, with a golden color that is very appealing. It is made with ingredients such as carp, lard, shiitake mushrooms, winter bamboo shoots, lean meat, peas, scallions, and ginger. The belly of the fish is stuffed full of shiitake mushrooms, fresh bamboo shoots, lean meat, and peas, creating a dish that is exceptionally delicious and leaves a long-lasting taste.

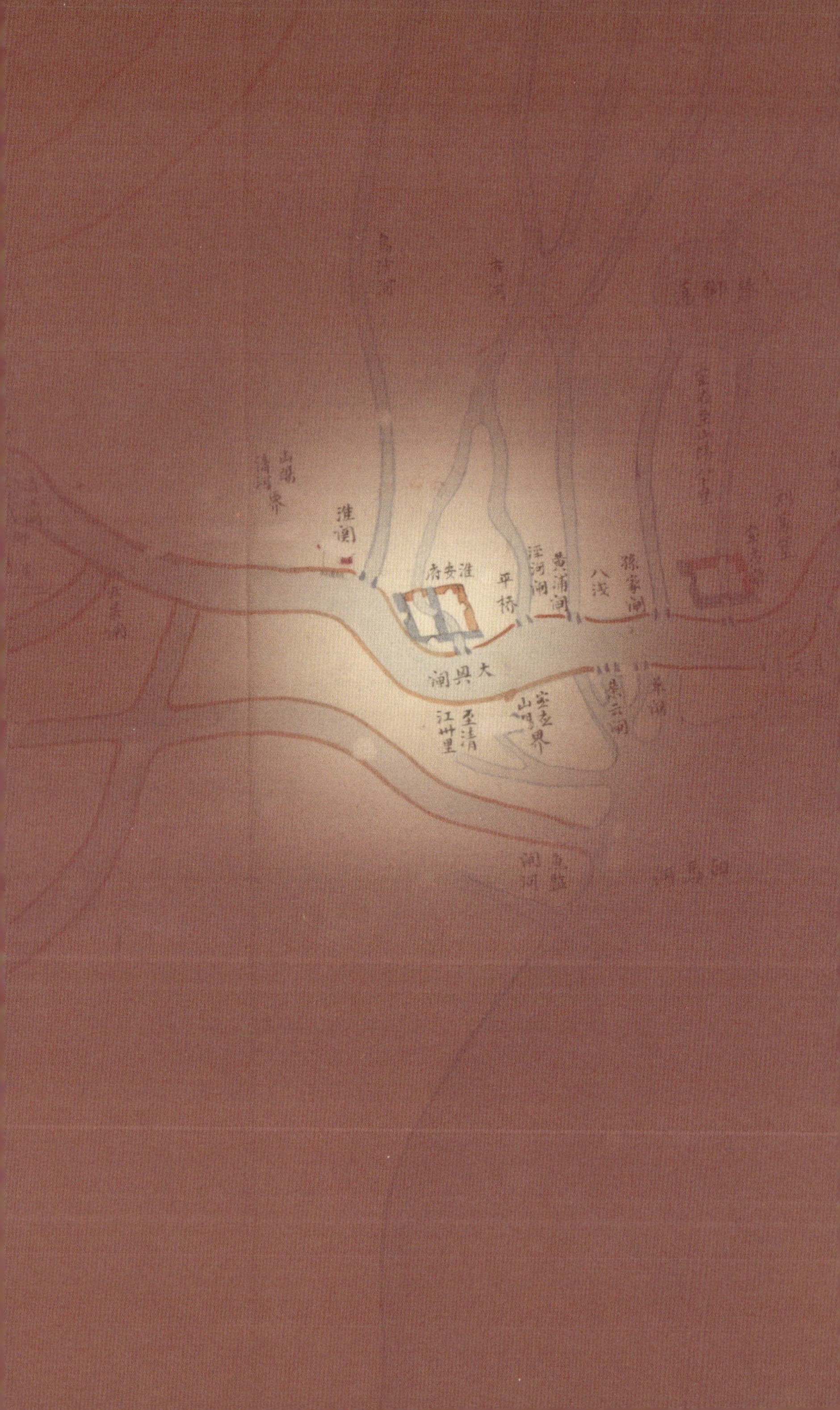
淮閘
淮安府
平桥
涇河閘
黄浦閘
八淺
孫家閘
大興閘
至清江卅里
山陽界

Huai'an:
A Strategic Point Connecting the North and South

The Magnificent "Southeast's Premier State"

A Strategic Junction of Water and Land Where North Meets South

The Huai River Must Be Properly Managed

Next to the Hongze Lake dike in Hongze District, Huai'an City, there stands a stele inscribed by Chairman Mao Zedong with the words "The Huai River Must Be Properly Managed." On May 4, 1951, the *People's Daily* reported that the Jianghuai area suffered another major flood, with most "entire villages submerged." Due to the fierce waters, the masses had no time to escape; some climbed trees, fell into the water by accident, and some were bitten to death by venomous snakes while on the trees ... Deeply moved, Chairman Mao immediately wrote these Chinese characters on the letterhead of the Chinese People's Revolutionary Military Commission, and then publicly published them in the *People's Daily* on May 15. These Chinese characters, written with full and forceful strokes, thick and strong, convey a majestic momentum, expressing a firm determination to manage the Huai River.

Throughout history, Huai'an has always been a key hub for canal transport, and rulers across the ages have been deeply concerned about canal transport here. After the Ming Dynasty, authorities set up a Canal Transport Governor's Office in Huai'an, responsible for managing canal transport affairs nationwide. Later, the Qing government moved the River Channel Governor's Office here to maintain the operation of the Grand Canal. At that time, there were only nine Governor's Offices in the whole country, and Huai'an alone hosted two of them, hence the saying, "Of the nine governors, Huai'an has two of them," which shows the significant status of Huai'an in the nation.

On October 1, 1952, the third anniversary of the founding of the People's Republic of China, in order to reflect the construction achievements after the establishment of New China, China Post issued the special postage stamps *The Great Motherland—Construction (Group II)*. The set consists of four stamps, of which the first stamp is "Huai River Water Gate," featuring an image of the Runheji Water Control Gate spanning across the Huai River, with Chairman Mao Zedong's inscription "The Huai River Must Be Properly Managed" above it.

Shanyang Bay

Shanyang Bay lies to the north of Huai'an City. It is not only a confluence of the Huai River but also meets the Si River, causing complex and winding river channels with swift currents here, posing a great risk of capsizing for the grain transport boats.[1] These boats only dared to enter Shanyang Bay by forming a long snake-like formation. Even then, the

1 Compiled by Institute of Historical Geography of Fudan University and Editorial Committee of the *Dictionary of Historical Place Names in China*, *Dictionary of Historical Place Names in China* (Jiangxi Education Publishing House, 1986), p. 55.

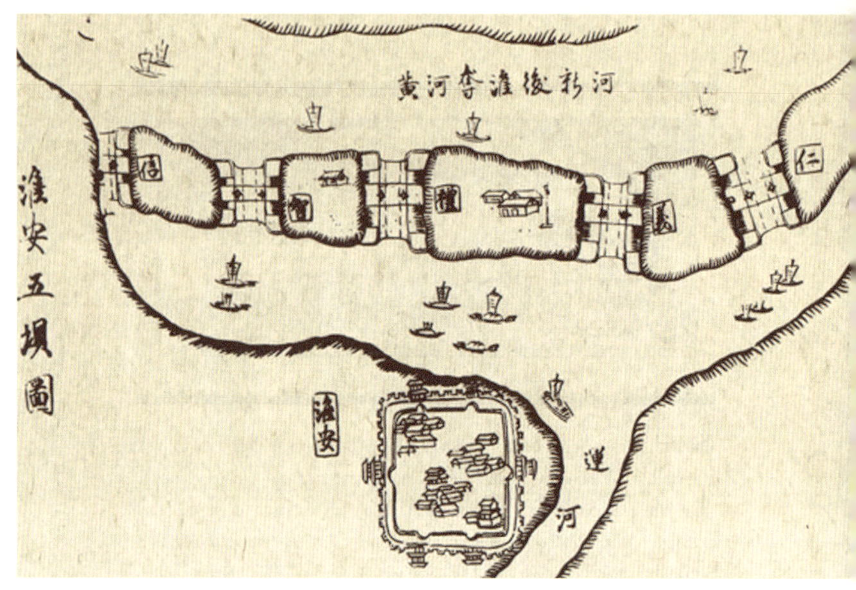

Map of the Five Dams of Huai'an (from Ji Xiangmeng and Du Tao, *The Five Dams of Huai'an*)

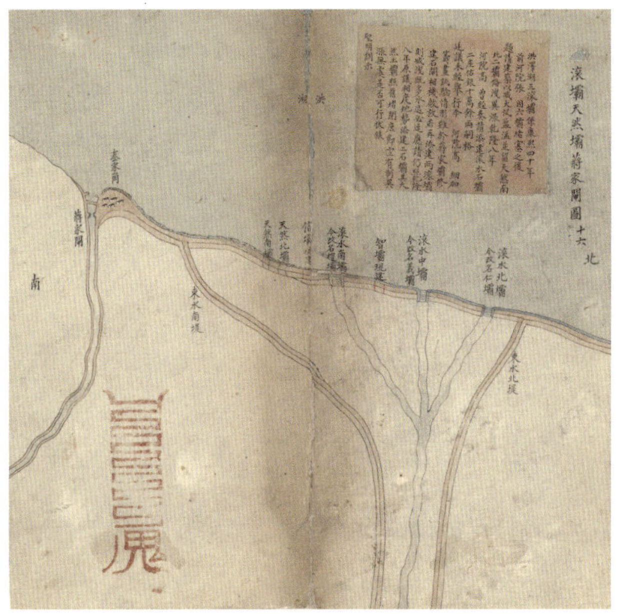

Map of the Dams and Barrages in the Lower Reaches of the Yellow River · Diagram of the Spillway Dams, Natural Dams, and Jiang Family Gate, No. 16

The diagram shows five dams named "Ren," "Yi," "Li," "Zhi," and "Xin," which were newly constructed rolling dams during the Kangxi and Qianlong periods of the Qing Dynasty. In the forty-third year of Kangxi (1704), three rolling dams named "Ren," "Yi," and "Li" were completed in this section. In the seventeenth year of the Qianlong (1752), the Zhi and Xin dams were added, and a "stonework" wall was built on the southern embankment, extending all the way to Jiang Dam.

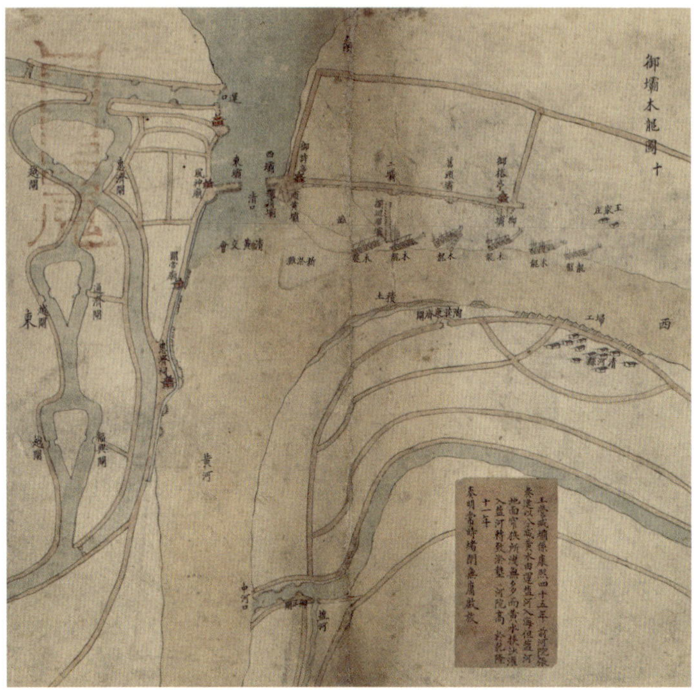

Map of the Dams and Barrages in the Lower Reaches of the Yellow River · Imperial Dam Wooden Dragon Diagram, No. 10

This diagram and the "wooden dragon" mentioned therein refer to a facility designed to force the river flow to change direction. This type of "flow-directing wooden dragon" channels the course of the Yellow River toward the northeast to lessen the impact of its powerful currents on the riverbanks. In the fourth year of Qianlong (1739), when Grand Secretary and Military Commission Minister Ortai inspected the river works in Jiangnan, he observed that the Taozhuang diversion canal was long and slightly curved, experiencing cycles of opening and silting. He decided to place wooden dragons below the Imperial Dam to further force the mainstream of the Yellow River toward the northern bank. Initially, one was built, followed by four more, respectively named the First Wooden Dragon, Second Wooden Dragon, Third Wooden Dragon, Fourth Wooden Dragon, and Fifth Wooden Dragon. The so-called "Imperial Dam," also known as the "Yellow River Control Dam," was constructed to resist the turbulent currents of the Yellow River.

danger was only halfway through. There were five dams named "Ren" (仁, Benevolence), "Yi" (义, Righteousness), "Li" (礼, Propriety), "Zhi" (智, Wisdom), and "Xin" (信, Trust). Grain transport boats would enter the Huai River via the Ren and Yi dams, while merchant ships would enter through the Li, Zhi, and Xin dams.[2] When passing each dam, the boats had to unload the grain and tow the vessel over the dam using manpower or animal power, then reload the grain and continue sailing northward. Furthermore, the boats had to sail against the current for sixty *li* on the Huai River, where the waves were tumultuous, making the journey extremely perilous and laborious for the crew.

The Qingkou node in Shanyang Bay is a hydraulic engineering heritage area. Historically, the Qingkou node was one of the most technologically sophisticated projects on the Grand Canal of China. Within its area of 49 square kilometers, there are 53 different types of cultural heritages. Over the Ming and Qing dynasties, a great number of financial, material, and human resources were invested continuously for its maintenance and management, ensuring the transport capacity of the Grand Canal and the smoothness of the canal shipping. In 2014, the Grand Canal of China was designated as a World Cultural Heritage Site, with the Qingkou node included as an important heritage area in the listing.[3]

Chen Xuan

In the thirteenth year of the Yongle era (1415) of the Ming Dynasty, Chen Xuan, the Earl of Pingjiang and the General of the Grain Transport, excavated the Qingjiang River following the old course of the Sha River of the Northern Song Dynasty (960–1127). The reason for doing this

---

2 Ji Xiangmeng and Du Tao, *The Five Dams of Huai'an*, http://wshuaian.org/show.asp?id=3074.

3 Hu Mengfei, *An Introduction to China's Canal Cultural Heritage* (The Yellow River Water Conservancy Press, 2020), p. 73.

Portrait of Chen Xuan

was both simple and very important. The Ming Emperor Zhu Di was eager to shift the political center from Nanjing to Beijing, urgently needed to transport grain from the south to the north. Was maritime transport an option? No, it wasn't. The specific reasons are widely debated. For example, the historian Huang Renyu believed that the Ming emperors, concerned with security, neglected commerce and foreign trade,[4] despite Zheng He's magnificent voyages to the Western Seas, which were more about diplomacy in the political arena. After all, before the founding of the Ming Dynasty, the grain transport by sea of the Yuan Dynasty was often cut off by local warlords like Zhang Shicheng. Therefore, Chen Xuan was ordered to be responsible for transporting grain from the Yangtze River basin to the garrisons in Beijing and Liaodong every year. From 1403 to 1415, Chen Xuan dedicated himself to the management and dredging of the canal, eventually terminating maritime transport and transporting an amount of grain far exceeding the emperor's request, even reaching five million *dan* (a traditional Chinese unit of volume and weight, 1 dan ≈ 60 kg in the Ming Dynasty).[5] Six years after Chen Xuan completed the canal management project, Zhu Di moved the capital to Beijing.

---

[4] [American] Huang Renyu, *Taxation and Transportation in the Ming Dynasty* (Jiuzhou Press, 2019), p. 190.

[5] [American] Luther C. Goodrich and Fang Chaoying (original editors), eds. Li Xiaolin and Feng Jinpeng, *Biographies of Prominent Figures in the Ming Dynasty (Volume 1)* (Beijing Times Chinese Press, 2015), pp. 222–223.

Plank Sluice

The Yifeng Sluice is one of the four major sluices built at the opening of Qingjiangpu (the others being Qingjiang Sluice, Fuxing Sluice, and Xinzhuang Sluice). These sluice gates were overseen and constructed by Chen Xuan in 1415 to adjust waterways such as Shanyang Bay, facilitating grain transport. In 1416, a plank sluice was added downstream of the Yifeng Sluice. Initially, it was quite rudimentary, using wooden planks as the gate. A year later, it was rebuilt as a stone sluice, but the name "Plank Sluice" has remained to this day. Three miles northwest of Plank Sluice is Yifeng Sluice. The two sluices are very close to each other, and Plank Sluice was also managed by the officials of Yifeng Sluice, hence Plank Sluice was also called Upper Yifeng Sluice, and Yifeng Sluice was called Lower Yifeng Sluice.

In the 17th year of the Wanli era (1589) of the Ming Dynasty, the intrusion of silt from the Yellow River made it difficult for grain transport ships to pass through the sluices. Consequently, the Yuehe Sluice

The ruins of Plank Sluice

was opened to facilitate passage. During the reign of Emperor Chongzhen in the Ming Dynasty, the main channel of the Plank Sluice became silted and was subsequently abandoned. Ships passing through the area were diverted to the Yuehe Sluice instead. In the Qing Dynasty, during the Shunzhi era, the Yuehe Sluice was also abandoned due to silting. Today, the ruins of Plank Sluice are located in the ecological and cultural tourism area of Huai'an City, enclosed by Meigao Road, Xiangyu Avenue, and the Li Canal.

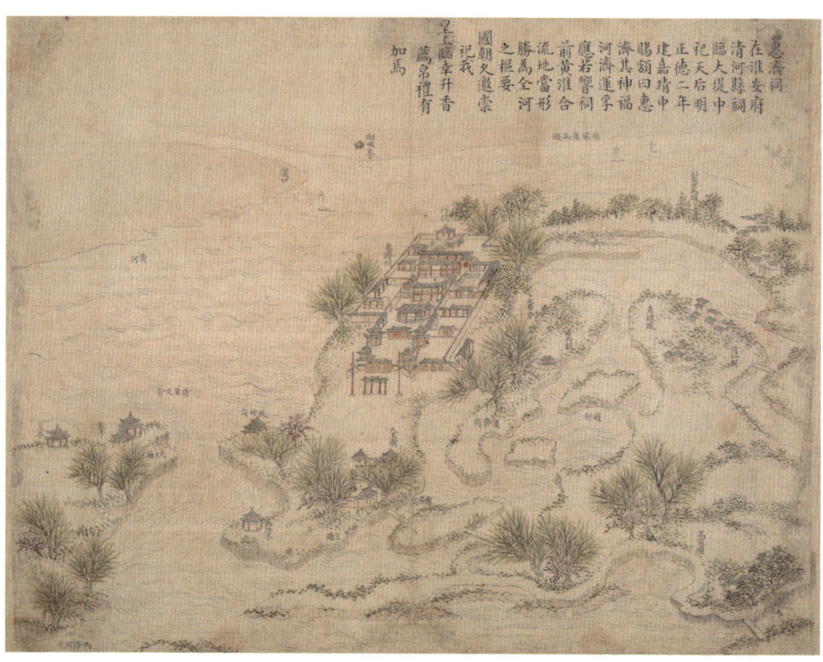

Map of Qianlong Emperor's Southern Tour and Stops (The image depicts Huai'an Huiji Temple.)

The Granary of the World

"The granary of the world" is one of the nicknames for Qingjiangpu. Huai'an boasts four famous granaries, among which Changying granary is one of the most important of the five major granaries near the canal during the Ming Dynasty.[6] It had a vast storage capacity, consisting of 40 areas, 80 warehouses, totaling 800 storage rooms, which could hold 1.5 million *dan* of grain for transport,[7] equivalent to 114,800 tons of grain. "The tribute from all counties is stored here to supply the capital's needs, with the entries amounting to no less than a million."[8] The function of Changying granary extended beyond just transferring and storing grain. At the time, officials' salaries were not solely paid in currency such as silver but also compensated with grain. Additionally, the stationed troops across various locations also required military rations, so Changying granary also served the purpose of distributing official salaries and supplying military rations. Furthermore, the storage of grain played a stabilizing role in local prices. It could even serve as a relief granary in times of disaster.

---

6 "Canal-side granary" refers to granaries near the canal used for the transfer of grain tributes. During the Yongle period of the Ming Dynasty, the canal-side granary was established in five locations: Huai'an, Xuzhou, Dezhou, Linqing, and Tianjin.

7 Huai'an Municipal Political Consultative Conference Cultural and Historical Committee, *A Brief Study of Qingjiangpu Town*, http://zx.huaian.gov.cn/col/14069_277241/art/16725024/1674888031218EA8W2zEn.html.

8 Yang Hong and Xie Chun, *Comprehensive Records of Grain Transport*, annotated by Xun Delin and He Zhenhua (Local Records Publishing House, 2006).

Map of the Salt Fields in North and South Huai River Region and Salt Transport Routes in Four Provinces (section of Huai'an)

This map was approximately created in the early years of the Qianlong era of the Qing Dynasty, and it lacks a title. *Map of the Salt Fields in North and South Huai River Region and Salt Transport Routes in Four Provinces* is temporarily named according to the legend provided on the upper part of the map. Accompanied by its legend, the map describes the transportation routes of the salt ships in the south and north of the Huai River, along with the salt production and distribution situations of twenty fields in the south of the Huai River and three fields in the north of the Huai River.

The map presents the transportation routes of salt ships in the Huai'an area and the distribution of river channels during the early Qianlong era of the Qing Dynasty.

How Does Huai'an "Clear and Control the Huai River"?

Huai'an Prefectural Government Office

The Huai'an Prefectural Government Office was originally built during the Southern Song Dynasty as the Wutong Temple, and during the Yuan Dynasty, it became the Yitan Wanhu Prefecture. In the third year of the Hongwu era (1370) of the Ming Dynasty, the prefect of Huai'an, Yao Bin, based renovations on this foundation, transforming it into the Huai'an Prefectural Government Office, which continued to be used until the end of the Qing Dynasty. The main gate of the government office faced south toward the street, with a screen wall in front and archways to the east and west. The columns were made of Phoebe zhennan, with the east archway inscribed with "important town along the Huai River" and the west one with "famed state facing the sea." During the Ming Dynasty, the jurisdictional scope of the government office included Haizhou (present-day Lianyungang), Pizhou, and nine counties: Shanyang, Qinghe, Andong (present-day Lianshui), Yancheng, Taoyuan (present-day Siyang), Shuyang, Ganyu, Suqian, and Suining, with the seat of government established in Shanyang County (present-day Huai'an District), making it the largest prefecture in Jiangsu Province by area. The government office has undergone several

Inside the Huai'an Prefectural Government Office

renovations and is essentially laid out in a symmetrical form along a central axis, covering a total area of nearly 20,000 square meters, with more than 50 buildings and over 600 rooms. "Without governance, the people cannot be managed; without officials, the policies cannot be carried out; without the office, no official can stand." The Huai'an Prefectural Government Office encompassed multiple functions including official workspaces, living quarters, and a prison as a political institution. It is the only remaining government office along the Grand Canal from Beijing to Hangzhou, and it is also one of the two best-preserved government offices in the country.

The Grand Canal Governor's Office Site

The original Huai'an Prefectural Government Office has now been divided into sections including the Huai'an Prefectural Government Office, the China Grand Canal Museum, and the Grand Canal Governor's Office Site. Zhenhuai Tower marks the southernmost end, its name embodying the wishes of the people of Huai'an for stability within the Huai River. Historically, the transportation hub for the south-to-north grain transfer and the north-to-south salt transportation was located in Huai'an, which thereby became the command center for the canal transport. During the Sui Dynasty, grain from the southeast was transported to Chuzhou and then transferred to the Tongji Canal heading north; a special canal transport office was established in Huai'an. By the Song Dynasty, grain from the six routes of the southeast entered the Bian River through Huai'an and flowed directly to the capital. During the Ming and Qing dynasties, the Grand Canal Governor's Office was set up in Huai'an. The *Revised Annals of Shanyang County* from the Qing Dynasty records: "All the grain ships from Huguang, Jiangxi, Zhejiang, and Jiangnan arrive at Shanyang in succession. After inspection and categorization by the canal governor, they proceed one by one through the Grand Canal. Even though the grain ships from Shandong and Henan do not pass through this place, they also adhere to its regulations from afar. Thus, the canal administration extends through seven provinces, with Shanyang being a strategic throat and key point." The official name of the Grand Canal Governor's Office in the Qing Dynasty was "Zongcao Buyuan Yamen" (总漕部院衙门), and the Grand Canal Governor was referred to as "*caotai*" (漕台, governor of grain transport) or "*caoshuai*" (漕帅, marshal of grain transport). From the collection of grain taxes to the storerooms, the progression of the grain boats northward, inspections, and suppression and transportation efforts were all personally supervised by the governor. Politically, the Grand Canal Governor's Office established the central status of Shanyang in canal transport and economically, it promoted the prosperity of the region. Today, the site of the office, as one of the World Cultural Heritage sites of the Grand Canal of China, houses the China Grand Canal Museum to the north. The museum displays a multitude of relics related to canal transport, serving as an excellent place for people to learn about the history of canal transportation.

Qingyan Garden

In the middle and later periods of the Ming Dynasty, the management of river regulation and grain transportation was chaotic and complex, with unclear distribution of powers and responsibilities resulting in power struggles and inefficiencies. Consequently, during the Qing Dynasty, these two matters were placed under the management of different ministers. As previously mentioned, the Grand Canal Governor's Office managed only the transport of grain, while the regulation of rivers was overseen by the River Transport Governor. The early River Transport Governors were responsible not only for the Grand Canal but also for the Yellow River. The original Governor's

Office was established in Jining and later relocated to Qingjiangpu (present-day Qingjiangpu District, Huai'an City). Qingyan Garden was the River Transport Governor's Office and its attached garden in the Qing Dynasty. "*Qingyan*" (清晏), meaning "clear rivers and peaceful seas" in Chinese, originates from the seventeenth year of the Kangxi Emperor (1678) when Jin Fu became the first River Transport Governor stationed there. Throughout the Qing Dynasty, there were 56 tenures held by 45 River Transport Governors in Huai'an over 183 years. In the eleventh year of the Xianfeng Emperor (1861), the Qing government abolished the position of the River Transport Governor, and the duty of managing river affairs was combined with that of the Grand Canal Governor, who relocated to Qingyan Garden for 43 years. In the thirtieth year of the Guangxu Emperor (1904), the canal governor's role was also abolished, and the office was converted into the Jiangbei Governor's Office. In the following year (1905), the Jiangbei Military Governor took over the site. Qingyan Garden was initially constructed in the fifteenth year of the Yongle Emperor (1417) as an office for the Ministry of Revenue during the Ming Dynasty. It was expanded by subsequent River Transport Governors, and by the Qing Dynasty, it had become a garden featuring attractions such as the Hefang Academy, Zhan Pavilion, Ye Garden, and Qingyan Boat, embodying both the exquisite beauty of the south and the grandeur of the north, earning the reputation as the "finest garden in the Jianghuai region."

Huai'an Tax Station

In ancient times, the central government often established tax stations at key water transport intersections and goods distribution centers to collect transit taxes on passing goods, vehicles, and ships. In the fourth year of the Xuande reign of the Ming Dynasty (1429), the court began to set up institutions specifically for collecting ship taxes along the

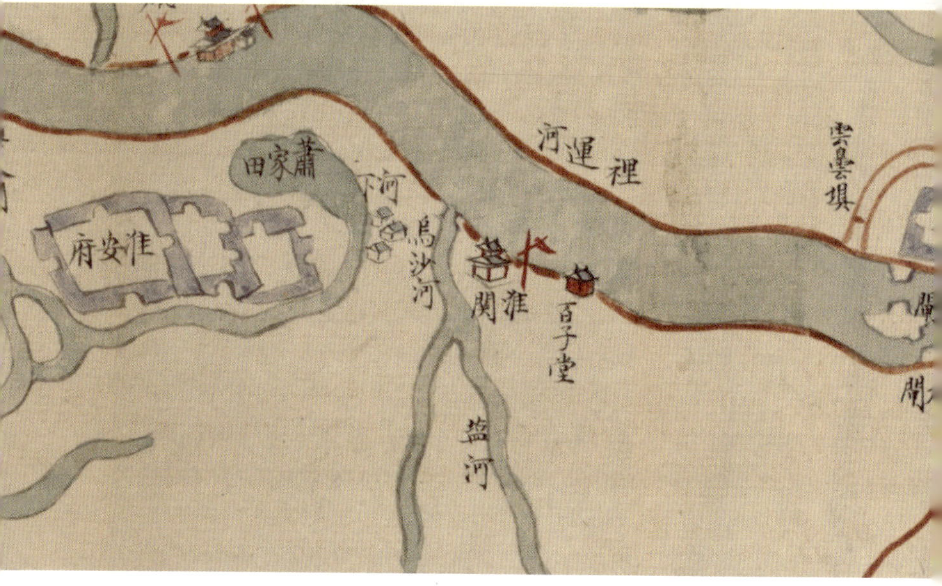

Complete Map of Canal Transport Routes (partial)

From the map, it can be seen that in ancient times, Huai Station was located close to the Salt River and was established adjacent to the Li Canal. Its location was not far from Huai'an Prefecture, where the higher-level administrative unit was located.

inland waterway routes, known as "tax stations." At that time, tax stations were widely distributed along the Grand Canal, the Yangtze River, and the Huai River basin. By the Wanli period of the Ming Dynasty, the most important eight tax stations were retained, of which seven were located along the Grand Canal. These were, from north to south, Chongwenmen, Hexiwu, Linqing, Huai'an, Yangzhou, Hushuguan, and Beixinguan (Hangzhou), with only Jiujiang in Jiangxi not situated along the Grand Canal. These tax stations were all under the jurisdiction of the central court's Ministry of Revenue and were managed uniformly by it. The Huai'an Tax Station was the largest of the eight major tax stations, commonly known as Huai Station among the populace. The ancient town of Banzha formed a market surrounding the customs office during the Ming and Qing dynasties, gradually evolving into a town. It declined along with the abolition of the customs office during the Republic of China period. The Huai'an Tax Station was restored in 2006 and has now become a part of the Li Canal Cultural Corridor.

Qingjiang Shipyard

Since the Yongle period of the Ming Dynasty, the Qingjiang Shipyard in Huai'an has prospered greatly. As the Grand Canal gradually became navigable, the demand for cargo ships increased dramatically. Huai'an, located in the middle section of the canal, was a crucial hub between the Yangtze River and the Huai River. Additionally, the grain transportation from the southern regions would pass through Huai'an's warehouses for transfer. Therefore, the imperial court decided to establish the Qingjiang Shipyard in this location.[9] During the Ming Dynasty, shipbuilding was strictly regulated by the government, and only two shipyards were authorized, with the other one located in Weihe, Shandong Province.

[9] The site is located between Shanyang (present-day Huai'an District) and Qinghe (present-day Qingjiangpu District).

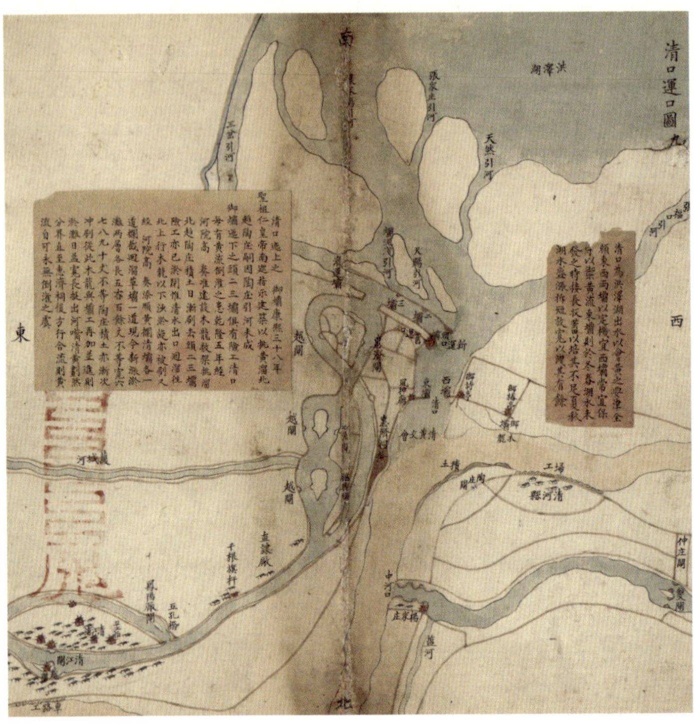

Map of the Dams and Barrages in the Lower Reaches of the Yellow River · Qingkou Port, No. 9

The location of the Qingjiang Sluice can be found in the bottom left corner of the map. This area is characterized by a complex network of waterways and turbulent currents. However, due to its strategic position at the confluence of rivers and lakes, it is of great importance. In ancient times, it was regarded as a vital node for water management. The Ming and Qing governments invested significant human and material resources to maintain their operation. Furthermore, due to its convenient transportation, both the Ming Dynasty's Qingjiang Shipyard and grain warehouses were established in this area.

Private shipbuilding was not permitted. The Qingjiang Shipyard was even more important than the Weihe Shipyard, and it accounted for over 70% of the country's ship production.[10] This laid the foundation for the thriving shipbuilding industry in Huai'an.

Intangible Cultural Heritage: Ten-*Fan* Drums

The ten-*fan* drums (十番锣鼓) originated in the Ming Dynasty and are a highly unique form of folk instrumental ensemble performance. The term "ten-*fan*" refers to the use of ten percussion instruments to alternately produce various drum patterns (drum scores). Due to the numerous patterns, there is a historical saying in Huai'an: "Ten *fans*, ten tunes." The performance of ten-*fan* drums is primarily associated with folk religious rituals and customary ceremonies. The performance can be categorized into two styles: seated and mobile, with techniques including blowing, pulling, plucking, singing, striking, and beating. The performance seeks complexity and variation in its musical forms using drums and gongs.

The ten-*fan* drums gained popularity during the Wanli era in the late Ming Dynasty, particularly in the Jiangnan region centered around Suzhou and Wuxi. The Chuzhou ten-*fan* drums were recreated by the folk musician Sun Yuqing of Chuzhou during the Jiaqing period of the Qing Dynasty. He boldly integrated drums and gongs with Kunqu opera, altering the rhythms and adding lyrics that reflected social life. By 1939, there were several groups performing ten-*fan* drums in Huai'an, known at the time as "*tangzi*" (堂子).

---

[10] According to the Ming-era scholar Xi Shu's *Records of Grain Transport Ships*: "In the seventh year of Yongle, Qingjiang and Weihe factories began construction in Huai'an and Linqing … All shallow-draft ships from Nanjing, (Nan) Zhili, Jiangxi, Huguang, and Zhejiang were built at Qingjiang, while ocean-going ships and shallow-draft ships from Shandong and Northern Zhili were built at Weihe." "In the third year of Jiajing … all ships previously built at Weihe were consolidated and produced at the Qingjiang factory."

The instruments used in Chuzhou's ten-*fan* drums are divided into two categories: civil and martial. The performance blends singing, striking, and playing, with drum patterns and tunes interspersed throughout, culminating in a finale with a drum tune. Additionally, there are purely instrumental pieces where drums are incorporated at the musical climax to enhance the atmosphere and intensify the expressive power.

Soft-Shelled Eel

"Huai'an, a city that satisfies every palate from the south to the north." The top culinary delight of Huai'an is the "soft-shelled eel." The dish is prepared using the spine of an eel, known as "pen-holder green," about one foot long, cooked in a rich broth. The finished dish has a dark, glossy appearance, with a tender and delicious taste that is intensely flavorful. When served, the eel's spine coils around the plate like the flowing sleeves of Chang'e, the moon goddess, hence the alternative name "Chang'e dancing gracefully."

Kaiyang Reed Shoot

Kaiyang reed shoot is a classic representative dish of Huai'an. Reed shoots, also known as grass shoots, are the tender stems of cattails. They have a fresh, crisp taste and are very refreshing. They can be used in soups, cold dishes, stir-fries, or be steamed. In Huai'an, "no banquet is complete without reed shoots," and they are an essential dish for entertaining guests.

Xuyi Crayfish

Xuyi crayfish is a famous specialty and delicacy from Xuyi County in Huai'an City. The crayfish meat is tender, plump, and juicy. The primary flavor profile for cooking Xuyi crayfish is spicy, blending the freshness of the river with a spicy kick, leaving a lingering fragrance and an unforgettable taste.

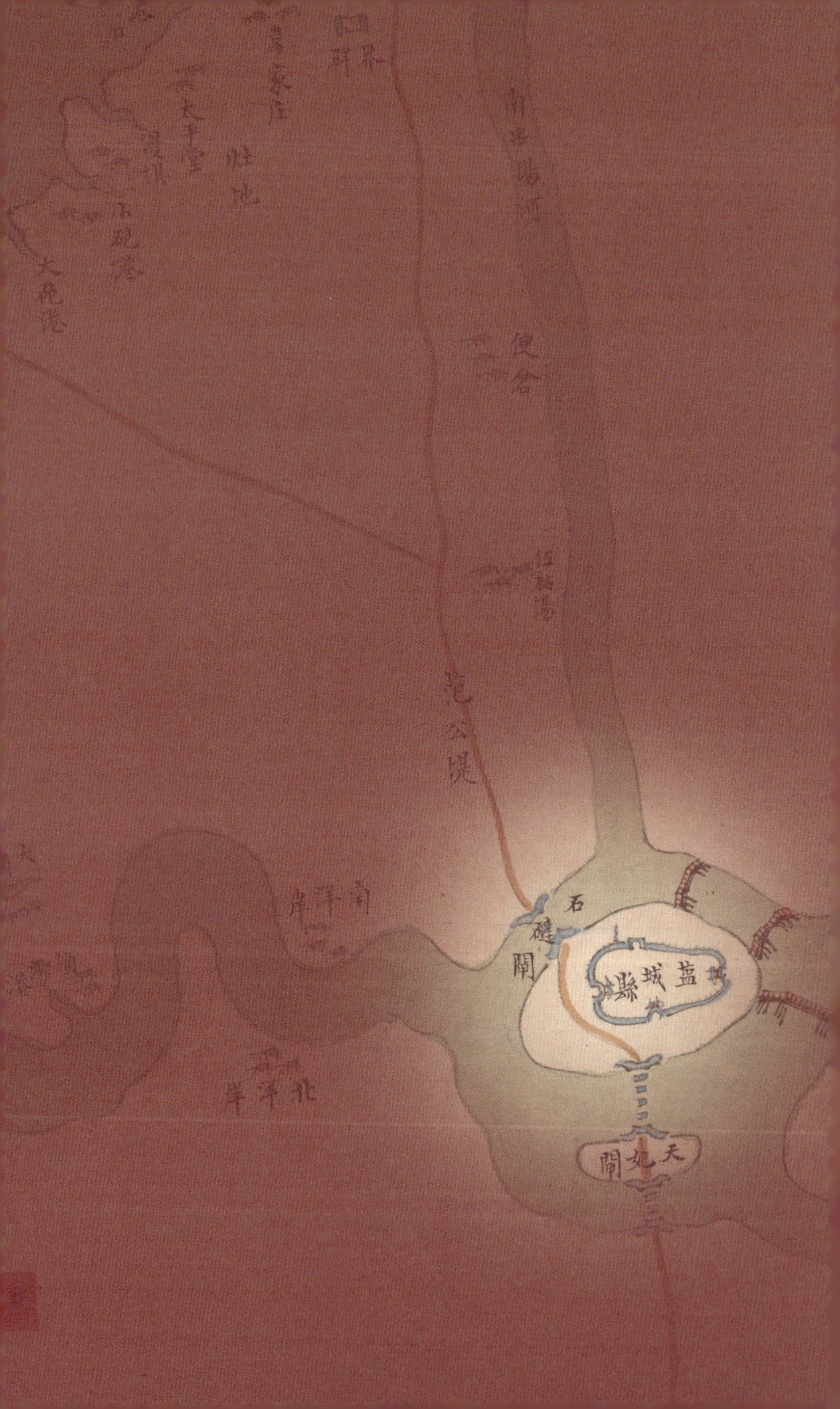

南串場河
便倉
伍祐場
范公堤
南洋岸
北洋岸
石䃮閘
盐城縣
天妃閘

Yancheng:
The City of a Hundred Rivers

The Salt Culture of "Salting the World"

Boiling Salt

Yandu County and Rivers Crossing Salt Fields

The Grand Canal does not pass through Yancheng. However, in the city, canals are not rare. According to statistics, Yancheng now has 410 county-level rivers and 4,192 township-level rivers. Surprisingly, most of these rivers were not naturally formed. Instead, they were dug as branch roads in the Han Ditch, the predecessor of the old Tongyang Canal. These rivers connect rivers and lakes and also facilitate food transportation, trade, travel, and even the local culture. The earliest name of Yancheng is "Yandu County," for in ancient Chinese, canals were called "渎," pronounced as "*du*." Large-scale canal excavations like this, lasting for thousands of years, are mostly unknown.

During the dynasties of Tang and Song, Yancheng was a flood-stricken coastal town. To protect the city, Fan Zhongyan led the construction of a dam, which is now named as Fan Gong Causeway ("Fan Gong" [范公] is the honorific title for Fan Zhongyan). The local people excavated the sites of Fan Gong Causeway and found that the then ditches connected with all salt fields, providing favorable conditions for the transportation of salt products and the local people's lives as well. Therefore, these rivers are also named as "Rivers Crossing Salt Fields."

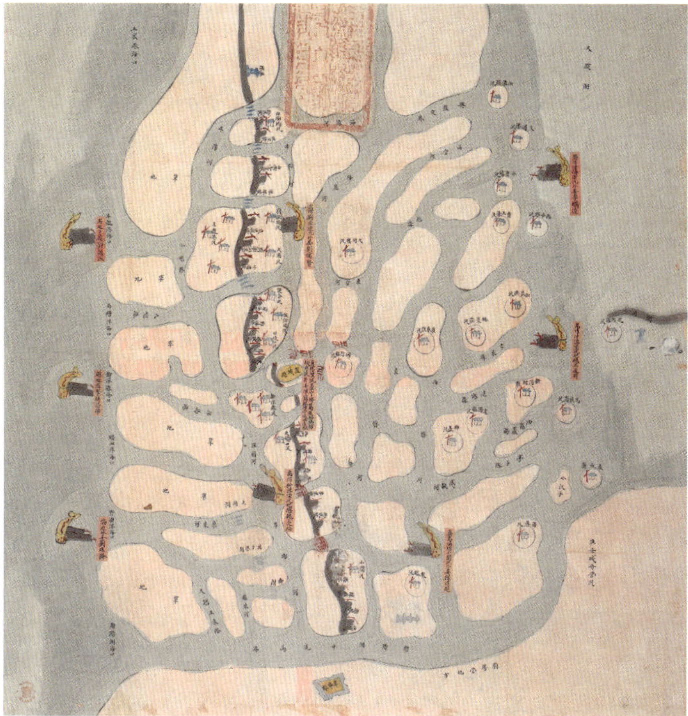

Map of Rivers and Seas of Yancheng

The picture was made after the 19th year of Daoguang (1839). The specific year is unknown and the original picture cannot be identified. Based on the contents, the map is named as *Map of Rivers and Seas of Yancheng*. The full map shows the distribution of rivers, seawalls and barracks under the jurisdiction of Yancheng Camp. In the picture, the canals are crisscrossed, vividly presenting the rivers crossing salt fields accessible in all directions in the town.

According to the *Annals of Yancheng County* during the Guangxu period in the Qing Dynasty, the jurisdiction of Yancheng Camp, consisting of both water and land, covers an area of about 200 *li*. Its north borders the ocean opposite Sheyang Lake, with 120 *li* long. Besides, the jurisdiction of Yancheng Camp includes 51 smaller camps, including those of Liuzhuang, Xiaoguan, Xinyang, and Shagou, to name only a few. All these can be found on the map.

The Rebellion of the Seven Vassal States

At the beginning of the establishment of the Western Han Dynasty (206 BC–AD 25), in 201 BC, Liu Bang, the founding emperor of the Han Dynasty, established Yandu County in the northwest of Yancheng and appointed his nephew Liu Bi King of Wu, who was in charge of this place.[1] According to Sima Qian (a famous official recording history in the Western Han Dynasty), Liu Bang felt regret when he summoned Liu Bi and said that he found Liu Bi looked like to rebel.[2] After all, Yandu County was a treasure land, tempting enough for any ruler to grab it for himself. After Liu Bi arrived, he dug the east Han Ditch and connected Rugao and other places to Yangzhou. The rivers and canals were only used to deliver salt products, not for transportation.[3] According to Sima Qian, Liu Bi, over 60 years old, cast money in the mountains and boiled the sea for salt, preparing to rebel against the central government by assembling those "heroes." During the rebellion of the seven vassal states that broke out under the reign of Emperor Jing of the Han Dynasty, Liu Bi was the prime victim of the policy of cutting the vassal states. Consequently, Liu Bi became the head of the rebellious troops. After the rebellion had been suppressed, Emperor Wu of the Han Dynasty decisively implemented the policy in a strict manner that the trade of salt and iron should only be conducted by the authority, and any form of private salt trafficking was illegal.

---

1 Feng Yanjun, "A Textual Research on the Time of Yandu County in the Early Han Dynasty and Yancheng County in the Late Jin Dynasty," *Pictorial Geography*, no. 10 (2020).

2 Sima Qian, *Records of the Grand Historian · A Biography of King Bi of Wu.*

3 Liu Wenqi, *Records of Yangzhou Waterway.*

Changxin Palace lamp of the Western Han Dynasty

The Salt Industry of the Huai River Region: The Finest in the World

As a Chinese goes, "All the people are hustling for profits and benefits."[4] The "profits and benefits" of Yancheng come from salt. In all past dynasties, Yancheng served as an important town to produce salt, mostly traveled by water. As a coastal town in the Han Dynasty, Yancheng is famous for the production of salt. In the Ming Dynasty, the production and sales income of salt in the Huai River estuary bay and the Yangtze River Delta reached as high as 680,000 taels of silver, plus that of the Qinhuangdao area, the 180,000 taels of silver, exceeding two-thirds of

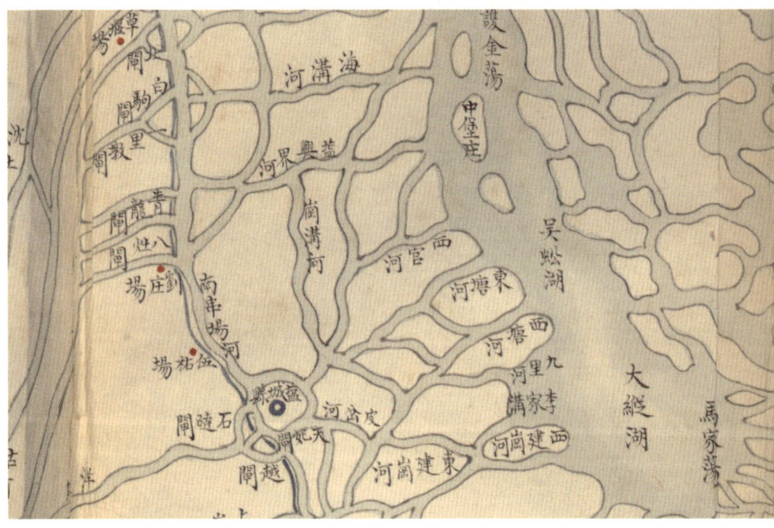

Map of the Salt Fields in North and South Huai River Region and Salt Transport Routes in Four Provinces (section of Yancheng)

Surrounded by rivers, lakes, and numerous water gates, Yancheng enjoys a favorable condition in salt production and transportation.

4 Sima Qian, *Records of the Grand Historian · Biographies of Merchants.*

the country's total revenue. Most of the salt first passes through the canals before being dispersed to the national markets.[5]

The Yellow River Altered the Runways of the Huai River

The capture of the Huai River refers to the historical events in which the inflow from the Yellow River occupied the waterways of the Huai River into the sea. Among them, the capture of the Huai River in the Southern Song Dynasty changed the fate of Yancheng. In October, the first year of Jianyan (1127) in the Southern Song Dynasty, Emperor Gaozong, despite the dissuasion of his ministers, fled to Yangzhou in the name of his visit to the southeast, leading to a massive offensive by the Jin (a kingdom northern to the Song Dynasty) army. In October 1128, Jin generals Wanyan Zonghan and Wanyan Zongfu joined forces in Puyang on the north bank of the Yellow River. In order to block the Jin Army, Du Chong, acting defensive general in Kaifeng, dug the Yellow River dam to divert the water to attack the enemy. Instead of stopping the enemy, the move drowned more than 200,000 local people. Therefore, the Yellow River flooded and diverted to the Huai River, changing the landform of today's northern Jiangsu region. Before the Southern Song Dynasty, Yancheng, adjacent to the sea, was well-known for its flourishing salt industry. The famous Fan Gong Causeway in the city was originally a seawall. Due to the diversion of the Yellow River with a large amount of sediment deposited, a vast alluvial plain has been formed on the shore. Nowadays, the coastline of Yancheng has retreated 50 or 60 kilometers from the Fan Gong Causeway, which has greatly changed the way of life of Yancheng people. The original coastal rivers crossing salt fields have has evolved into rivers connecting the inside of the city.

---

5 [American] Huang Renyu, *The Grain Transport of the Ming Dynasty* (Jiuzhou Press, 2019), p. 161.

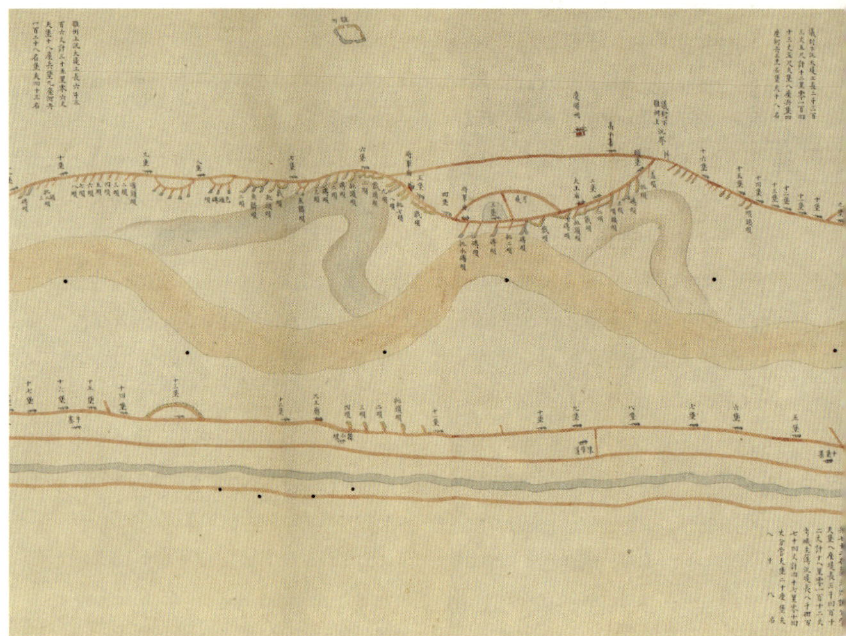

Map of Dams in the Waterways of the Yellow River in Six Provinces **(partial)**

The map is made from the fourth year to the fifth year of Daoguang's reign (1824–1825) in the Qing Dynasty. The picture clearly shows the Yellow River channel, as well as its changing old and new river roads in the areas of the Yangtze River and the Huai River. In fact, over the past thousand years, the Yellow River has been diverted more than 20 times. Therefore, the lower reaches of the Yellow River were often thought of as "going east or west, having no sense of direction."

A Gourd Ladle City

Yancheng is also called a "gourd ladle city." During the reign of Yongle (1403–1424) in the Ming Dynasty, officials rebuilt the wall on the basis of the wall base of the Song and Yuan dynasties. Overlooking the whole city, they found it shaped like a gourd ladle, so they called it a "gourd ladle city." Ouyang Xiu (1007–1072) said, "There are all mountains around Chuzhou," but the reason why the people of Yancheng built a "gourd ladle city" was that "the salt farms around the city" would scoop salt with a "gourd ladle" and flourish. In addition, Yancheng has been plagued by floods since ancient times, so a "gourd ladle" expresses the expectations of the locals for an everlasting peaceful and well-being life.

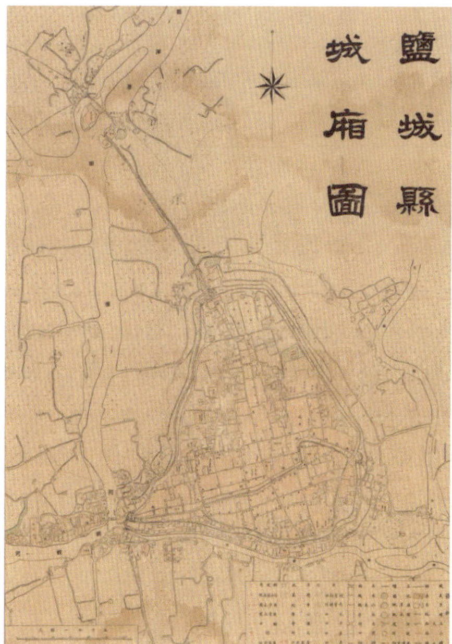

Map of Yancheng County (1922)

Measured in the seventh year of the Republic of China (1918), the map was printed in the eleventh year of the Republic of China (1922). On the map, the urban outline of Yancheng looks like a gourd ladle.

Salt Worker

Salt laborers were historically referred to as "salt workers," "salt pan laborers," or "salt-producing households." During the Ming and Qing dynasties, the management of salt laborers (those engaged in salt production) was the most stringent in history. In the early Ming Dynasty, the court established a system where criminals, vagrants, or refugees were relocated to coastal areas to produce salt. They were registered as salt-producing households in their household registries, meaning that their descendants were also required to engage in salt production, with no other career options available. These salt workers registered as salt-producing households were considered "lowly people" in the Ming and Qing dynasties, yet these so-called "lowly people" were responsible for producing the majority of China's wealth at the time.

Making Salt

There are six processes in making salt: crushing, drying ash, pouring brine, testing lotus, boiling salt, and picking flowers. Although the names sound good, every process involves very intense physical labor. In ancient times, spring and summer were the salt seasons, during which the salt workers had to expose themselves to the scorching sunshine. In addition, they soaked in brine all year round and lived in the smoky air from the stoves. The brine had a strong irritation to the skin, resulting in cracking. When the wound was in touch with the brine, blood flowed in unbearable pain, for the fingers were closely connected with the heart. Therefore, salt production, a highly intensive physical labor, is also known as "toil." Among the salt workers, some were farmers living nearby, who made salt in spring and summer, and worked back in the fields in autumn and winter.

The Picture of Boiling Wave · Boiling Salt with Brine

It is the first monograph on sea salt production in China, compiled by Chen Chun, from Tiantai County in the Yuan Dynasty. According to the book, the author of the paintings was a man named "Shou Yi" (also called "Heshan"). The book has 52 pictures and 52 poems (47 pictures and 47 poems existing), first included in the *Yongle Canon* from the Ming Dynasty, and then incorporated into the *Siku Quanshu* from the Qing Dynasty, describing in detail the operation method of each process in salt making. The picture illustrates the process of boiling salt with brine mentioned in the book. Meanwhile, the book depicts the scene of the struggling salt workers. In 2019, the book *Annotation of Boiling Wave* was published by the Commercial Press.

Dispersion by Emperor Hongwu

A historical incident or a legend, the dispersion by Emperor Hongwu, is also called the migration by Emperor Hongwu, the first emperor in the Ming Dynasty. During the Hongwu period (1368–1398) of the Ming Dynasty, there was a large-scale population migration, widely spread in the form of folklore. Zhu Yuanzhang, Emperor Hongwu of the Ming Dynasty, forced 400,000 people from the south of the Yangtze River to migrate to northern Jiangsu for reclamation, which was thought of as revenge and punishment for the gentry who supported his opponent, Zhang Shicheng, the King of Wu. Among the migrants, many became later salt laborers. In Yancheng, Taizhou, and other areas, there are still many people who think that their ancestors come from Suzhou, Huzhou, or Hangzhou.

Facing the Sea

A Plank Road Leading to the Sea

More than 2,000 years ago, the east of Xixi (near Xixi Ancient Town, Dongtai, Yancheng City) was still a vast ocean. Day after day, the ancient wind pushed the sea back and forth, cutting out a small natural port on the east side of Xixi (commonly known as "a big mouth to the sea"). The unique geographical location provides a favorable and unique condition for salt production in Xixi. In the fourth year of the Yuanshou (119 BC) in the Western Han Dynasty, Emperor Wu of the

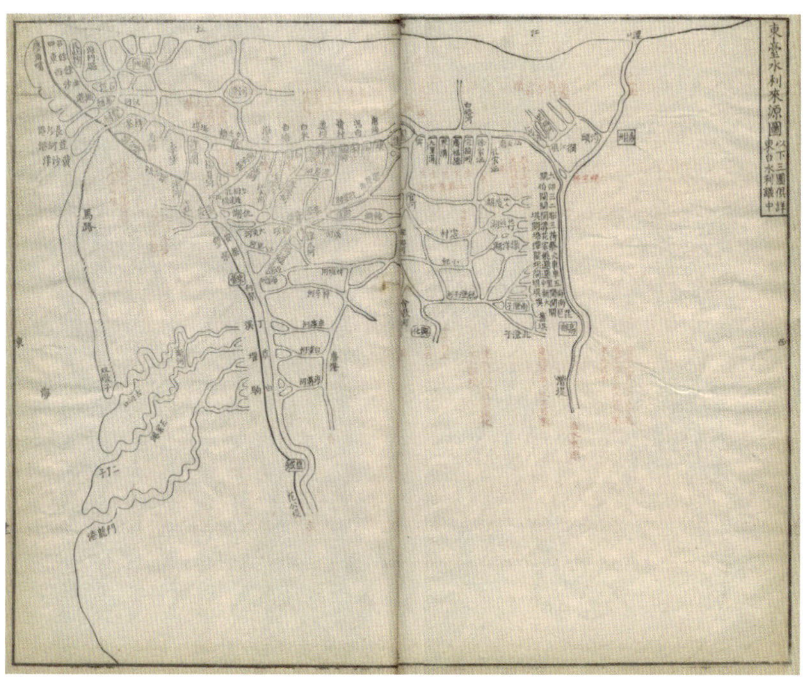

Map of Dongtai Water Conservancy Source (from *Map of Huaiyang Water Conservancy* of the Daoguang period)

Han Dynasty issued an edict, advocating that his subjects participate in salt production, thus promoting the early prosperity of the salt industry in Yancheng. During the Tang Dynasty, Xixi became an important place of salt production in Huainan salt fields.

In order to facilitate salt transportation, the Xixi people built a man-made earth plank road, over 1,600 meters long. The road leads to the sea, forming the original appearance of this plank road. From the completion of the construction to the end of the 1980s, the building materials had changed from earth to blue bricks. What is unchanged is the desire of the Dongtai people to earn a living from one generation to another. No matter where the Dongtai people rush about, this main road still stretches quietly on the land of their hometown, carrying their strongest homesickness.

Fan Gong Causeway

There is a long coastline in the east of Yancheng. Since ancient times, if the water back poured and eroded the land, the fields would be damaged and the people would be displaced. In the eighth year of Dazhong Xiangfu (1015) in the Northern Song Dynasty, Fan Zhong-yan supervised Xixi Salt Warehouses and witnessed this situation. In the first year of Tiansheng (1023), he wrote to Zhang Lun, Deputy Envoy of Jianghuai Shipping. Zhang Lun asked the court to appoint Fan Zhongyan as Magistrate of Xinghua County to preside over the repair of the weir. The project began in the second year of Tiansheng (1024), undergoing innumerable toils and challenges. Two years later, Fan Zhongyan returned to his home to memorize his dead mother. Then he again requested Zhang Lun to appeal to the emperor to allow him to go back to repair the weir, which was finally approved. In the sixth year of Tiansheng (1028), the construction of the weir was finally completed by Zhang Lun. It is recorded that the weir is about 71 kilometers long and 10 meters wide at the bottom, 3.3 meters

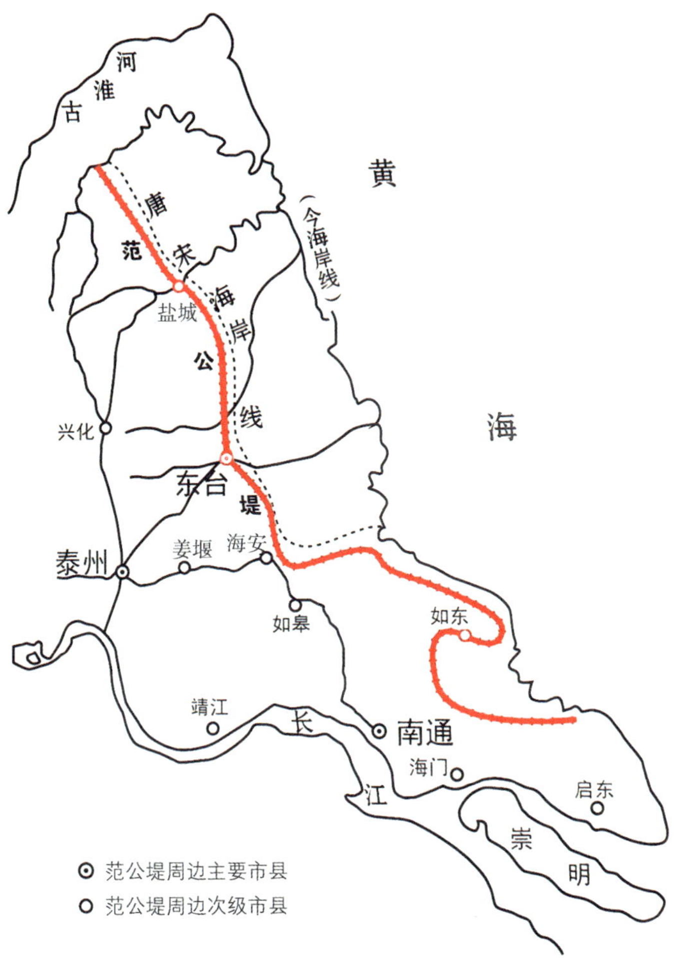

Schematic diagram of Fan Gong Causeway ruins

wide at the top and 5 meters high. After the weir was built, it turned Xinghua into a city invulnerable to floods and tides. From then on, the businesses here were thriving, and the local people all showed gratitude to Fan Zhongyan, naming the dike as "Fan Gong Causeway." The Yellow River swept down and its soil fell on the east coast, causing the causeway to leave away from the sea. In the twenty-first year of the Republic of China (1932), Fan Gong Causeway ended its mission as a sea weir and it was built into the Tongyu Highway, and later changed to a section of national highway 204, making new contributions to the local development with a completely new look.

The Spring Sea Tower

In the south of Xixi Stream in Dongtai County, adjacent to Taidong River, is standing Spring Sea Tower, a national key cultural unit. According to *Dongtai County Annals* of the Jiaqing period in the Qing Dynasty (1796–1820), and other records, the tower was built by Yuchi Jingde, a famous general in the early Tang Dynasty, for pacifying the rough sea and for navigating the vessels. Yancheng has prospered by salt production and shipment, and this tower serves as a sign of sea salt transportation, so it is also called the "needle to tranquilize sea," "tower to pacify sea," and "Yuchi tower." Constructed in bricks, the tower has seven floors, eight octagonal sides, and dense eaves. With no platforms, auxiliary steps, bucket arches, or corner columns, the hollowing tower looks very simple on its walls over the second floor. There is a Buddhist shrine on the eight sides of each floor. The decorations of the tower top consist of a combination of copper gourds, phase wheels, and cast-ironed inverted pots. In spring, the waving sea currents are booming and roaring from the tower. After weathering the seasons, the tower built in the Tang Dynasty remained standing high, looking over the city. While standing around the tower and looking up, the sounds of peddling in the Xixi City seafood market, of salt boats setting sail, of the garrison drill, seem to pass through thousands of intervening years and to linger in the ears again.

Intangible Cultural Heritage: Hair Embroidery Art

In China, as a common saying goes, "Our body hair and skin are all endowed with by our parents, so we dare not destroy them." Hair, a token of the highest etiquette, conveys loyalty, firmness, and infinite affection. The woman gave her hair to the most beloved person, vowing "I would always accompany my husband, in weal and woe." The newlyweds wrap their hair together, signifying that they will tie the knot and never desert or betray each other. Hair embroidery originated in Dongtai City. In the Tang Dynasty, under the flourishing Buddhism, the native devout women took hair and embroidered it on silk as the golden eikon and worshiped it day and night to show their piety. After that, what was embroidered gradually became all-encompassing, thus bringing about a wealth of fine works passed down from generations, such as the *Statue of Guanyin* embroidered by Guan Zhongji, a female painter of the Yuan Dynasty, and *Playing the Chord Under the Moon* during the Jiajing period of the Ming Dynasty. The techniques of hair embroidery, taking advantage of the hair that is tough, smooth, and lustrous, mainly adopt the black line against a white background, so that the products are characterized by a soft color and a plain style, endowed with an immortal artistic value. In general, hair embroidery shows the outstanding creativity of the ancient working people.

Dongtai Fish-Soup Noodles

Dongtai fish-soup noodles are a kind of traditional pasta in Dongtai, Yancheng, mainly with noodles as the most important raw material. The ingredients of the specialty also include the waters in the rivers crossing salt fields, grain in Nanxiang, and salt and fat carp in Dongxiang. The finished product has the characteristics of thick soup, white juice, bead-like drips, refreshing and delicious taste.

Funing Big Cakes

Enjoying a history over four centuries, the Funing big cakes are a traditional specialty in Funing area, Yancheng City. Cake slices easily roll up, and are as white as snow, as thin as paper, as sweet as honey, as soft as clouds.

Wuyou Drunken Snails

Originated in the Ming Dynasty, Wuyou drunken snails are a specialty of Wuyou, an ancient town in Yancheng City. It takes snails as raw materials, whose shell is soft and transparent, rich in wine aroma, tender and delicious, moderately salty and sweet. It is a delicacy with wine.

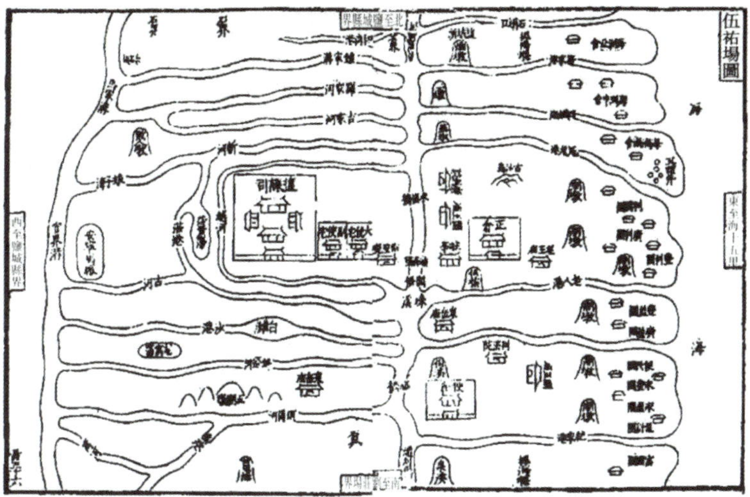

Wuyou Field of the Ming Dynasty (from *Records of Salt Laws in North and South Huai River Region* of the Jiajing period in the Ming Dynasty)

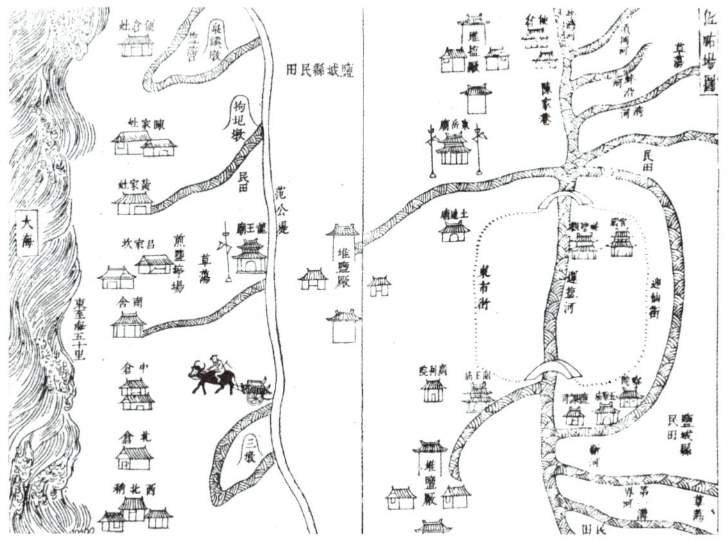

Wuyou Field of the Qing Dynasty (from *Records of Salt Laws in North and South Huai River Region* of the Qianlong period in the Qing Dynasty)

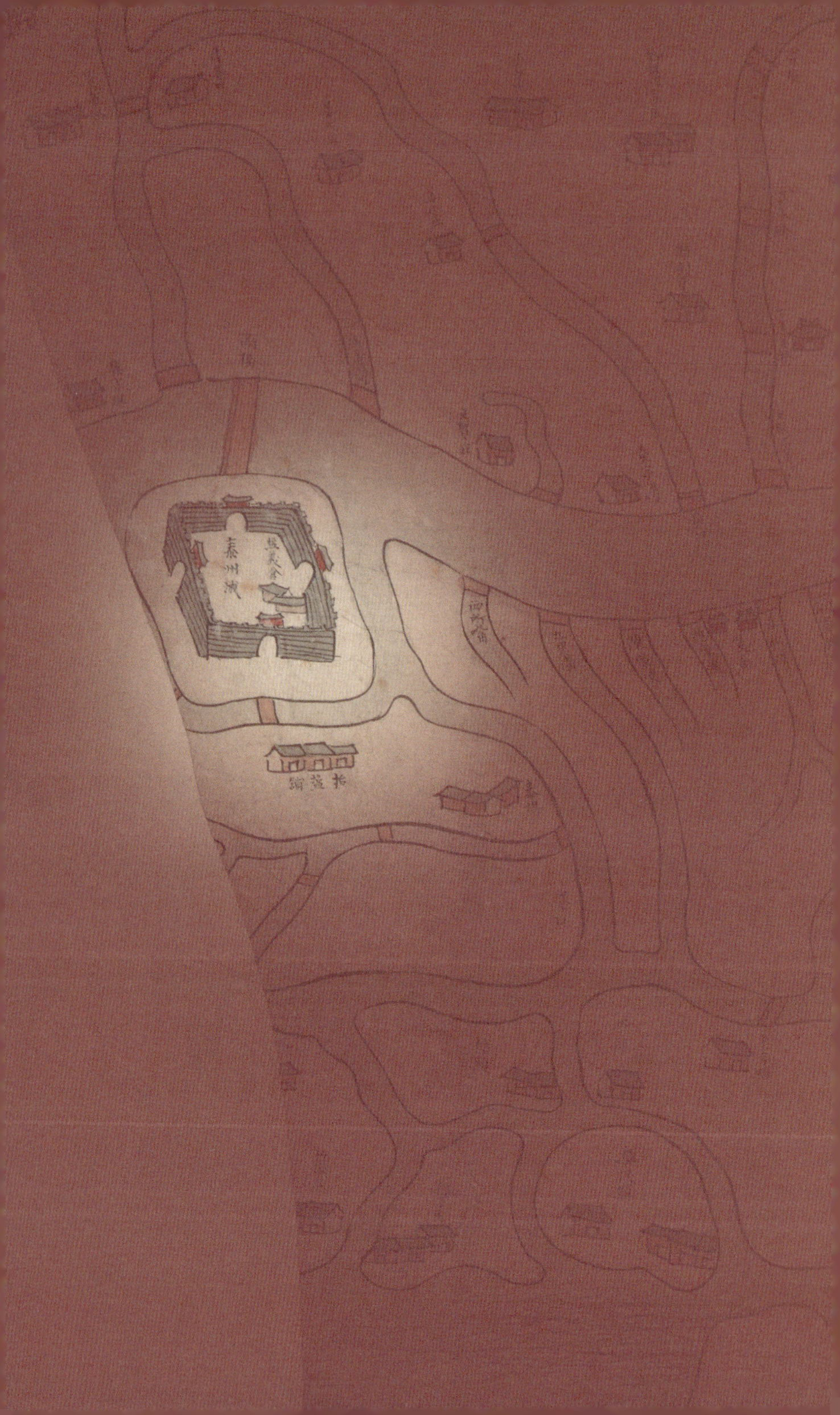
泰州城

Taizhou:
A Place of Peace and Prosperity

The Phoenix Land of Intersecting Waterways

The Treasure of Water Transportation

Hailing

Taizhou, located on the northern bank of the lower reaches of the Yangtze River and the northern wing of the Yangtze River Delta, faces Jiangyin and Zhangjiagang on the southern bank across the river. In the Zhou Dynasty, it was called Haiyang. In the Warring States period, the State of Chu set up Haiyang City. The Western Han Dynasty

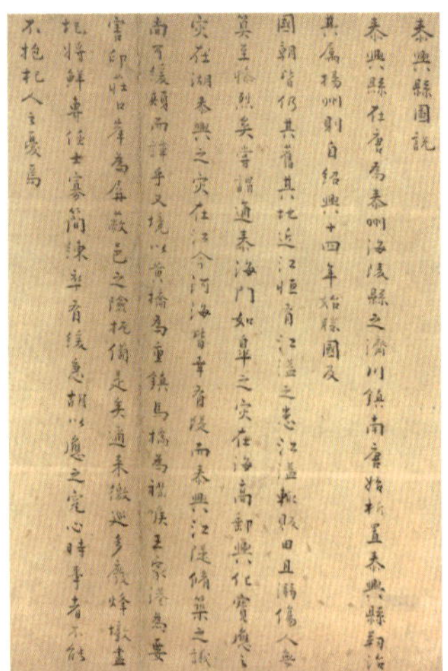

Illustrated Gazetteer of Yangzhou Prefecture · Taixing County **(illustration part)**

Illustrated Gazetteer of Yangzhou Prefecture · Taixing County (picture part)

named it "Hailing County." According to the *Unified Annals of the Qing Dynasty*, vol. 67, it was named as "Hailing" for its terrain was high while facing the sea. In the Western Han Dynasty, Liu Bi dug the Han Ditch. During the Western Han Dynasty, in the region, there were only three county administrations, including Hailing, Yancheng, and Sheyang. Therefore, Hailing County covered a large area.

In *Records of the Grand Historian · Biographies of Merchants*, Sima Qian depicted that in the Western Han Dynasty, in the south of the Yangtze River, which was wide and sparse, local people took rice and fish as food, conducting agricultural production with the burning land and the primitive rice farming technology, so they could lead a self-sufficient life without trading. The place was fertile with food, so the local people didn't worry about famine or other disasters. They were so contented that they were unwilling to make efforts for a better life. Consequently, far from accumulating enough wealth, many of them were still living in poverty. In the south of the Yangtze River and the Huai River, people seldom suffered from hunger or cold, nor did they enjoy a well-to-do life.

A City of Three Waters

Taizhou has no mountains but water. Moreover, different from other places, the waters from the Yangtze River, the Huai River, and the sea converge in Jiangyan District of Taizhou City, blending together three flavors: clear, muddy, and salty. It is precisely because of the above reason that Taizhou was also called in ancient times "A City of Three Waters."

Zhuyu Ditch

During the reign of Liu Bi, Zhuyu Bay, in Hailing County, was the main producing area of Huai salt, which was an important source of wealth for the whole state. At the same time, it also served as an essential grain

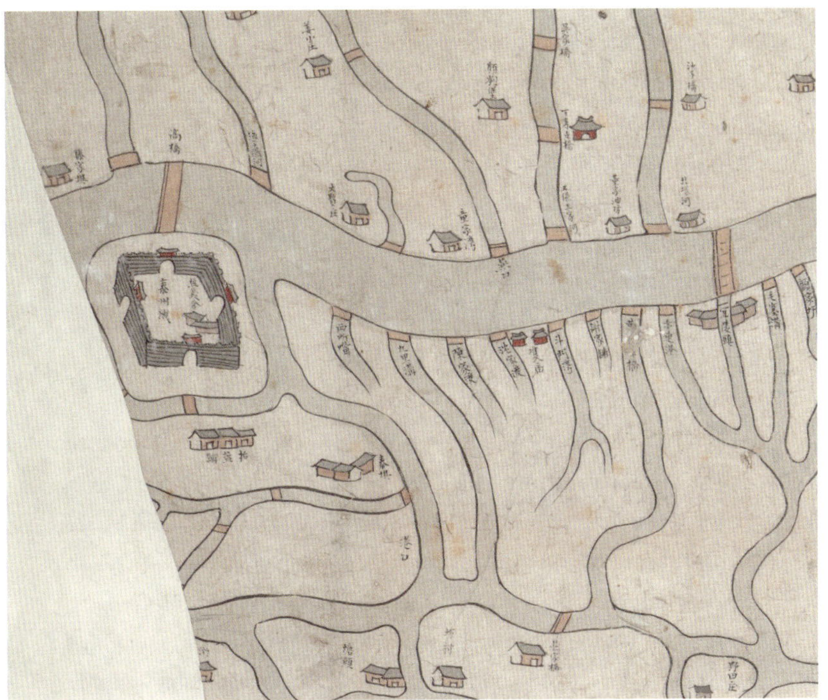

Map of Salt Rivers in North and South Huai River Region **(partial)**

The picture was made around the 22nd year of the Qianlong (1757). The whole picture now is incomplete. The title was also formulated according to the content of the picture. The above picture is about the regions in Taizhou, whose crisscross waterways are vividly shown.

area. In addition to the Han Ditch, Liu Bi also excavated a Zhuyu Ditch, starting from Zhuyu Bay (present-day Wantou Town, Yangzhou) in the west to Hailing Granary (now part of Taizhou) in the east, and then extended it to Panxi in Rugao.

Zhuyu Ditch is the predecessor of the old Tongyang Canal and also the famous salt transport river. Connected with Han Ditch, it is also called Han Ditch's Branch Road or King of Wu Ditch, with many other names such as Salt Canal and Salt Transport River, to name only a few. In the first year of the Xuantong period (1909) in the Qing Dynasty, it was renamed Tongyang Canal, with a total length of over 150 kilometers. Later, due to the excavation of the new Tongyang Canal, it was renamed the old Tongyang Canal.

Hailing Granary

Hailing Granary, at the eastern end of Zhuyu Ditch, is probably one of the most famous barns. In the *Book of Han · Biography of Mei Cheng*, it was remarked that "all the grain transported to Xixiang, both by sea and land, is still less than that stored in Hailing Granary." In "Ode to the Capital of Wu" by Zuo Si, a litterateur in the Western Jin Dynasty, acclaimed that the grain stored in Hailing Granary was so much that it even overflew to the outside, stale and rotten. Luo Bingwang, in the Tang Dynasty, was also amazed at the excessive storage of grain in the Hailing Granary. As an important source of grain provisions, Hailing Granary played a great role in supporting Liu Bi in launching the rebellion of the seven vassal states, which clearly demonstrates its abundance of storage.

Grain Transport Under the Institution of *Sanbang*

There were various institutions at different levels in charge of grain transport. In the capital of every province where grain transport took place, the title of the official in charge was Grain Circuit Intendant, under whom there were Guards, Corps, and Stations, a three-level (from high to low) institution system. For example, in Nanjing, the jurisdiction of Jiang'an Grain Circuit Intendant consisted of 15 Guards and 51 Corps, in which *Sanbang* (三帮) residing in Taizhou were under the governance of Yangzhou Guard. Taizhou Museum has collected some materials on *Sanbang* of Yangzhou Guard, showing that Taizhou *Sanbang* designated two officials in charge of grain transport, one for leading 95 vessels to the North while the other to the South. In Taizhou, there were 34 vessels, on which you could find the capital, assistant capital, and sailors, the total number of which was around ten. As a result, in Taizhou alone, there were three to four hundred people engaged in water transport. To put it in another way, the transport system supported the daily life of three to four hundred families. And nationwide, millions of households lived on water transport.

Seawalls

When Fan Zhongyan was in charge of Xixi Salt Warehouse in Taizhou and of the storage and marketing of salt, he presided over the construction of the famous Fan Gong Causeway. Since then, the rulers of the Song Dynasty had laid special emphasis on managing the seawalls. Once, a Song official appealed to the court that the seawalls should be ready to be repaired and restored whenever they were in danger of collapsing of being damaged, which was the only way that could keep the seawalls strong and solid. The reason for the stress on seawall construction was that the coastal areas, especially those along the Yangtze River and the Huai River, were mostly salt-producing areas. The construction of seawall projects, such as sea weirs, could protect not only the lives of local residents but also the salt-producing land from the sea.

Map of the Salt Fields in North and South Huai River Region and Salt Transport Routes in Four Provinces **(partial)**

The direction of the blue line in the picture guides the position and direction of Fan Gong Causeway, indicating that the waters of the Yellow River used to occupy the position of the Huai River into the sea through Jiangsu Province. After five or six centuries, the large amounts of sediment have forced the coastline back, leaving a large area of shoals.

Rivers to Transport Salt

The management of the seawalls has also affected the construction and operation of the rivers to transport salt. In Taizhou, there were two rivers to transport salt in ancient times, in which the upper river was the old Tongyang Canal, including the Nanguan River mentioned below, and the lower river referred to the rivers crossing salt fields system, "passing through the Zhaogong Bridge and Yanggong Causeway before converging into rivers crossing salt fields in the east city" (*Taizhou Annals* of the Daoguang period). The system consists of both natural channels and artificial waterways spontaneously excavated by locals. In ancient times, these rivers were mainly used for salt

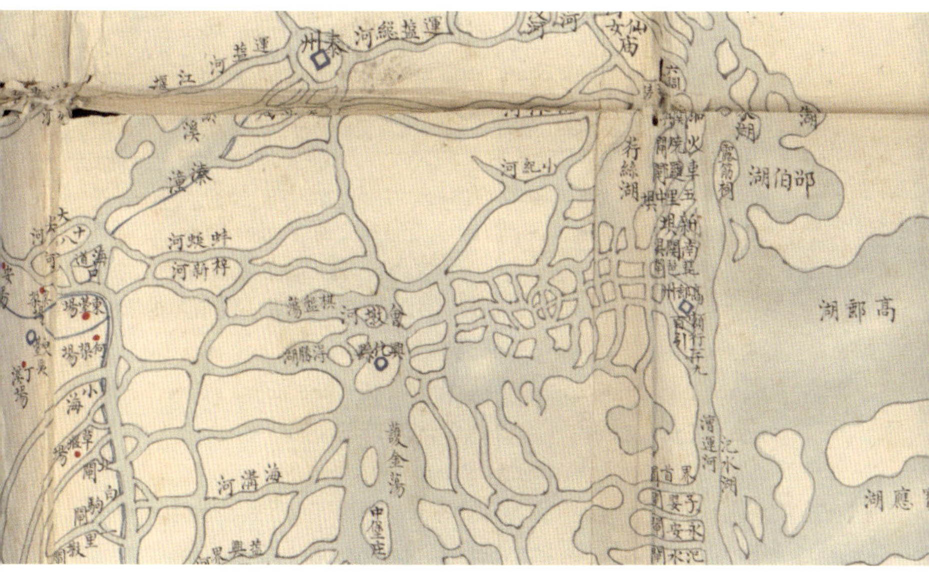

***Map of the Salt Fields in North and South Huai River Region and Salt Transport Routes in Four Provinces* (partial)**

It can be seen in the picture that on both sides of Taizhou there are the two salt transport rivers, which shows its crucial geographical position in salt transportation.

production, marketing, and transporting, so they were called Rivers to Transport Salt. In the first year of Shengyuan (937), the Southern Tang Dynasty, Hailing was renamed Taizhou (泰州) with the meaning "a peaceful country and well-being people." (The pronunciation of "*tai*" [泰] in Chinese means being peaceful and well-being.) Meanwhile, the Hailing Salt Supervision Agency was set up. It was not until the Hongwu period of the Ming Dynasty that the seat of the Salt Supervision Agency was removed to Yangzhou. Therefore, Taizhou has a history of about 450 years as the base of the highest administration agency and the transport center for the Huai salt. During the Ming and Qing dynasties, the Taizhou Salt Transportation Division was of great significance. Its jurisdiction was over ten salt farms, including those of Fu'an, Anfeng, Liangduo, Dongtai, Heduo, Dingxi, Caoyan, Xiaohai, Jiaoxie, and Bencha, and the salt production accounted for one third of the whole country.

The Nanguan River

The Nanguan River, also known as the Shangguan River, was called the Jichuan River in ancient times. In 1365, Zhu Yuanzhang, King of Wu State in the Yuan Dynasty, sent Xu Da to attack Zhang Shicheng in Taizhou. When he passed through Taixing County, he found that the waterway was blocked, so he dug a 7.5-kilometer-long river through the mouth of the Yangtze River to connect the Jichuan River. Since then, the Jichuan River, also known as the Nanguan River, was finally connected with the Yangtze River. The river flowing into the city changed the lives of the local residents, making it easier for vessels to reach the Yangtze River and to irrigate the fields on both sides. In the 25th year of Hongwu (1392) of the Ming Dynasty, the Ming government set up two dams outside the northern gate of Taizhou, which eliminated the danger that the river could not store water during drought and the river would flow back during the flood. However, the upper and lower rivers were no longer connected. After the founding of the People's Republic of China, the "Taizhou Ship Lock" was built and the new Tongyang Canal was excavated, connecting the Nanguan River and the Luting River, and the connection between upper and lower rivers was resumed after a 560-year-long separation. Later, China carried out three major renovations of the Nanguan River, so that the river played an essential role in activating the local economy and facilitating people's lives.

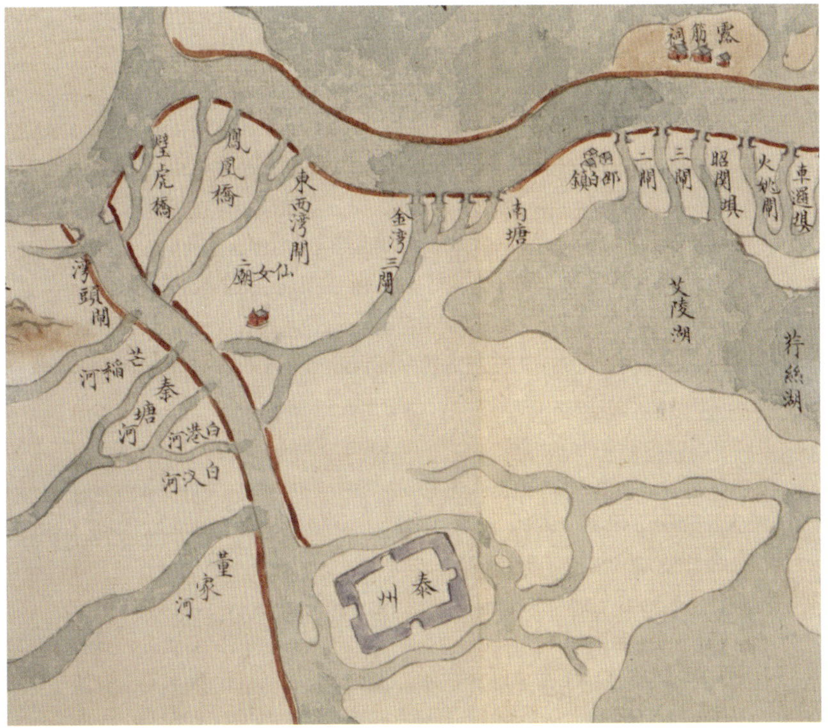

Complete Map of Canal Transport Routes (partial)

Phoenix Perching in Hailing

Where Does Phoenix Perch?

In ancient times, Taizhou City has a unique and elegant name: "Phoenix City." According to the *Taizhou Annals* of the Daoguang period, Hailing City was shaped like a phoenix, with its head and tail in the south and north, its left wing in the east and the right wing in the west. According to the documents, the High Bridge of the southern gate of Taizhou has 78 steps, looking like a high phoenix head. There is a long street, similar to the long neck of a phoenix, extending northward from High Bridge to the southern city gate. The phoenix body is composed of the main city of Taizhou. There are two tall mounds in the southeast and southwest corners of the city river, forming the phoenix wings. If you go further north from the north gate to the Zhaogong Bridge, you can see a phoenix-tail-like pagoda standing there. In short, from the south to the north, the whole city of Taizhou looks like a colorful phoenix spreading its wings to fly.

Taizhou is not surrounded by the sea, but there is a "Wanghai Tower" in the city. "*Wanghai*" (望海) in Chinese means "looking at the sea." The name was from that the altitude of Taizhou in the Western Han Dynasty was higher than that of the sea. Wanghai Tower was first built

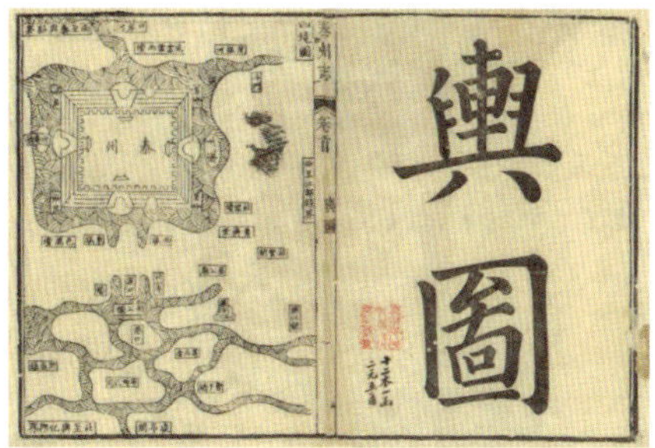

Map in *Taizhou Annals* of the Daoguang period (partial)

in the second year of Shaoding (1229) in the Southern Song Dynasty, repeatedly destroyed in wars but rebuilt in the prosperous periods.

Wanghai Tower was rebuilt in 2006. It follows the Song Dynasty system, with three floors of ring corridor, dark brown, green, and gray, simple and elegant. Wanghai Tower was built near the Fengcheng River, the moat running around the city in ancient times. Outside Taizhou, there are three "green belts," namely the Yinjiang River, Zhoushan River, and the new Tongyang Canal, forming a harmonious scenery between the city and the waters.

As a legendary ancient god bird, the phoenix represents the auspicious. Taizhou, whose first character, "*tai*" in Chinese, means being peaceful and well-being, was built in the Southern Tang Dynasty. Hailing County is under the jurisdiction of Taizhou, and it is also the seat of Taizhou Prefecture. It can be seen that whatever the name of the city is, "Phoenix City" or "Taizhou," what has never changed for thousands of years is the common wish of the local people for a peaceful and well-being country. In the Qing Dynasty, Wang Youqing spoke highly of Taizhou as a city "with deep waters and thick layers of soil" (*Taizhou Annals*, vol. 8). Therefore, blessed by both waters and transports, Taizhou has been a prosperous birthplace for not a few great men.

The Blooming Flower Sea on Waters: Cole Flowers in Qianduo Town

The Xinghua area is the location of the lake bed of the ancient Sheyang Lake. As early as 5,000 years ago, it was a waterfront of the East China Sea, then as the coastline moved east, it gradually became a swamp beach. It is the lowest land in Jiangsu Province, with an average altitude of only 1–2 meters, so the local people use the expression "pot bottom" to describe the Xinghua terrain. In addition, the climate there is characterized by flooded summers and dry winters. Since ancient times, the Xinghua area has had more water and fewer fields. Therefore, throughout history, protecting farmland has become the top priority in the struggle between farmers and nature in Xinghua.

In the Song Dynasty, Fan Zhongyan built "Fan Gong Causeway," whose remains can be seen from Xinghua to Yancheng. In addition, in the lake swamps area of Xinghua, small islands of different sizes were

Cole flower fields in spring (photographed by Pan Ruizhi)

formed under the impact of the upstream water and the top support of the downstream tide, which provided favorable conditions for the swamps to turn into lands. The earlier generations accumulated soil stacks to drain water out of the field, thus gradually forming the prototype of a "stack field." In the dry season, by small boats, the peasants collected the silt from the bottom of the river to pile upon the stack, so as to dredge the river and increase the height of the field and the soil fertility. In addition, they used bailing buckets to scoop water from the river to water the fields, dripping it evenly far away.

The stack fields are a unique landscape of farmland in Xinghua City. Xinghua has more than 60,000 mu of such arable land, in which the cole flower sea in Qianduo (千垛, literally a thousand stacks) Town is the most famous.

Nowadays, visitors can not only travel by boat across the stacked fields but also wander along trails to appreciate the sea of flowers and crisscrossed waterways. The stacked fields in the river are of various shapes and heights, just like the islands on the sea, basking in the sun and dotted with the golden color of cole flowers.

Intangible Cultural Heritage: Qintong Boat Festival

Qintong Boat Festival is an ancient traditional folk activity, which is originated from the Song Dynasty. Legend has it that the people in the Qin Lake area were grateful to the army led by Yue Fei, who fought against the Jin Army. On every Qingming Festival, the local people would go to the river by boat to pay tribute to the dead soldiers. Over time, the ceremony has gradually evolved into a folk cultural activity with a history of over 800 years. Before the festival, people throughout the area compete to decorate their tribute ships, which is the most important occasion in March and April. The performances at the Boat Festival express the expectations of the local people for a peaceful country, a wealthy life, a flourishing world, and a fertile land.

During the festival, the villagers row their tribute boats, showing off their fancy dressing. The most exciting activity is the race consisting of over one hundred boats. In the loud noise of the gong, the crew shouts in unison and spares no efforts to row, magically bringing about innumerable spoondrift. With hundreds of poles up and down, dozens of pole boats, like dragons, are charging into the heart of the river, forming a very spectacular and impressive scene. Nowadays, the annual Qintong Boat Festival, on the second day of the Qingming Festival, is one of the top ten folk cultural activities in China.

Zhongzhuang Liquor-Saturated Crab

Zhongzhuang liquor-saturated crab, involving 21 complicated production processes, originated in the Ming Dynasty, with the freshwater crabs of Wugong Lake and Dazong Lake as the best. With rich wine, liquor-saturated crab meat is tender, delicious, and tasty. It serves as not only a high-grade cold dish on the banquet but also an exquisite gift for relatives and friends.

Jingjiang Crab-Roe Soup Bun

A Jingjiang crab-roe soup bun in Taizhou is featured with its wrapped skin as thin as paper, prone to breakage after a small bite. The bun is made with unique procedures, appealing patterns and grotesque tasting ways. While making the buns, remember to simmer the pig feet with gentle heat, cool it into aspic, and then make the filling with it. The steamed soup bun is translucent and soft. When tasting it, you should "gently lift it, slowly move it to your mouth, effortlessly bite the wrapped skin and suck the soup."

Huangqiao Sesame Seed Cake

Huangqiao sesame seed cake is a traditional snack in Taixing City, named after the famous "Huangqiao Decisive Battle" in October 1940. After being baked, the cake body is yellow and soft, red as a crab shell. It is light yet crispy and tasty.

五台山
沙河埧
宝塔湾
天寧寺
揚州府
板桥
至高郵一百里

Yangzhou: The Renowned Capital to the East of the Huai River

Origin of the Grand Canal

"Shanghai" in the Tang Dynasty

A "Prequel" to the Story of Goujian

The legend about King Goujian of Yue lying on the firewood and tasting gall to defeat the State of Wu is well-known. However, it is less known how the State of Yue defeated the State of Wu. Apart from secretly forming alliances with the states of Qi and Chu, King Goujian induced King Fuchai of Wu to launch an attack on the Central Plains. While initiating the war, King Fuchai also mobilized a large number of laborers to build Han City as a base for northward march, and to dig the Han Ditch to facilitate military logistics. The Han Ditch, linking the Yangtze River and the Huai River, was the precursor of the Grand Canal. To encourage the State of Wu to march northward to the Central Plains, King Goujian had Wen Zhong lead numerous laborers to assist the State of Wu in digging the Han Ditch, in order to facilitate King Fuchai's northward march. While the State of Wu exhausted its national strength in warfare and water conservancy construction, the State of Yue preserved its strength and bided its time. After years of continuous wars and depletion of resources, Wu was unable to withstand Yue's strength and eventually fell, but the transportation facilitated by the Han Ditch has influenced the development of the region and even the entire China for thousands of years.

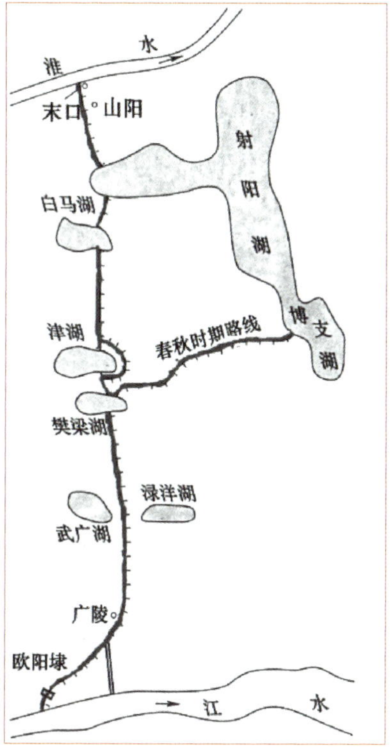

Diagram of the route of Huaiyang Canal from the Warring States Period to the Tang Dynasty

The Water Transportation Hub

The reason why Yangzhou could serve as a hub on the canal was primarily that Liu Bi built his capital here during the Western Han Dynasty. After Yangzhou gaining such a status, all kinds of goods from the State of Wu were gathered in Yangzhou before being distributed to the whole country. With its advantageous location by the water, Yangzhou became not only a water transportation hub for the canal but also one of the wealthiest regions in the country.

Yangzhou's Unique "God of Wealth"

Archaeological researches suggest that during the reign of Liu Bi, Wu's income over 30 years rivaled the national tax revenue of the Han Dynasty over 40 years due to its convenience of transportation and advantage in salt production.[1] To this day, Liu Bi together with Fuchai is still worshipped as the god of wealth by the local people at the Han Ditch's Great King Temple in the Hangou Community of Meiling Street, Hanjiang District, Yangzhou City.

The Heart of the Grand Canal

In the period of Emperor Yang of the Sui Dynasty, after being excavated, the Grand Canal connected the three major water systems of the Yellow River, the Huai River, and the Yangtze River in Jiangsu Province, turning Yangzhou into a crucial hub for water transportation. The Grand Canal facilitated the transportation and irrigation in the towns along the canal, playing an important role in promoting the economic and cultural development and exchanges in the Yellow River, Huai River, and Yangtze River basins, laying the foundation for the unprecedented prosperity of Yangzhou during the Tang Dynasty.[2] In

---

1 Ji Lizhen, ed., *Sea Symbols of China: Legend of Sea Salt* (China Ocean University Press, 2017), p. 26.

2 *The History of Yangzhou*, https://yangzhou.gov.cn/yangzhou/lsyg/lmtt_yz.shtml.

618, Emperor Yang of the Sui Dynasty was killed by his general Yuwen Huaji and was buried in Caozhuang, northwest of Yangzhou.

Yan Liben, *Emperors and Kings Through the Ages* (partial)

This picture shows Yang Guang, Emperor Yang of the Sui Dynasty.

"Shanghai" in the Tang Dynasty

During the Tang Dynasty, Yangzhou, considered as today's Shanghai, rose to prominence. Suzhou was the coastal city at the mouth of the Yangtze River downstream, but in terms of transportation location, it was far inferior to Yangzhou. The reason lies in the later excavation of the Han Ditch by emperors, such as Fuchai, Liu Bi, and Yang Guang. Consequently, Yangzhou actually became a convergent point of river, canal, and sea, with an exceptionally advantageous geographical location. At that time, Yangzhou served as not only a central city of domestic commerce and culture, but also a hub for international trade and cultural exchanges. The renowned monk Jianzhen in the Tang Dynasty embarked on his eastward journey from Yangzhou.

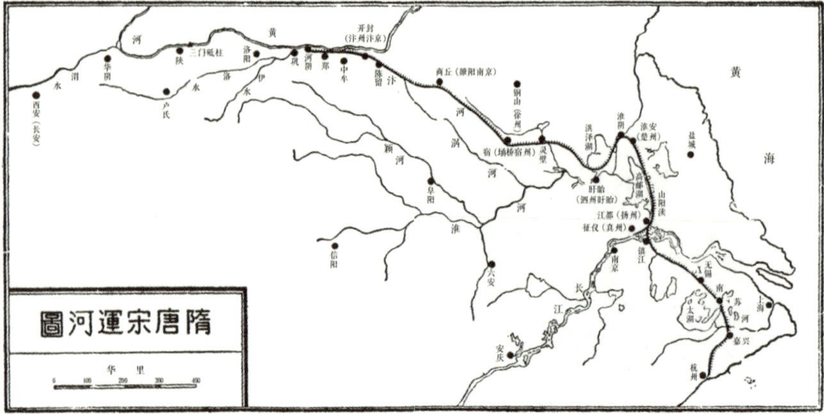

The Canal Map of the Sui, Tang, and Song Dynasties (according to Quan Hansheng, *Tang and Song Empires and Canals*)

The coastline depicted in the map is based on contemporary geography and does not represent the situation during the Tang Dynasty. In the map, Yangzhou is located at the intersection of the Grand Canal and near the Yangtze River, making its east-west transportation extremely convenient.

The Largest Metropolis in Southeast China

During the Tang Dynasty, agriculture, commerce, and handicrafts flourished in Yangzhou, giving rise to numerous workshops and artisanal establishments. It was the largest metropolis in southeastern China, often referred to as the "Yang First, Yi Second." ("Yi" refers to "Yizhou," the ancient name for Sichuan, lying in the southwest of China.) An ancient saying goes: "In the southeast, there are three key administrations, of water transportation, of salt, and of rivers."[3] Yangzhou happened to be strategically located at the nexus of these three key administrative areas, serving as a crucial water transportation hub

[3] Zhang Yiming, ed., *A History of Huaiyang Food Culture* (Qingdao Publishing Group, 2000), p. 13.

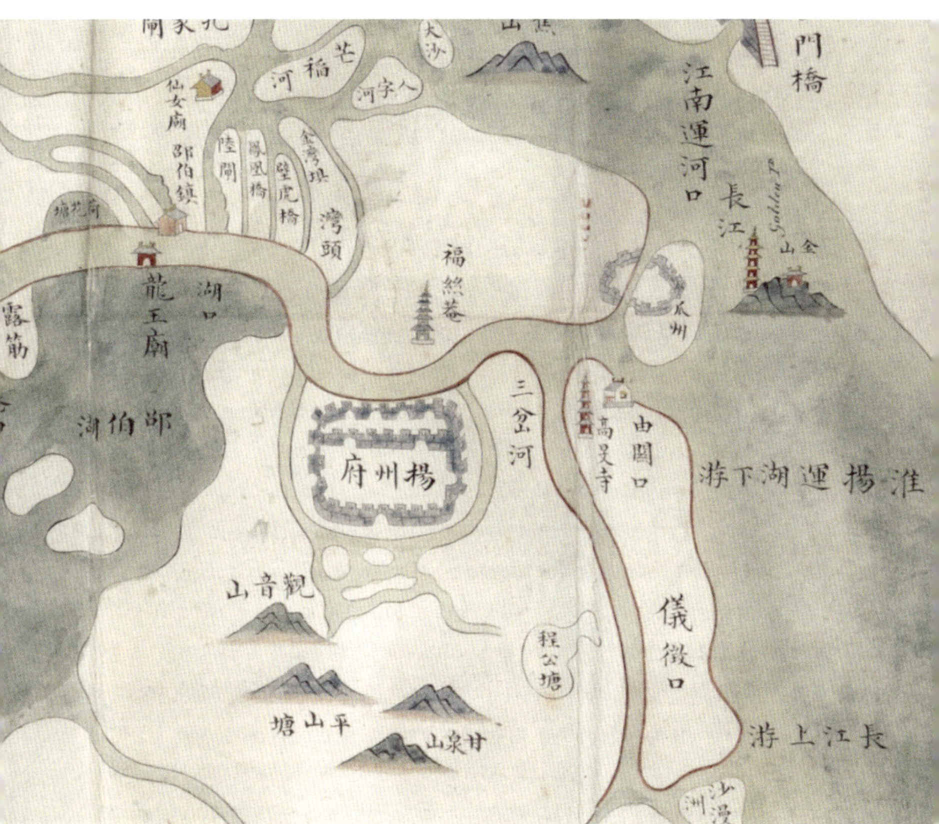

***Huaiyang Waterway Map* (partial)**

The *Huaiyang Waterway Map* was drawn during the 12th to 14th years of Jiaqing's reign (1807–1809) of the Qing Dynasty and was named after the content. The map has no scales or cutlines. The map depicts Hongze Lake, the canal, and the surrounding waterways and construction works. The section of the map above shows the distribution of waterways and construction works in the vicinity of Yangzhou.

from south to north and an important port for domestic and international trade. It was the seat of various administrative offices, such as the Governor's Office, the Grand Governor's Office, the Inspection Commissioner of Huainan Circuit, and the Military Commissioner of Huainan Circuit, overseeing the provinces of Huainan and the northern bank of the Yangtze River.[4] In the water and land transportation network centered around Chang'an, Yangzhou consistently played a pivotal role.

The Fall of the Tang Dynasty

Chen Yinke, a great historian, once said: "Since the An Lushan Rebellion in the Tang Dynasty, the regime in Chang'an has been able to continue by relying on the supply of the eight southeast provinces, in addition to the cultural forces. During the Huang Chao Uprising, the economy of the southeast region was almost destroyed, and the transportation of the Bian River and the Grand Canal was cut off. Consequently, the regime of Chang'an that lived on the southeast financial resources collapsed, marking the doom of the Tang Dynasty."[5] Not only the Tang Dynasty, but also the Song, Ming, and Qing dynasties that followed, all made the Grand Canal the lifeblood of their capitals. The Southern Song Dynasty took Hangzhou, the southernmost point of the canal, as its capital, and continued the history of the Song Dynasty for more than a hundred years; the Southern Ming Dynasty (1644–1662) resisted the attack of the Qing soldiers in Yangzhou but was defeated, and eventually retreated to the southwest; and the British swam upstream along the Yangtze River, occupying Zhenjiang and approaching Nanjing, and forcing the Qing government to sign the

---

4 Jia Bingqiang, *The Direction of the Grand Canal and the Rise and Fall of Cities Along the River*, https://news.ncwu.edu.cn/info/1013/13392.htm.

5 Chen Yinke et al., *National History Classes at the Southwest United University* (Tiandi Publishing House, 2021), p. 165.

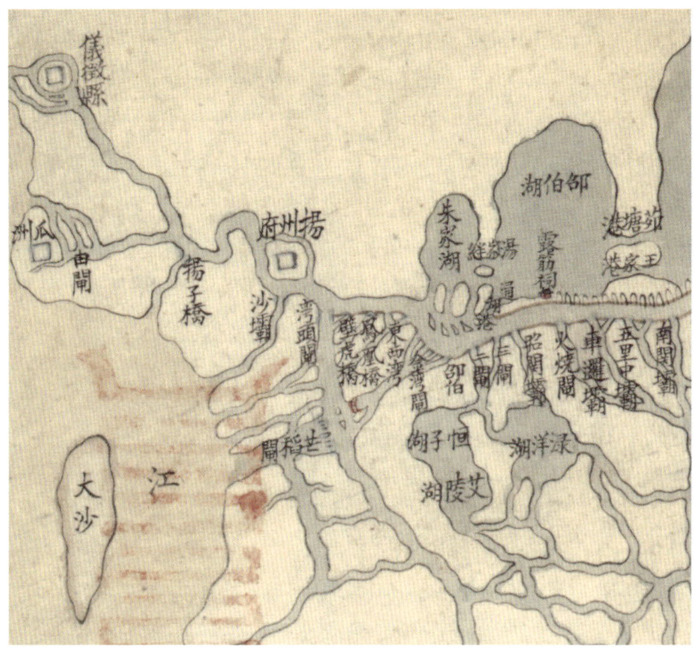

Map of the Dams and Barrages in the Lower Reaches of the Yellow River · The River Below Dams of Gaobao, No. 12 (partial)

Treaty of Nanjing. All these show that the prosperity and decline of the Grand Canal is not only a symbol of the rise and fall of past dynasties but also a witness to the glory and disgrace of the whole country.

The Emperor Kangxi and Qianlong's Favorite City to Visit

In Jin Yong's novel *The Deer and the Cauldron*, Emperor Kangxi traveled south of the Yangtze River many times to look for Wei Xiaobao. In reality, Yangzhou was the city he visited most frequently. Later, his grandson, Emperor Qianlong also made many visits to Yangzhou, making the city more prosperous than ever. By then, Yangzhou, with a population of more than 500,000, became one of the eight largest cities in China, and one of the ten largest cities in the world around the end of the 18th century and the beginning of the 19th century.

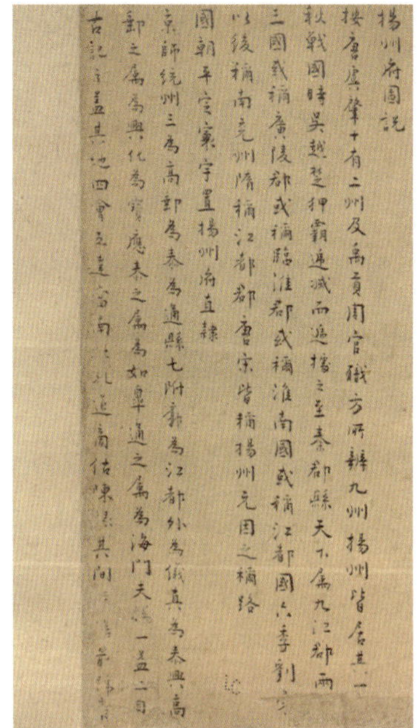

揚州府圖說
按唐虞肇十有二州及禹貢周官職方所辨九州揚州皆居其一
秋戰國時吳越楚爭霸迭滅而遞據之至秦郡縣天下屬九江郡兩
三國或稱廣陵郡或稱臨淮郡或稱淮南國或稱江都國六季割之
以後稱南兗州隋稱江都郡唐宋皆稱揚州元因之稱路
國朝平定寰宇置揚州府直隸
京師統州三為高郵為泰為通縣七附郭為江都外為儀真為泰興高
郵之屬為興化為寶應泰之屬為如臯通之屬為海門天[illegible]一並二[illegible]
古記之盖其地四會五達當南北之道商估陳集其間[illegible]

Pictorial Volume of Yangzhou Prefectur· Yangzhou Prefecture (illustration of Yangzhou Prefecture)

***Pictorial Volume of Yangzhou Prefecture · Yangzhou Prefecture* (map of Yangzhou Prefecture)**

Color-illustrated book *Pictorial Volume of Yangzhou Prefecture* in the Ming Dynasty was published in one volume, bound in folds. The title on the book spine reads *A Folded Pictorial Volume of Yangzhou Prefecture*. The content of the book in 24 folded pages is divided into Yangzhou, Jiangdu, Taixing, and other regions, in which the maps and illustrations account for two halves. The two pictures are the map of Yangzhou Prefecture (only half of which exists) and the corresponding illustration of Yangzhou Prefecture (only half of which exists).

Money Order

In the past, Yangzhou, located at the transportation hub, rich in salt and fisheries, provided enormous salt tax and revenue to the governments of all dynasties. Especially in the Ming and Qing dynasties, trade in Yangzhou was more prosperous, and merchants from all over the world established "guildhalls" here, whose business scope, with strong local characteristics, was extensive. At the same time, the money order, namely credit remittances, was on the rise. The pioneering initiative in the economy lies in that money deposited in the exchange shop in Nanjing could be exchanged in Beijing, which greatly facilitated currency circulation and merchants' travel.

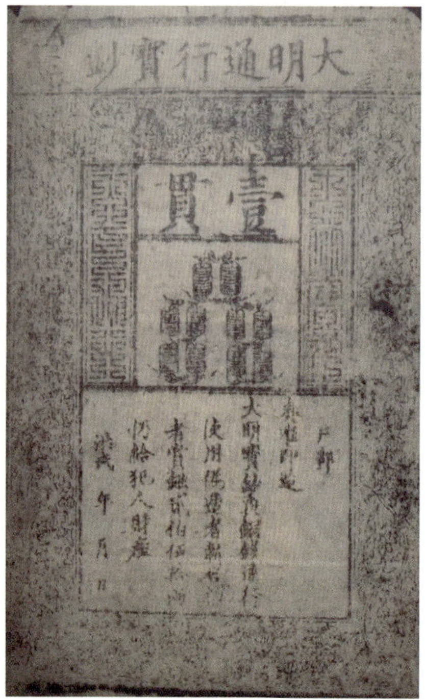

Circulated currency in the Ming Dynasty

Ye Yanlan, *Scholars of the Qing Dynast · Yuan Mei*, colored on paper

Yuan Mei (1716–1798), courtesy name Zicai, was known as Jianzhai, and in his later years was known as Recluse of Cangshan, the Host of Suiyuan, and the Old Man of Suiyuan. His work on food, *Recipes from Suiyuan*, is a classic "menu" focusing on Huaiyang cuisine and covering other cuisines, such as Anhui, Shandong, and Hangzhou cuisines.

Salty Flavor in Huaiyang Cuisine

"The salt of the whole country is derived from the North and South Huai River Region." Salt from the North and South Huai River Region is first gathered in Yangzhou before being distributed. Salt has become the most popular seasoning used by Yangzhou people in cooking. Therefore, Huaiyang cuisine is mainly salty. In addition, as the area is located beside the Yangtze River and the sea, there are many aquatic products, full of fresh flavor. Huaiyang cuisine is one of the four traditional Chinese cuisines (Sichuan, Shandong, Huaiyang, and Cantonese cuisines), and it was also the second most important Chinese imperial cuisine in the past. To this day, Huaiyang cuisine is still the mainstay of state banquets.

The River Town Veiled in Green Willows and Red Flowers

The Graceful and Elegant Slender West Lake

It is not widely known that the Slender West Lake was originally excavated for military purposes. Formerly known as Safeguard Lake, the Slender West Lake was also named as the Paoshan River and was created for the defense of the city. During the Tang and Song dynasties, the Safeguard River was a north-south channel on the west side of Yangzhou, connected to the canal, with its northern and southern trenches at its two ends. After the Tang and Song dynasties, its military defense function weakened and gradually evolved into a flood-discharge and shipping waterway, extending from Shugang to the Grand Canal. The present name of the Slender West Lake comes from a poem with the same name of Wang Hang, a poet of the Qing Dynasty. The general meaning of the poem is that the West Lake in Yangzhou, smaller and slimmer than that in Hangzhou, enjoys impressive prosperity and has become an ideal destination for people to enjoy themselves, so it should be called Slender West Lake.

Slender West Lake's long and narrow surface embodies the delicate charm of the Jiangnan region. As early as the Southern Song Dynasty, the literati and scholars of Yangzhou extended their recreational activities to this area. Historical records indicate that Xu Zhanzhi of the

Southern Song Dynasty built structures, such as the wind pavilions, moon-viewing pavilions, blowing terraces, and harp chambers,[6] some of which still exist today. Over the following dynasties, the site was further expanded and developed into a grand spectacle. By the middle and late Qing Dynasty, it had essentially taken its present form. In his *Visiting to Beautiful Yangzhou*, vol. 1, Wang Zhenshi wrote: "Slender West Lake … its winding and meandering waters extend for over twenty *li*. Surrounded by lakes and mountains, painted boats come and go, and the boatmen paddle and strike the oars, creating a deep sense of enjoyment." Slender West Lake is renowned worldwide for its unique scenic beauty and rich cultural connotations.

The Five Pavilion Bridge over the Slender West Lake

[6] In *The Book of Song · Biography of Xu Zhanzhi*, there is a record of Xu Zhanzhi's administration of Yangzhou at that time: "In the old days, there were tall buildings in Guangling, which Xu Zhanzhi further repaired. Looking south, there was Zhongshan Mountain; to the north of the city, there were pools and marshes, abundant with water and wildlife. Xu Zhanzhi built wind pavilions, moon-viewing pavilions, blowing terraces, and harp chambers. With lush bamboo and blooming flowers, he gathered scholars to enjoy leisure activities, making it a flourishing scene for a time."

From Here Set Sail the Flourishing Culture of the Tang Dynasty: The Daming Temple

Yangzhou is home to eight renowned temples, with Daming Temple being the most prominent. It was constructed during the Daming era of Emperor Xiaowu of the Southern Song Dynasty. Before entering the temple, visitors encounter a stone inscription from the Yongzheng period, which reads "The First View in Eastern Huai," derived from a poem by Qin Guan, a poet of the Northern Song Dynasty: "If tourists are to discuss the beauty of the sights, / They must consider this the first view in Eastern Huai" ("Five Poems of Guangling II · In Response to Ziyou's Inscription on Pingshan Hall"). Inside the temple, there are numerous scenic spots, including the Decorative Archway, Xiyuan Garden, Kangxi Imperial Stele Pavilion, and "The Fifth Spring." The most famous ones, however, are the Qiling Pagoda and Pingshan Hall. Historically, the temple is also notable for the internationally-known Master Jianzhen.

In the first year of the Kaiyuan period (713), the reign of Emperor Xuanzong of the Tang Dynasty, after completing his studies, Jianzhen returned to his hometown, Yangzhou. From there, he was engaged in religious and social activities throughout the Jianghuai region. The Qiling Pagoda, built during the Sui Dynasty, served as a place where Jianzhen taught and transmitted Buddhist precepts before his journey to Japan. After five unsuccessful attempts, Jianzhen finally succeeded on his sixth voyage to Japan. He brought with him numerous Buddhist scriptures and medical books. Under his influence, Japanese Buddhism gradually became more structured and complete. The Yangtze River, the Yellow River, and the Grand Canal form the lifeblood of the Chinese nation, linking vast territories and developing the economy. Chinese culture has flowed and spread along these waterways, maintaining an unbroken and enduring legacy. The mention of the Grand Canal inevitably brings up canal culture. Daming Temple, located beside the canal, was also a crucial hub for maritime cultural exchange during the Tang Dynasty. "Though mountains and rivers divide us, we share the same sky and moon." Jianzhen's outstanding contributions to cultural exchange between China and Japan during the Tang Dynasty are eternally remembered by the people of both nations.

Qiling Pagoda in Daming Temple

"Flowing to the Ancient Ferry Crossing at Guazhou"

During the 200 years from the Southern Dynasties to the Sui Dynasty, Guazhou (literally "melon-like shaped town") was an underwater sandbank at the mouth of the Yangtze River, named for its melon-like shape. By the middle Tang Dynasty, Guazhou gradually silted up into an island. Located at the intersection of the Grand Canal and the Yangtze River, it became a commercial hub. The Tang poet Bai Juyi's verses, "The Bian River flows, the Si River flows, they flow to Guazhou's ancient ferry landing" ("Longing for Each Other"), indirectly describe the linking and operational function of the Grand Canal. From Guazhou, one could travel upstream directly to the Bian and Si Rivers. Guazhou was not only a crucial point on the canal but also a strategic military location. It served as a front line of resistance against the armies of the Jin and Yuan dynasties in the Southern Song Dynasty and against Japanese pirates in the Ming Dynasty. During the Taiping Rebellion (1851–1864), Guazhou served as the frontline as well. An ancient saying goes, "Though Guazhou is a small place, it overlooks Jingkou, connects to Jiankang, reaches the sea, and stays close to the Yangtze River, serving as the throat of seven provinces and the shield of Yangzhou."[7] During the Qing Dynasty, the continuous erosion by the Yangtze River led to the collapse of the Guazhou riverbank. In the 21st year of Guangxu's reign (1895), the entire city of Guazhou sank into the Yangtze River, and the once-prosperous scene was swept away by the waters. The current Guazhou City was rebuilt in the early period of the Republic of China and is located to the northwest of the original city. In the 1950s, the rectification works of the Beijing-Hangzhou Grand Canal began, straightening the section passing through Yangzhou. Consequently, the Guazhou Canal wasn't

---

7 Compiled by Qing scholars Wu Qide and Wang Yangdu and edited by Qing scholars Feng Jin and Chang De, *The Chronicle of Guazhou During the Jiaqing Period*.

the major transportation artery anymore, leading to a further decline in Guazhou's status.

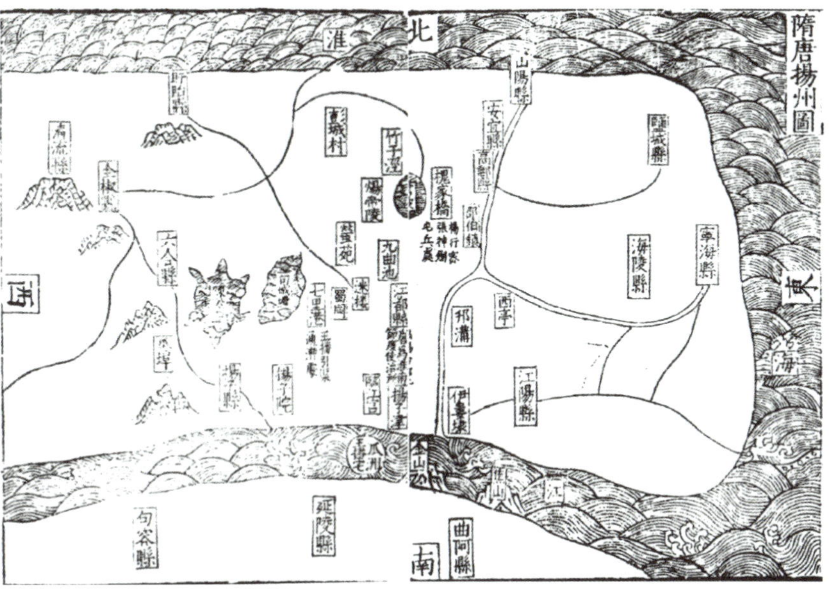

The Map of Yangzhou During the Sui and Tang Dynasties (from *Chronicle of Yangzhou During the Jiajing Period*)

Why Visit Yangzhou in the Misty Flowery Late Spring?

"In the world's three parts of moonlit nights, / Two parts are mercilessly in Yangzhou" (Xu Ning, "Remembering Yangzhou"). Yangzhou frequently appears in the writings of poets throughout the ages. In their verses, Yangzhou is depicted as a uniquely enchanting paradise on earth. When modern people think of Yangzhou, several keywords often come to mind, such as "blossoming willows in March," "the renowned capital to the east of Huai River," and "twenty-four bridges." Li Bai, wrote to a friend leaving for Yangzhou, "For River Town veiled in green willows and red flowers," a seemingly simple yet richly evocative line, which has become a timeless and widely celebrated verse. The prosperity of Yangzhou during the Tang Dynasty was closely tied to the excavation of the Grand Canal.

After the excavation of the Grand Canal was completed in the Sui Dynasty, Yangzhou, a natural junction of the canal and the Yangtze River, became a crucial hub for north-south transportation and a central marketplace for goods. *The Complete Tang Prose* describes Yangzhou's status as a transportation hub: "Yangzhou, the secondary capital, is a rich and fertile land in the southeast. It encompasses the advantageous terrain of the North and South Huai River Region and is a crucial point between Wu and Yue. The streets of Yangzhou are bustling, and the boats and carts are numerous." With the economic development around the Yangtze and Huai Rivers, Yangzhou became the "Shanghai" of the Tang Dynasty. At that time, it was said that "merchants and traders come and go to Guangling," and "rich merchants and great traders are always in the hundreds." A contemporary saying, "Yang first, Yi second,"

Yuan Jiang, *The Scroll of a View on the Garden of Separation* (partial)

highlighted Yangzhou's prominent status. In the blossoming spring of March, Yangzhou's flowers are as splendid as brocade, and the misty rain creates a dreamlike atmosphere, making it irresistibly attractive.

Intangible Cultural Heritage: Jade Carving

Although Yangzhou itself was not a jade-bearing area, its convenient transportation and great wealth in ancient times created favorable conditions for the formation and development of jade carving. Jade carving in Yangzhou is a major school of Chinese jade carving craftsmanship. Historically, Yangzhou jade artifacts developed unique local characteristics and artistic styles in terms of themes, types, and craftsmanship. Modern Yangzhou jade works combine the styles of "southern elegance and northern grandeur," showcasing an artistic charm that is graceful, delicate, and exquisitely translucent. In the middle Qing Dynasty, Yangzhou jade carving reached an unprecedented level of artistic achievement, with the reign of Emperor Qianlong marking its peak. Nearly ten large jade mountains weighing thousands of catties were crafted in Yangzhou for the Qing court. Yangzhou craftsmen excelled in creating large jade pieces and adeptly combining jade carving with painting and calligraphy. They employed perspective effects from painting in their designs and decorations, carving multi-layered patterns that transitioned from nearby to deep, and from large to small, of the general appearance of a picture, presenting vivid scenes with narrative elements. Among these, the jade mountain, called "Yu the Great controlling the waters," weighing over ten thousand catties and known as the "king of jade artifacts," became a world-renowned treasure.

Yangzhou Fried Rice

Yangzhou fried rice is renowned at home and abroad. It is rigorous in the selection of ingredients, meticulous in cooking and processing, and concerned with color coordination. The fried rice has distinct and fluffy grains, moderate in texture, glossy in color and irresistible in aroma.

Wensi Tofu Soup

Wensi tofu soup is made with the finest ingredients and exquisite knife skills. The tofu shreds are tender and silky, melting instantly in the mouth, accompanied by other fresh ingredients. The soup is flavorful, leaving a lingering aftertaste.

Three-Diced Steamed Bun

Three-diced steamed bun stands out for its traditional fermentation method and savory fillings. The "three dice" refers to diced chicken, pork, and bamboo shoots, which are harmonized. The bun's exterior is as white as snow, and the filling is juicy. The dish "boasts ample nutrition yet not excessive, a delightful flavor yet not overwhelming, rich oiliness yet not greasy, a crisp texture yet not hard, tender ingredients yet not mushy." It is a frequent delicacy on the breakfast tables of Yangzhou locals.

象山
甘露寺
小閘
大閘
鎮江府
南閘
銀山
昭關
南門橋
泰運橋
羅公廟
蒜山
高資港
金山寺

Zhenjiang: A Vital Transportation Hub

The Scenic Beauty of Beigu Mountain

Pacifying the Yangtze River

Dantu

Since ancient times, Zhenjiang has been closely related to the canals, and even its original name, "Dantu," is derived from them. The *Records of Jingkou* (an early monograph detailing the scenic sights of the Jingkou region) written by Liu Sun in the Southern Song Dynasty, documents a legend about Emperor Qin Shi Huang's eastern inspection tour and mountain excavation. It is said that upon Emperor Qin's arrival in the Zhenjiang area, he witnessed the rare colored clouds, or the so-called "*qi* of the sovereign," emanating from Longmu Lake. To disrupt the "*qi*," he dispatched a group of prisoners attired in red ("*dantu*," 丹徒 in Chinese) to carve a passage through the mountains, allowing the water to flow into the Yangtze River. Thus, the area around Longmu Lake came to be known as "Dantu."

Jingkou

"Between Jingkou and Guazhou is a stretch of water, / Zhongshan Mountain stands right there beyond a few folded hills." These two lines from the poem "Anchoring in Guazhou" by Wang Anshi (a politician, reformer, and poet in the Northern Song Dynasty) just reveal the highly convenient transportation between Zhenjiang (Jingkou), Yangzhou

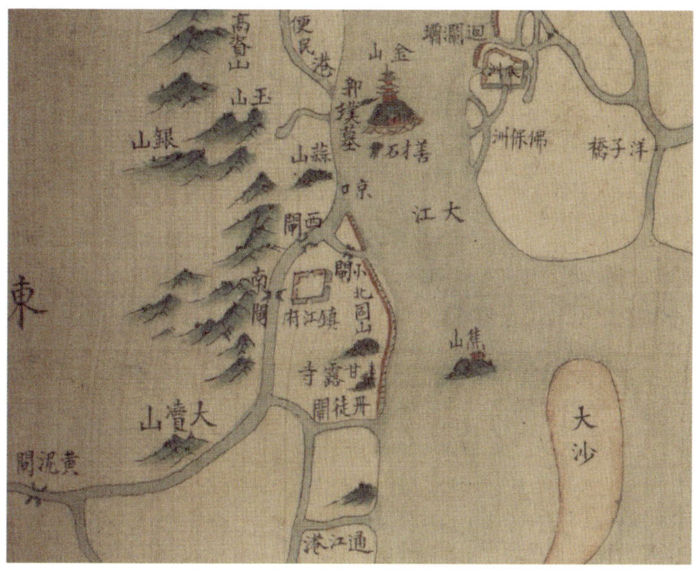

Complete Map of the Yellow River, Grand Canal, Lakes, and Rivers (partial)

(Guazhou), and Nanjing (Zhongshan Mountain). Zhenjiang and Yangzhou are situated respectively on the southern and northern banks of the Yangtze River, while Nanjing can be easily reached by sailing upstream along the river. Sun Quan once chose Zhenjiang as his capital and renamed it "Jingkou," a designation that lasted until the Song Dynasty. It was not until 211 that, driven by military considerations, Sun Quan relocated his capital to Moling and renamed it "Jianye."

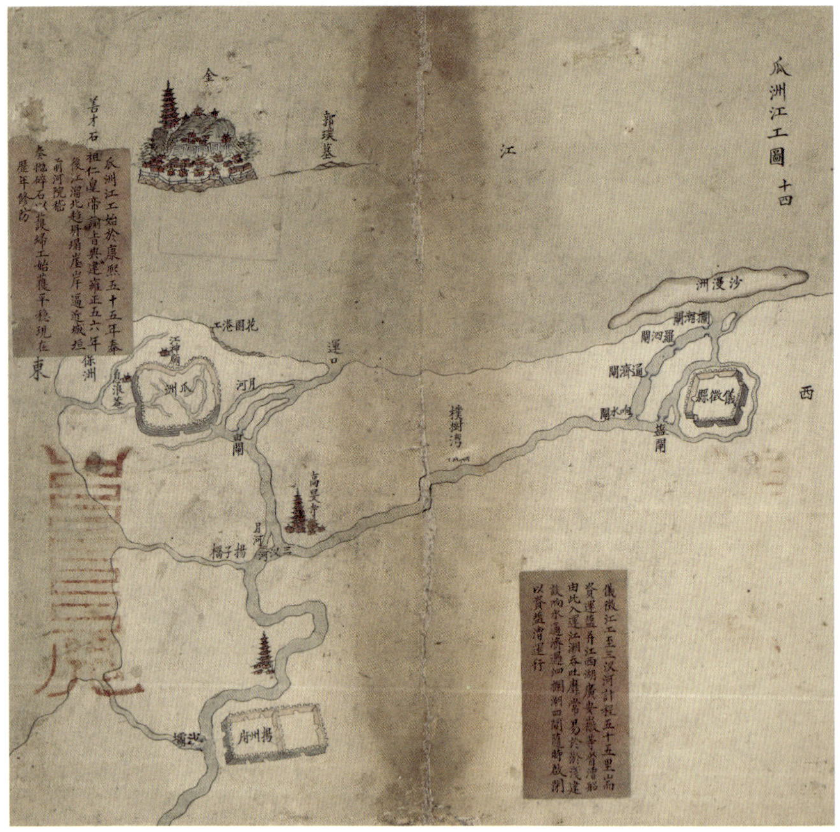

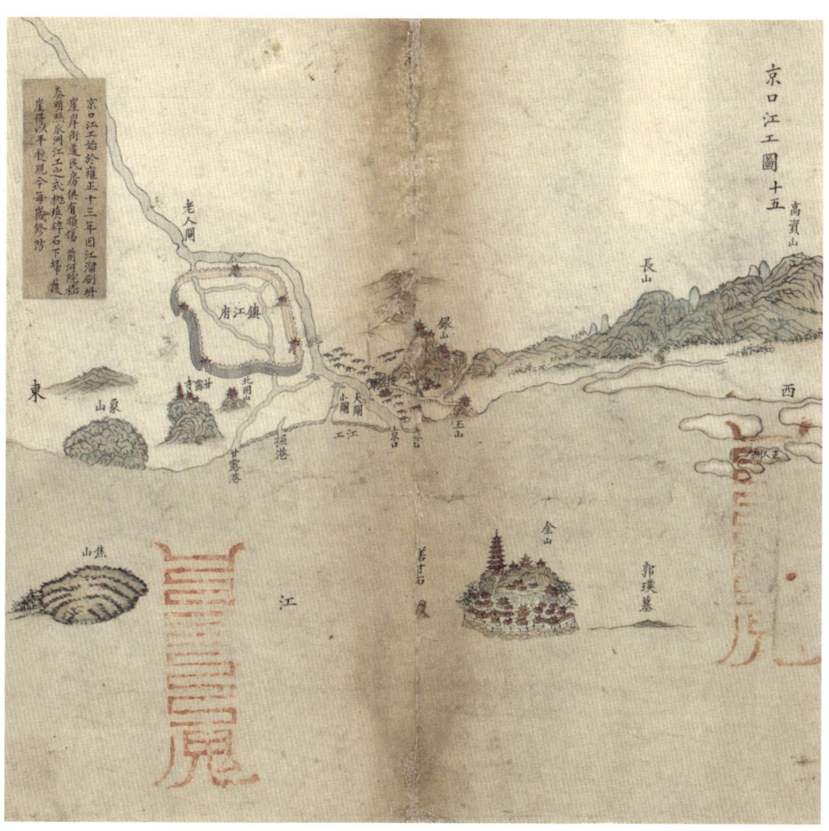

ABOVE: *Map of the Dams and Barrages in the Lower Reaches of the Yellow River · Jingkou River Engineering Map, No. 15*

LEFT: *Map of the Dams and Barrages in the Lower Reaches of the Yellow River · Guazhou River Engineering Map, No. 14*

In both maps, Jinshan Mountain can be seen amid the Yangtze River, indicating that Jingkou and Guazhou are within visible distance.

Pogangdu Canal

After Sun Quan relocated his capital to Nanjing, somehow the military status of Zhenjiang was strengthened. For one thing, due to that "between Jingkou and Guazhou is a stretch of water," stationing troops in Zhenjiang allowed for a northward view of Yangzhou, reinforcing the Kingdom of Wu's Yangtze River defense line. For another, Zhenjiang was the northern gateway to the capital of Wu, thus its significant position in military and defense could not be neglected. In addition, the fiscal revenue and taxes of Wu government all came from the three counties (Wu, Wuxing, and Kuaiji), so Sun Quan ordered his commander Chen Xun to excavate the Pogangdu Canal to connect Zhenjiang and Nanjing, facilitating the transportation of materials to Nanjing. "The river mirrors the crescent moon, while the Qinhuai River swells with the spring tide. It's the perfect time to travel along the Pogangdu Canal, as the spring waters are high."[1] Yan Zhenqing, a famous calligrapher in the Tang Dynasty, once praised the spring waters of the Pogangdu Canal in the Jurong section with such words.

The Ancient Zhenjiang Canal

The Zhenjiang section of the Grand Canal is 42.6 kilometers long, including a section called the ancient Zhenjiang Canal which is 16.69 kilometers long, from the Pingzheng Bridge, lying at the mouth of the canal, to the mouth of the Sancha River in Jianbi.[2] This section of the ancient canal, known as Dantu Waterway in the past, was excavated as early as in the Spring and Autumn Period and Warring States Period. In the 37th year of Qin Shi Huang's reign (210 BC), he excavated the Jingxian Mountain and initiated the Dantu River mouth, extending

---

1 Zhou Shaoliang, ed., *New Edition of the Whole Collection of Tang Dynasty Literature*, bk. 2, vol. 2 (Jilin Literature and History Press, 2000), p. 3865.

2 Liu Zhixiang, *Geographical Exploration of Zhenjiang* (Gansu People's Publishing House, 2012), p. 265.

the canal westward over ten *li*, and the aforementioned Pogangdu Canal was dug in order to connect the Dantu Waterway.[3] After the Sui and Tang dynasties, this waterway became an important part of the Jiangnan Canal system.

Zhenhai Army and Zhenjiang Army

During the Tang Dynasty, Jingkou was renamed as Runzhou, and it was also one of the seats of the commander of the Zhenhai Army. At the same time, Zhenjiang was not far from the Yangtze River estuary, so it was called "Zhenhai" (镇海, literally "pacifying the sea"). Han Huang, a famous minister in the middle and late Tang Dynasty, led the Zhenhai Army to rescue the Tang Court by transporting grain and rice to Luoyang on several occasions. When Zhao Kuangyin, the founder of the Song Dynasty, unified the country by destroying the Southern Tang Dynasty, he also reorganized the Zhenhai Army which had been in use for 200 years during the Tang Dynasty into the Zhenjiang Army,[4] from which the name Zhenjiang (镇江, literally "pacifying the river") came. In the third year of the Zhenghe period (1113) during the Northern Song Dynasty, Runzhou was elevated as Zhenjiang Prefecture. Zhenjiang, acting as a place name, never changed its name since then.

---

3 Zhang Qiang, *Studies on Chinese Canals and Transportation: Three Kingdoms, Jin Dynasty, and Southern and Northern Dynasties* (World Publishing Corporation, 2021), p. 99.

4 The book titled *Complete Records of Chinese Emperors (Volume 3) · Selected Writings of Emperor Taizu* of Song, edited by Lin Li, contains the imperial edict *Decree to Change Zhenhai Army to Zhenjiang Army*, "The name 'Zhenhai' refers to the former army stationed in Dantu. Since the unsettled situation in western Zhejiang, they were ordered to relocate to Yuhang, whose situation had been resumed in order since then. As a result, this military unit should be given a new name. In order to permanently safeguard border security, the old name Zhenhai Army should be changed to Zhenjiang Army."

A seated portrait of Emperor Taizu of Song (founding emperor of the Song Dynasty)

Throat of Water Transportation and Gateway to Wuyue Kingdom

After the Sui and Tang dynasties, Zhenjiang's position grew dramatically important. It became a pivotal location for transferring grain and rice tributes from the Qiantang River basin and the Taihu Lake region, and even that from Fujian, Guangdong, and Guangxi provinces would be transshipped through Zhenjiang. The grain transported via Zhenjiang from the Liangzhe Region[5] accounted for 25% of the nationwide shipments, and at its peak, the volume of grain passing through Zhenjiang comprised 68% of the entire country's grain transportation.[6] It can be said that the Zhenjiang Canal played a vital role in influencing the economic lifeline of the nation during ancient times. A famous verse written by Zha Shenxing, a poet of the Qing Dynasty, vividly describes the former glory of water transportation in Zhenjiang: "Ships stretch three thousand miles, laden with grain, / Lanterns light the riverbanks, ten thousand homes aglow."

Zhenjiang Opened as a Trading Port

In July 1842, a British force of more than 12,000 people attacked Zhenjiang. The defending officials and soldiers engaged in fierce combat with the British army, known as the Zhenjiang Defense War Against the British. After the First Opium War, the British invaders coveted the prosperous Zhenjiang. From 1849 to 1852, the British Consul in Shanghai, Rutherford Alcock, suggested to the British Governor of Hong Kong and Minister of China three times to "replace the trading ports of Fuzhou and Ningbo with Hangzhou, Suzhou, and Zhenjiang."[7]

---

5 In the Song Dynasty, the Liangzhe Region governed the areas south of the Yangtze River in present-day Jiangsu Province and the entire territory of Zhejiang Province.

6 Liu Zhixiang, *Geographical Exploration of Zhenjiang* (Gansu People's Publishing House, 2012), p. 265.

7 Xu Xu, *The Brief History of Zhenjiang* (Jiangsu University Press, 2020), p. 175.

The Dagukou Fort in the mid-19th century

Despite the frequent activities of the Taiping Army in Zhenjiang at that time, the British invaders still chose Zhenjiang as a trading port after the Second Opium War. Finally, on May 10, 1861, Zhenjiang was opened as a trading port. Subsequently, with significant trade, the city witnessed the development of finance and industry. At that time, Zhenjiang, Wuxi, and Hankou were collectively known as the "Three Ports of the Yangtze River."

Xijin Ferry

During the Three Kingdoms period, Xijin Ferry was originally named Suan Mountain Ferry, renamed as Jinling Ferry in the Tang Dynasty, and was not called Xijin Ferry until the Song Dynasty. Xijin Ferry is one of the main ferry crossings on the southern bank of the Yangtze River. It faced the famous Guazhou Ferry in Yangzhou across the river, with Wang Anshi's famous verse, "Between Jingkou and Guazhou is a stretch of water," referring precisely to Xijin Ferry. Xijin Ferry was not merely a simple port for crossing. It was a place where people waited for boats, transported goods, and consequently, settled down to live.

During the Sui Dynasty, ships sailing from Yangzijin (the mouth of the Grand Canal at that time) to Jingkou (present-day Zhenjiang) on the southern bank saw a constant stream of merchants coming and going. In the 26th year of the Kaiyuan period during the Tang Dynasty (738), the prefect of Runzhou, Qi Huan, altered the route for water transportation and opened up the Yilou River, which extended for 25 *li*. Since then, ferries from Jingkou could directly reach Yangzhou, with Jinling Ferry facing Guazhou, thus turning over a new page in the history of Jingkou as a key hub for water transportation.

During the Northern Song Dynasty, Xijin Ferry Ancient Street emerged at the foot of Yuntai Mountain and preserved the architectural features of the Tang and Song dynasties, such as bluestone streets. By the Ming Dynasty, as the Yangzhou riverbank shifted southward, the span of the Yangtze River between Zhenjiang and Yangzhou gradually narrowed, making Jingkou and Guazhou increasingly closer. As Gu Zuyu (a historical geographer of the early Qing Dynasty) wrote in his *Summary of Historical Geography Reading: Volume 23*, "The stretch from Guazhou Ferry to Jingkou was still eighteen *li* in the Song Dynasty; while it is no more than seven or eight *li* today." After the Qing Dynasty, the riverbank shifted northward by more than 300 meters, transforming the once bustling waterfront ferry into a dry dock. Here, shops of various trades lined up alongside the ancient ferry, and on Xijin Ferry Street, remnants of the past can still be seen, including the waiting pavilion where passengers once awaited their boats and the stone stairs used for embarking and disembarking.[8]

[8] Shao Rulin, *Luoyang: The Heart of the Grand Canal* (China Travel & Tourism Press, 2015), pp. 296–297.

Map of Kangxi Emperor's Southern Tour, vol. six (partial)

The Jinshan Temple Flooded by White Snake Is Not in Hangzhou

How Did the Water Flood Jinshan Temple?

There are three mountains in Zhenjiang: Jinshan Mountain, Jiaoshan Mountain, and Beigu Mountain.

Jiaoshan Mountain is an island surrounded by water in the Yangtze River, named after Jiao Guang who retreated to the mountain for seclusion during the Eastern Han Dynasty. The tale of Bai Suzhen dueling with the monk Fahai, leading to the legendary "flooding of Jinshan Temple," has made Jinshan Temple in Zhenjiang and Leifeng Pagoda in Hangzhou equally renowned.

The *Legend of the White Snake* is one of the four great Chinese ancient folk love stories. Its origins can be traced back to the periods of the Tang and Five dynasties, and it took its basic form during the Southern Song Dynasty. By the Yuan Dynasty at the latest, scholars had adapted it for *zaju* (杂剧, a traditional Chinese art form that combines songs, spoken dialogue, and dance) and storybooks. Compiled by Feng Menglong during the Ming Dynasty, the vernacular novel *The White Snake Bound Forever in the Leifeng Pagoda* is the earliest and most complete version of this legendary tale. From the Ming and Qing dynasties to the present day, the legend has been adapted and performed in various forms of folk literature and popular arts, including stories, songs, *baojuan* (宝卷, a kind of telling and singing literature), novels, operas, vernacular novels, dramas, and *tanci* (弹词, fiddle ballads in Chinese southern dialects), as well as films, television, cartoons, dance, and comic books. Its influence has expanded continuously, spreading throughout China and reaching many countries in Asia, including Japan, Korea, Vietnam, and India.

Illustrated Compendium of the Three Realms · Illustrations of the Three Mountains of Jingkou[9]

Jinshan Temple, steeped in history, traces its origin to the Eastern Jin Dynasty under the reign of Emperor Ming. Today, visitors to Jinshan Temple are greeted by a grand avenue leading directly to the temple gates, offering unobstructed views of the majestic structure standing tall against the backdrop of the Yangtze River. However, in ancient times, this serene landscape was vastly different. Jinshan

9 Compiled by Wang Qi (1529–1612) and his son Wang Siyi, *Illustrated Compendium of the Three Realms* was first published in 1609 during the 37th year of the Wanli period of the Ming Dynasty.

Temple, true to its name, was once an island situated amid the mighty Yangtze River, accessible only by boat. It was not until the early Tongzhi period of the Qing Dynasty that Jinshan Temple was connected to the southern mainland, transforming the once waterborne wonderland into a landbound paradise. As Guo Xiangzheng, a renowned poet of the Song Dynasty, aptly captured in his poem "Jinshan Journey": "Amid the boundless azure, Jinshan Mountain stands, / Snow-capped peaks and icy pillars, where the immortal palace expands." Little wonder is that the ancients bestowed upon this island amid the waters the elegant moniker "floating jade," and often associated its description with the fabled realms of "Penglai" and "Yaojing." Even Emperor Kangxi of the Qing Dynasty, once gazing upon Jinshan Mountain, couldn't help extolling its grandeur in his poem "Rainscape of Jinshan Mountain": "Endless river mists and boundless trees, / Rival even the peaks of Penglai and Yingzhou." The temple's grand entrance bears the inscription "Jiangtian Zen Temple," a testament to Kangxi's imperial calligraphy. Nestled against the mountainside, Jinshan Temple is further accentuated by the towering Cishou Pagoda, which stands resolutely atop Jinshan Mountain's summit. From afar, one might only perceive the temple, seemingly enveloping the mountain itself, giving rise to the local adage: "At Jinshan Temple, one sees the temple and the pagoda, but not the mountain."

Contrary to popular belief, the monk Fahai in history did not live in the Song Dynasty but in the Tang Dynasty. He is said to be the son of the then-famous statesman Pei Xiu. Within the temple grounds lies "Fahai Cave," which is said to be the very spot where Abbot Fahai engaged in his ascetic meditation. Throughout the ages, the mighty Yangtze River has witnessed the ebb and flow of its tides, including the fluctuation of the water levels surrounding the solitary island. As Su Shi, a renowned poet of the Song Dynasty, penned in his poem "Visiting Jinshan Temple": "I hear the tidal waves rise one *zhang* high, / Even in winter's chill, sandy traces remain. / South of Zhongling, the stone slabs lie, / Emerging and submerging with the ancient tide."

Thus, the notion of "flooding of Jinshan Temple" seems more akin to a romantic fantasy bestowed upon a natural phenomenon by the ancients. Yet, it is precisely such rich imagination and remarkable creativity that have shaped the long and illustrious history and culture of the Chinese nation.

Wen Zhengming, *Jinshan Mountain*

Beigu Tower: A Panorama of Historical Resonance

As Xin Qiji, a renowned poet of the Southern Song Dynasty, penned in his poem "Nanxiangzi: Ascending Beigu Pavilion with Thoughts of Home": "Where to gaze upon the vast land? / A panorama unfolds from Beigu Tower."

In 1205, during the first year of the Kaixi period of the Southern Song Dynasty, the patriotic poet Xin Qiji ascended the Beigu Tower. Gazing upon the mighty Yangtze River surging eastward, he was overwhelmed with a surge of emotions, both nostalgic and melancholy, leading him to compose the famous poem: "A thousand years of rivers and mountains, no trace of heroes to be found, save for the domain of Sun Quan" ("Yongyule: Recalling the Past in the Beigu Pavilion of Jingkou").

Although Beigu Tower was actually named by Emperor Wu of the Southern Liang Dynasty in 544, Xin Qiji's poems firmly established the association between Beigu Tower and the image of Sun Quan in the public mind. Sun Quan once established a short-lived capital here, named Tieweng (铁瓮, iron fortress) City. According to the *Records of Geography* compiled by Gu Yewang of the Southern Liang Dynasty, this city "had a circumference of 630 paces, with two gates in the south and west, both inside and outside were solidly built with brick walls." The ruins are located at the front peak of Beigu Mountain. In 211, out of military considerations, Sun Quan moved the capital to Moling, renaming it as "Jianye." To ensure the supplies for the new capital, the excavation of the canal, known as "Pogangdu," once again captured Sun Quan's attention.

Beigu Mountain in the Three Kingdoms period was quite extensive, encompassing the front, middle, and rear peaks. Today, only the rear peak overlooks the river remains, serving as the main peak of Beigu Mountain. Today, visitors can still appreciate its rugged terrain with the Yangtze River to the north and cliffs on the other three sides.

Jinshan Temple's Water-Land Buddhist Ritual

The water-land Buddhist ritual, also known as the "water-land dojo" or "water-land assembly," is an ancient Buddhist ceremony dedicated to offering prayers and supplications for the deceased. It also serves as a means for self-cultivation, repentance, and accumulation of merit. Jinshan Temple's water-land Buddhist ritual is one of the most grand and elaborate ceremonies in Chinese Buddhism, with a history of over 1,500 years.

Water-Land Buddhist Origins Attributed to Empress Dowager Ci Sheng (Ming Dynasty)

The water-land ritual paintings, a unique genre of religious art, emerged and flourished alongside the water-land Buddhist ritual, a grand ceremony dedicated to spiritual renewal and the supplication for the deceased. The imagery depicted in these paintings draws inspiration from the water-land ritual's procedures and folk beliefs.

The words in the painting above describe the legendary narrative of Emperor Wu of the Southern Liang Dynasty receiving divine guidance from a monk in a dream, leading to the creation of the water-land ritual. Embedded within its intricate details is a profound yearning for spiritual purification, the accumulation of merit, and the aspiration for universal peace. This painting holds immense religious significance, showcasing a harmonious blend of art forms, including music, painting, language, and ritual, making it a source of profound inspiration for generations to come.

This comprehensive ritual emerging during the process of Buddhism's sinicization is said to have originated from a dream of Emperor Wu of the Southern Liang Dynasty. Upon awakening, he consulted with the esteemed Zen Master Baozhi, leading to the creation of the ritual's procedures. In 508, during the seventh year of the Tianjian period, the first grand universal salvation ceremony was held at Jinshan Temple.

Today, the water-land Buddhist ritual at Jinshan Temple follows a meticulously structured sequence, including missions, such as establishing the sacred space, sending forth emissaries and issuing talismans, inviting the Buddhas and Bodhisattvas to ascend, making offerings, seeing off the deities, offering prayers for the deceased, bestowing blessings, and sending forth the enlightened beings. These ceremonial activities can last for a minimum of 7 days and nights, with some extending to as long as 49 days. The number of monks participating in the ritual can range from 48 to over 100, reflecting the grand scale of the event.

The music accompanying the Jinshan Temple's water-land Buddhist ritual harmoniously blends musical elements from various dynasties following the Northern and Southern Dynasties, indicating the rich cultural heritage embedded within this sacred tradition.

Zhenjiang Vinegar

Zhenjiang vinegar is renowned for its five distinctive qualities: color, aroma, acidity, mellowness, and richness. It boasts a clear and bright hue, a gentle tartness, a smooth and harmonious mouthfeel, a subtle sweet undertone, and a deep, savory flavor that intensifies with age. The consistent quality of the vinegar makes it an ideal dipping sauce for a variety of meat-filled snacks.

Pot Cover Noodles

Its preparation involves replacing the large lid of a soup pot with a smaller one, creating a makeshift cooking vessel within the larger pot. This unique cooking method yields noodles of unparalleled excellence—delightfully fragrant, bathed in a clear, savory broth, with a perfectly soft texture that resists clumping or sticking. Vibrant greens add a touch of freshness, while the noodles themselves boast an ideal balance of softness and elasticity, ensuring a delightful bite with every mouthful.

Crystal Salted Pork

This dish features pork trotters, meticulously cured using a brine made with niter, a salt substitute. The resulting pork is a symphony of textures and flavors, a feast for the eyes and the palate. Upon being cooked, crystal salted pork unveils its splendor: the meat, a vibrant shade of red, contrasts beautifully with the pristine white skin, both glistening with an extraordinary sheen. The aspic, a translucent masterpiece, resembles the purest crystal. The crystal meat is fat yet not greasy. Dipped into ginger vinegar, it offers a unique and mellow taste, crispy and fresh.

Nantong:
The First City of Modern China

Well-Known Langshan and Jinghai

Water Transportation of Nangtong and Zhang Jian's Industrial Salvation

The End of the Yangtze River and the Beginning of the Sea

On the bell tower of Nantong, there is a couplet written by Zhang Jian: Once a prefecture and now a county, / The end of the Yangtze River and the beginning of the sea. The second line refers to the geographical location of Nantong. During the pre-Qin and Eastern and Western Han dynasties, most areas of Nantong were still submerged in the sea. In the Han Dynasty, the flow of the Yangtze River slowed down, and the silt it carried gradually formed sandbanks which eventually connected to form land. It was the terrain vividly described as "the end of the Yangtze River and the beginning of the sea" that the Yangtze River surged into the Yellow Sea and the East China Sea.

South Tongzhou Prefecture

"South Tongzhou Prefecture, North Tongzhou Prefecture, South and North Tongzhou Prefectures connect the South and North." It is said that this line of the couplet was written by Emperor Qianlong who was inspired by the scenery when he passed by Nantong during his southern inspection tour. Some say it was written by Ji Xiaolan. North Tongzhou Prefecture refers to the present-day Tongzhou District in Beijing, while South Tongzhou Prefecture refers to modern-day

Nantong City. This couplet actually illustrates that Nantong was already a city with convenient transportation, connecting the south and north at that time.

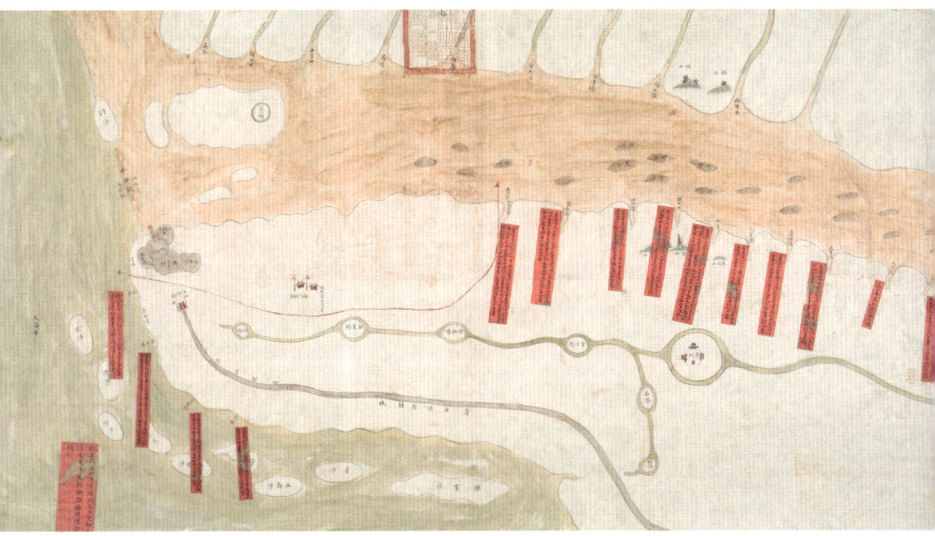

Coastal Map of Tongzhou **(partial)**

The *Coastal Map of Tongzhou* was approximately devised in the 20th year of the reign of Emperor Daoguang (1840). The map is annotated with such terms as "water salinity levels" and "fresh water from the river, salty water from the sea." In addition, the river and the sea are marked in different colors. The map features 15 red markers that indicate the depth of rising water, shoals, sunken reefs, and the distance to the ocean at various ports of the Yangtze River.

The Total Annals of the Qing Dynasty documents that Tongzhou prefecture "strategically guards the river and sea, firmly controls the islands, borders the sea on the northeast, and is situated at a critical port. The Langshan Mountain rises high, serving as a major sea defense at the north of the Yangtze River," highlighting the topography, terrain, and importance of Nantong. Therefore, in the second year of the reign of Emperor Yongzheng (1724), Tongzhou Subprefecture was separated from Yangzhou Prefecture and elevated to a prefecture directly under the provincial government.

Nantong-Yangzhou Canal

The Nantong-Yangzhou Canal runs through the cities of Yangzhou, Taizhou, and Nantong in Jiangsu Province and has two routes. The northern route is the old Nantong-Yangzhou Canal, which has a history of over 2,000 years. It was originally called Zhuyu Ditch, dug by Liu Bi, during the Han Dynasty. Initially, it did not reach the territory of Nantong, only connecting Taizhou and Yangzhou. Later, it extended to Hai'an and Rugao, eventually reaching Nantong. The old Nantong-Yangzhou Canal is also known as the Salt Transport Canal. Successive rulers after Liu Bi gradually extended this waterway to the southeastern coastal areas, which were newly formed, to obtain more salt taxes, eventually connecting it to the Yangtze River in Nantong. The old Nantong-Yangzhou Canal is approximately 150 kilometers long and is still navigable today. The other route is the new Nantong-Yangzhou Canal, which was excavated after the founding of the People's Republic of China.

The two Nantong-Yangzhou canals run almost parallel to each other. The most straightforward reason for constructing a new Nantong-Yangzhou Canal is that the old one is somewhat narrow for modern ships.

Nantong-Lüsi Canal

Nantong-Lüsi Canal, originally named as Salt Transport Canal, was excavated in the first year of the Xianchun period (1265) of the Southern Song Dynasty. It was a grand canal that ran from Tongzhou to the sea via Jinsha and Yuqingchang (present-day Yudong). It was dug by civilians mobilized by Li Tingzhi, Governor of North and South Huai River Region. This canal was initially meant to facilitate the movement of military boats, marking the early form of the Nantong-Lüsi Canal.

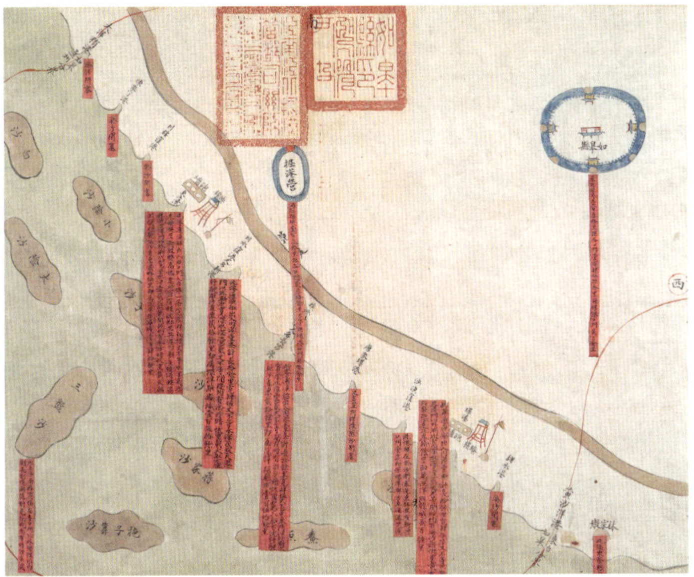

***Coastal Port Map of Rugao County* (partial)**

This map was devised during the reign of Emperor Daoguang. Due to the incomplete red labels, it is tentatively titled *Coastal Port Map of Rugao County* based on its content. The map bears seals inscribed in Han characters, reading "Seal of Rugao County" and "Seal of the Commanding Officer of Jiangnan and Jiangbei Juegang Camp," indicating that this map was an official military map. The map does not include a legend or scale, with orientation which was marked around its edges showing south at the top and north at the bottom. The map features detailed lookout towers and cannon walls at the ports, while other elements are roughly sketched with lines; various ports and sandbanks are annotated with text.

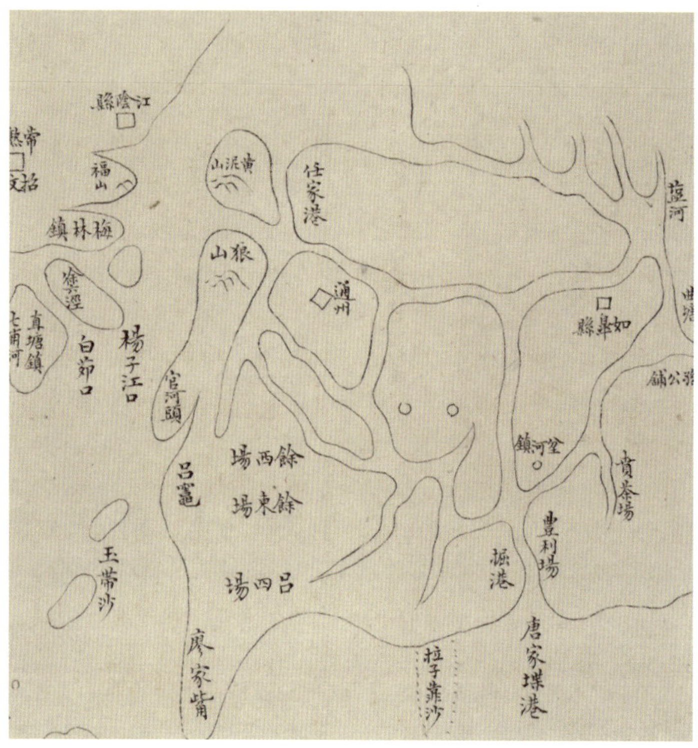

Coastal Map of the Seven Provinces **(partial)**

This map was copied and devised by Jin Baoyi in the seventh year of the reign of Emperor Guangxu (1881) of the Qing Dynasty. The original cartographer's life details are unknown. This map is one of the six series. All maps are hand-drawn copies, depicting landscapes, such as mountains, coastlines, islands, and sunken reefs, as well as marking administrative divisions like prefectures, subprefectures, and counties. Each map is accompanied by texts explaining coastal defenses, hydrology, and navigation routes at that time.

Dasheng Cotton Mill

Why did Zhang Jian start his industrial salvation with a cotton mill? After the Opium War, cotton yarn became a major commodity that Britain exported to China. Over the span of thirty to forty years, the quantity of imported cotton yarn in China increased significantly. Compared to 1881, the quantity of imported cotton yarn in China surged more than sixfold by 1891. In 1892, it reached a peak of 1.304 million *dan*.[1] At that time, most of the imported cotton yarn came from India, with high production and low prices. As a result, the price of domestically produced cotton yarn in China increased, and the domestic market was almost entirely occupied by imported cotton yarn. Against this backdrop, Zhang Jian decided to establish the Dasheng Cotton Mill, aiming to use industry to resist the economic invasion by foreign powers. The name "*dasheng*" (大生) was derived from *The Book of Changes*, "Caring for life is the greatest morality within the world." He took the words "greatest" (*da*, 大 in Chinese) and "life" (*sheng*, 生 in Chinese) from this sentence. Zhang Jian's view on modern industry was: "The greatest path to nourish the people and the wonderful technique to enrich the nation is not only for the sake of defense against humiliation, but defense is inherently within it."[2]

Zhang Jian

---

1 Compiled by Institute of Economics, Shanghai Academy of Social Sciences, and Academic Committee of Shanghai International Trade Association, *Shanghai Foreign Trade (1840–1949)*, vol. 1 (Shanghai Academy of Social Sciences Press, 1989), pp. 47–48.

2 Li Shujin, *Research on China's Modern Foreign Trade Thought* (Henan University Press, 2001), p. 88.

Tangjiazha

Zhang Jian's selection of the site for the Dasheng Cotton Mill at Tangjiazha is actually closely related to the canal. The water gate of Tangjiazha is located at the intersection of the old Nantong-Yangzhou Canal and the Gangzha River.[3] Zhang Jian referred to this place as "between the inland canal and the outer river."[4] This canal has been responsible for transporting salt and grain since the era of Liu Bi. Later, it was extended to Nantong, making the area accessible to both the north and the south. Thus, Tangjiazha, with its unique water transport advantages, became one of the birthplaces of modern Chinese national industry, and it quickly developed as a result. Today, Tangjiazha, known as the "first town of modern industrial heritage," has welcomed a new life through preservation.

Hohai Civil Engineering School

Zhang Jian was not only an advocate of saving the country through industry but also the founder of modern hydraulic education. Among his achievements, Hohai Civil Engineering School, the first higher education institution for hydraulic engineering in China, was established upon the initiative of Zhang Jian, who was then the President of the National Water Conservancy Bureau.[5] Educators Huang Yanpei and Shen Enfu responded to this initiative and founded the school in Nanjing, which is the predecessor of today's renowned Hohai University.

---

[3] Compiled by the Jiangsu Province Compilation Committee and edited by Shan Shumo, *Dictionary of Place Names of the People's Republic of China, Jiangsu Province* (The Commercial Press, 1987), p. 155.

[4] Zhang Jian, *Autobiography of Zhang Jian*, ed. Wen Mingguo (Anhui Literature and Art Publishing House, 2014), p. 132.

[5] Chen Guoda et al., ed., *China Geology Encyclopedia* (Shandong Science and Technology Press, 1992), p. 609.

The opening ceremony of Hohai Civil Engineering School in 1915 (Zhang Jian is in the tenth position from the left in the first row.)

Library of Hohai Civil Engineering School

Governance of the Huai River by Zhang Jian

At that time, as the President of the National Water Conservancy Bureau, Zhang Jian pioneered many innovative approaches to water governance. His *Jianghuai Water Conservancy Construction Plan* fully reflects his emphasis on advanced concepts of engineering design in water conservancy projects. He stressed the use of more scientific and precise modern surveying and calculation techniques for conceptual design. In this book, he began by presenting empirical measurement data, describing the "actual measurement of the heights of mountains" and "the lengths of rivers." He also stated: "In the second month of 1911, I established the Water Conservancy Survey Bureau in Qingjiangpu. The initial step was to measure the existing widths, depths, and heights of such main rivers as the Huai River, Yi River, Si River, and Shu River. Next, we moved on to lakes and ponds, and then to farmland, to determine the true shape of the entire terrain. Only with a true understanding of the terrain can we properly determine the course of rivers and the distribution of canals."[6] It is precisely because of this approach that Zhang Jian's strategy of "70% of the Huai River leading to the Yangtze River and 30% to the sea" proposed in the *Jianghuai Water Conservancy Construction Plan* was highly forward-thinking, as this strategy was derived based on various measured data and calculations.

In addition, Zhang Jian broke away from the traditional approach of focusing on post-disaster relief rather than long-term prevention and control. He advocated for prioritizing disaster prevention and management over relief efforts, aiming for a comprehensive strategy to

---

[6] Compiled by the Compilation Committee of *The Complete Works of Zhang Jian*, *The Complete Works of Zhang Jian*, vol. 4 (Shanghai Lexicographical Publishing House, 2012), pp. 387–398.

fundamentally eliminate flooding. He believed that the control of every flood required a substantial amount of government and private charitable relief funds, yet "the disaster was still not resolved, and the relief funds were quickly exhausted," which ultimately was not a sustainable solution. He stated: "To manage the Huai River, it is necessary to find an appropriate course, almost of an initiating nature." This remark not only referred to the specific route to guide the river but also indicated the need for a fundamental change in the principles and methods of managing the Huai River.

Zhang Jian's selected works on water governance

The "River Breeze and Sea Charm" of Nantong

The Hao River: The "Emerald Necklace" of Nantong City

The Hao River, originally an ancient moat, has been recorded in history since the fifth year of the Xiande period (958) in the Later Zhou Dynasty (951–960) when Nantong was established. A city with water has a certain charm. With the Hao River, Nantong exudes grandeur and subtlety. The Hao River is one of the only four ancient moats left in China. For centuries, it has played crucial roles in defense, drainage, and transportation, earning the nickname "the human circulatory system." Its orderly width, clear waters, meandering flow, and beautiful landscape where gulls fly and fish swim have earned it the reputation of the city's "emerald necklace."

Along the banks of the Hao River are significant historical and cultural sites, including the Nantong Museum, the first museum founded by Chinese people; Tianning Temple, an ancient temple of the Tang Dynasty; Arctic Pavilion, the only remnant of Nantong's ancient city wall; and Wenfeng Pagoda of the Ming Dynasty. The love for the river reflects the deep attachment of the Nantong people to their hometown. Over the years, the banks of the Hao River have been renovated multiple times, with pavilions and bridges blending into the scenery. Pleasure boats and yachts add to the enchanting atmosphere.

The nightscape of the Hao River in Nantong

Tianning Temple and Temple Street

Temple Street, as the name suggests, exists because of a temple. This temple is Tianning Temple, an ancient temple of the Tang Dynasty renowned as "the grand spectacle of the prefecture." Initially named as Guangxiao Temple, Tianning Temple faces south with its back to the north, with a layout featuring the main gate, the Hall of the Four Heavenly Kings, the Mahavira Hall, and the Medicine Buddha Hall (present-day Sutra Library) along its central axis. The west side houses the meditation hall and monk quarters, arranged with strict symmetry. In the northwest corner of the temple stands Guangxiao Pagoda, a five-tiered, octagonal structure made of brick and wood mix. In front of the main gate, there is a screen wall and a pair of stone lions for protection. Tianning Temple was established in the fourth year of the Xiantong period (863) in the Tang Dynasty, while Tongzhou was built in the fifth year of the Xiande period, nearly a hundred years later. Hence the saying in Nantong goes like this, "First there was the temple, then the city."

Temple Street is located in the northwest corner of ancient Nantong City. The main street runs north-south orientation, paved with square stones, and interspersed with east-west alleys. Although called "street," Temple Street is quite narrow and not the "commercial street" one might imagine. Instead, it is an old neighborhood filled with the flavor of everyday life, where many residents still live. Temple Street is rich in history and culture. Besides Tianning Temple, it features the Ziwei Academy built in the Song Dynasty and the Zilang Academy of the Qing Dynasty, which had the longest operating time during that period. The street boasts the former residences of one top scholar, one second-place scholar, and eighteen successful candidates in the highest imperial examinations. It also includes the first female teacher training college with undergraduate courses in China, founded by Zhang

Jian and his associates, Nantong's first higher elementary school, the only provincial elementary school, and the first elementary school for commoners. Nantong Middle School, which has educated countless students, is also located here, along with a contact point for the underground Communist Party of China and the former residences of revolutionary martyrs during revolutionary times. Within this 14-hectare ancient neighborhood, buildings from the Ming and Qing dynasties and the Republic of China are scattered. The daily life of ordinary people intertwines with the weight of history, creating the unique cultural atmosphere of Temple Street.

Temple Street in the snow

Nantong Blue Calico: A National Intangible Cultural Heritage

Nantong blue calico, also known as "medicine pattern cloth" or "sprinkled flower cloth," originated from the Qin and Han dynasties and flourished during the prosperous commercial periods of the Tang and Song dynasties. In the massive work *Complete Collection of Illustrations and Writings from the Earliest to Current Times* compiled by Chen Menglei, a scholar of the Qing Dynasty, it recorded: "Medicine pattern cloth was first dyed blue by applying ash medicine to the cloth. When it was dry, the grey medicine was removed, and then it was green and white, with figures, flowers, birds, and poems in various colors, and it was used to fill the coverlets and curtains." Nantong is renowned as the home of blue calico. The production of modern blue calico involves several steps: pattern design, template making, stencil printing, dyeing with plant-based dyes, starching to reveal the patterns, and washing. All these processes are done by hand. The combination of blue and white aligns with traditional Chinese aesthetic standards, and these two colors alone can create a simple yet natural, ever-changing, and vibrant world of blue and white art. The patterns are inspired by popular folk stories, theatrical characters, and especially by auspicious motifs composed of plants and animals. These motifs often use metaphors and puns, with simple and elegant designs reflecting the common people's longing for a happy life and their straightforward aesthetic taste, making it a unique form of Chinese folk art.

Langshan Chicken

Langshan chicken is an ancient local breed originally from Rudong County of Nantong. It is characterized by its black feathers and red comb, robust physique, thin skin, tender meat, and large, abundant eggs. There are various ways to cook Langshan chicken, including stir-frying, roasting, braising, deep-frying, stewing, and simmering, but it is best when simply stewed.

Hibiscus-Shaped Patchouli Dumplings

Hibiscus-shaped patchouli dumplings use the leaves of the aromatic herb patchouli as the dumpling wrapper and sweet osmanthus bean paste as the filling. They are lightly fried to make patchouli dumplings. The appearance of the dumplings resembles a hibiscus bud about to bloom, white as snow with a hint of green. They have a refreshing and fragrant taste, helpful to dispel heat and remove dampness. After eating them, the mouth feels cool and the fragrance lingers for a long time. They are particularly suitable for hot summer.

Rudong Clam

Rudong County of Nantong boasts a vast coastline and extensive tidal flats, rich in countless seafood delicacies. Among these, the most renowned is Rudong clam, celebrated as "the freshest delicacy in the world." Autumn is the best season for these clams, as they are at their plumpest and most flavorful times. The clam meat is succulent and juicy when prepared, offering a tender and smooth texture. It stands out for its exceptional freshness, making it a true gourmet treat that is visually appealing and delicious in flavor.

泰興
靖江
鎮江
丹陽
常州
金壇
江陰
金匱
昭文
常熟
溧陽
宜興
荆溪
九龍
任公釣臺
元墓

Changzhou:
The Key Support of the Central Wu Region

A Prosperous and Abundant Cornerstone of the Southeast

Suzhou and Changzhou: The Land of Abundance in the Country

Ji Zha's Assignment to Yanling

King Shoumeng of Wu believed that Ji Zha was the most capable of his four sons and should succeed to the throne. However, Ji Zha believed that he should pass the throne to his elder brother. Therefore, he refused. His elder brother died not long after ascending to the throne, and his second brother proposed to Ji Zha again, but Ji Zha declined. In 547 BC, his second brother, who had become the new King of Wu, gave Ji Zha the largest piece of land around the capital, that is, Yanling, present-day Changzhou, Wuxi, Jiangyin, Danyang, Yixing, and other large areas. Yanling, Changzhou's original name, has been carried down.

Yan City

A saying goes that you have to visit Beijing to learn about the Ming and Qing dynasties, Hangzhou to learn about the Southern Song Dynasty, Xi'an to learn about the Sui and Tang dynasties, and Yan City to learn about the Spring and Autumn Period. Yan City ruins were discovered in the 1970s. The records of the Yan City in ancient books vary. Some say it was Ji Zha's dominion, while others say it was where the State of Yue's hostages were held. The general shape of Yan City is three

Map of Townships and Bridges in Wujin and Yanghu Counties, Changzhou Prefecture

The map was made around the middle of the Daoguang period to the Xianfeng period of the Qing Dynasty.

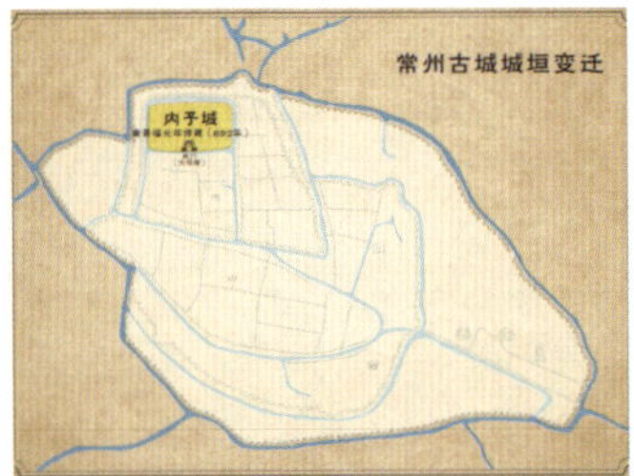

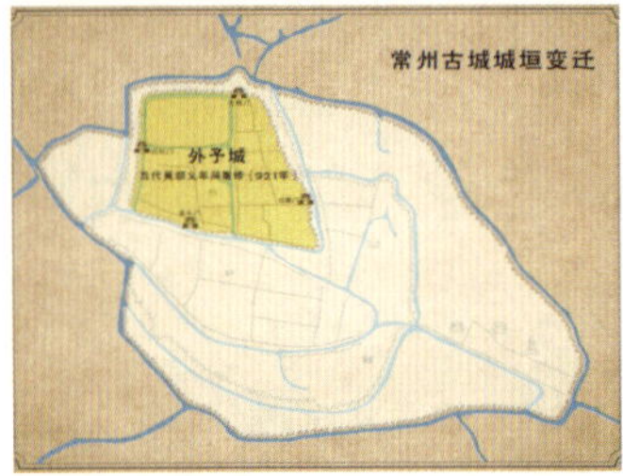

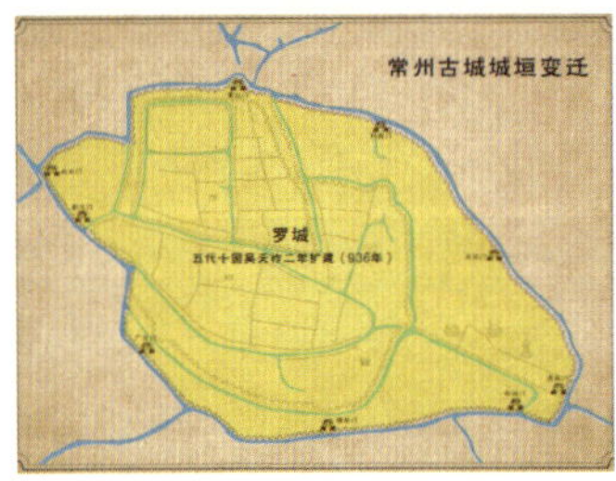

Map of Changzhou Ancient City Wall Changes

Source: Changzhou Mapping Institute

cities and three rivers; outside the city, there was a river; outside the river, there was the city. The structure is extremely distinctive. The three rivers outside the Yan City are human-made canals. You will know the reason why the ancients always spoke of cities and rivers together when you see Yan City.

Changzhou: The Most Important City in the Eastern Yangtze River

During the Tang Dynasty, Changzhou was listed as one of the ten most *wangzhous* (望州).[1] After the completion and opening of the Beijing-Hangzhou Grand Canal, Changzhou's geographical advantages became even more significant, as it was connected to the Yangtze River on the left and Taihu Lake on the right, with the canal running through the city. After being sent to Changzhou as the prefectural governor, Dugu Ji, a poet of the Tang Dynasty, and his wife took the initiative to thank the emperor, saying that "Changzhou was the greatest of all cities in the eastern part of the Yangtze River," and that it was a great honor to be the prefectural governor of Changzhou.

[1] The *wangzhou* is similar to today's municipalities with independent planning status.

The Fourth Largest City of the Song Dynasty

Unlike other cities that thrived along rivers, Changzhou was bisected by the Beijing-Hangzhou Grand Canal, and the ships that floated down the canal passed through the city. During the Sui and Tang dynasties, the Jiangnan Canal entered the city through the Guangji Bridge outside the Chaojing Gate, then exited from the Dongshui Gate via the Xishuiguan. The merchants and boatmen came one after the other to Changzhou. Changzhou's economy became increasingly prosperous and its population grew rapidly. During the Song Dynasty, the size of Changzhou City was second only to Kaifeng, Suzhou, and Hangzhou. As a result, Changzhou is also known as "a land of strategic location in Wu region and a meeting of boats and carriages in Baiyue."

The Canal Diversion

The Grand Canal has been constantly re-routed for thousands of years, resulting in the city of Changzhou changing and expanding in size along with the canal. After the Sui Dynasty, Changzhou was an important stagecoach station for the water transportation of grain to the capital, and the canal moved south three times from the Yuan Dynasty to the 21st century, resulting in the present "three rivers and four cities" of Changzhou, in which "the city was built on the river, the river moved with the city, and the river and city were intertwined."[2] During the Song Dynasty, Changzhou was the fourth largest city in China. When Tang He, the founding general of the Ming Dynasty, was appointed to Changzhou, he suggested to Emperor Zhu Yuanzhang that Changzhou should be shrunk in size, as it was even larger than the capital, Nanjing. Zhu Yuanzhang heeded the advice and shrank Changzhou to a quarter of its original size.

---

2 "Look at Changzhou's Role in National Strategic Opportunities," *Changzhou Daily*, September 30, 2019, A04 ed.

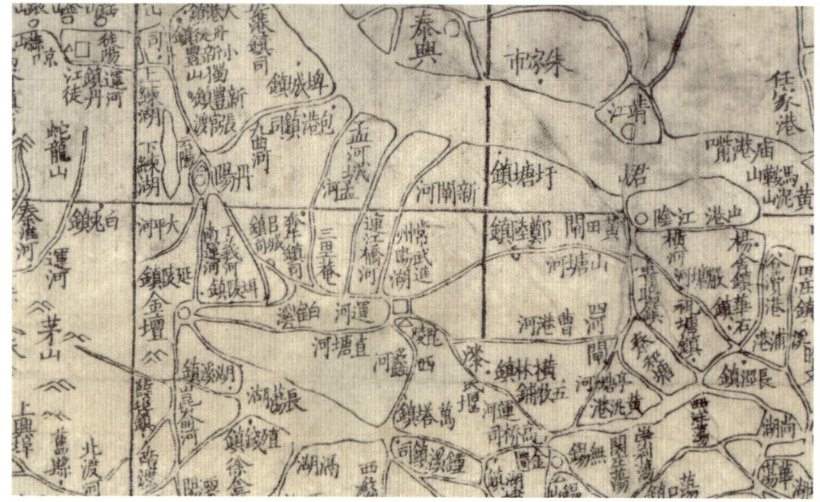

Complete Map of Jiangsu (section of Changzhou)

Benniu Sluice

The Changzhou section of the Grand Canal is 45.8 kilometers long, from the entrance of Jiuli Village in the Benniu Town to the exit of Guhuaitan in the Henglin Town. The Benniu Town has been a very famous place since ancient times. The *Annal of Piling During the Xianchun Period* written in the Song Dynasty recorded: "During the Han Dynasty, a golden ox came out of Shichi in Shandong Province and went to Qu'e. Its path was blocked by a fence, causing the ox to charge forward wildly, hence the name 'Benniu' [Charging Ox]." It is also quoted from the *Chronicle of Sifan*: "There was a bronze ox in the Wance Lake, which was chased by people, and it went up the east mountain into the soil cave and walked to this fence, and hence the name of today's fences and weirs." According to this statement, the name of Benniu Town has a history of more than 2,000 years since the Han Dynasty.[3]

The Benniu Sluice in the Benniu Town is a well-known water conservation landmark. As for the time when the Benniu Sluice was built, there were three statements. The first one refers that the Benniu Sluice was built in the Spring and Autumn Period, the second one refers to the Qi and Liang dynasties, and the third one refers to the Sui Dynasty. *The Book of Southern Qi Dynasty · Biography of Quan Jingwen* had remarked that "if you arrive at Benniu Town, you can rest on the bank." It can be seen that the Benniu Sluice appeared in the period of the Northern and Southern Dynasties. The Benniu Sluice was well-known during the Tang and Song dynasties due to its significance in water transport and people's livelihood. During the Xining period of the Song Dynasty, the Japanese monk Cheng Xun, who journeyed throughout China, documented the operation of the Benniu Sluice in *A Journey to Tiantai and Wutai Mountain*: "On September 8, I arrived

3 Hu Qiwei, Zhou Chen, and Jiang Hao, *A Reading of Canals* (Shanghai Jiao Tong University Press, 2014). p. 243.

***Map of Kangxi Emperor's Southern Tour*, vol. 6 (partial)**

Map of Kangxi Emperor's Southern Tour is a masterpiece of art and history painted by a painter of the Qing Dynasty named Wang Hui (1632–1717), totaling 12 volumes and over 200 meters in length. It shows the mountains, rivers, cities, and places of interest that Emperor Kangxi passed along the way from the time he left the capital on his second southern inspection tour (1689). More than 10,000 figures, thousands of cattle, horses, dogs, sheep, and other livestock, mountains and rivers, the city government offices, streets and villages, pawnbrokers, and merchants are all depicted.

The above is a portion of the sixth volume of *Map of Kangxi Emperor's Southern Tour*, which depicts Kangxi's journey from the Benniu Town to Changzhou Prefecture via the Grand Canal. Unlike the other volumes which are either in the Palace Museum or in foreign art museums, the sixth volume is divided into seven parts, each in the hands of a different private collector. The bridge in the picture above is the Wanyuan Bridge, which is still in use now.

Map of Garrison Area in Changzhou

The map was made during the reign of Emperor Qianlong and Jiaqing of the Qing Dynasty. The whole map is not attached with the legend and scale, but marks the neighboring county boundaries and the distance between them. The map graphically depicts the hills, rivers, garrison areas, bridges, etc., and has notes in each place, marking the posts of soldiers stationed in each garrison area.

at the Benniu Sluice and slept there. At dawn on September 9, as I crossed the weir, I saw there were five windlasses each to the left and to the right, with sixteen water buffaloes, eight on the left and eight on the right."[4] However, there were times when the Benniu Sluice was abandoned and neglected. When Su Shi passed by the Benniu Sluice in the Northern Song Dynasty, he lamented, "There is no water in the well in June, and I look up to see the ancient weir across the Benniu."[5]

The sluice had been abandoned many times, but due to the important role it played, it was often rebuilt. The *Annal of Piling During the Xianchun Period*, the earliest surviving chronicle of Changzhou, contains an article by the great poet Lu You titled "The Record of the Benniu Sluice in Changzhou." It recorded the process of rebuilding the Benniu Sluice by governor Zhao Shanfang and discussed the importance of the waterway transportation.[6] It also mentioned the familiar saying that Suzhou and Changzhou are the "bread basket" of China.

The Southward Exodus During the Period of Yongjia in the Western Jin Dynasty

The southward exodus during the period of Yongjia was the first large-scale migration of people from north to south in Chinese history. Most of the Sima clan of the Western Jin Dynasty and their royal family and officials moved to Nanjing for the construction of their new capital. Present-day Jiangsu Province received 70% of the population of this migration, and Changzhou received 70% of this 70%, indicating that

4 Zhai Guangzhu, *Standardization in Ancient China* (Shanxi People's Publishing House, 1996), p. 221.

5 Compiled by Zeng Guofan, *Notes to Eighteen Schools of Poetry* (Yuelu Shushe, 2015), p. 645.

6 Compiled by Cheng Guozheng, *Selected Literatures of Ancient Chinese Architecture in Song, Liao, Jin, and Yuan Dynasties* (Tongji University Press, 2010), p. 46.

almost half of the immigrants stayed in Changzhou, according to the *History of Chinese Migration*. According to the research, the famous calligrapher Wang Xizhi's family settled in the Changzhou area in the late Western Jin Dynasty.

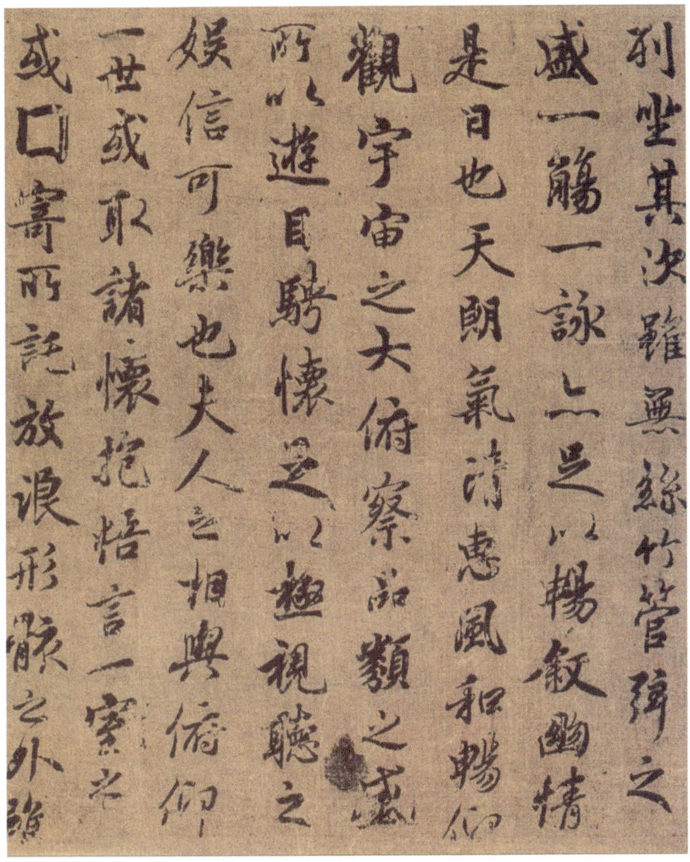

Wang Xizhi, *Lanting Xu* (copied by Chu Suiliang, partial)

Grain Transportation in Changzhou

With the opening of the Beijing-Hangzhou Grand Canal, Changzhou rapidly developed. By the Song Dynasty, the annual grain transportation volume in Changzhou reached a peak of 7 million *dan*. "From Suzhou and Songjiang to the seven prefectures of Fujian and Zhejiang, all travelers going between the northern and southern capitals must pass through this route."[7] In the 26th year of the Hongwu era (1393) of the Ming Dynasty, Changzhou Prefecture actually levied more than 530,000 *dan* of grain, close to the combined total of Guangxi and Yunnan provinces. In the second year of the Yongzheng era of the Qing Dynasty (1724), Wujin County had over 120 grain transport ships (referring to the fleet for transporting military and civilian grain), moored outside the west gate of the city in the area of Yongfengli by the Great King Temple, and later moored to the area around Baijia Bridge, until the early years of the Daoguang era of the Qing Dynasty.[8]

---

7 Yang Peng, *Channel Economy: An Emerging Model for Regional Economic Development* (China Economic Press, 2012), p. 17.

8 Xiang Si, *The Story of Emperor Qianlong's Southern Tour* (Forbidden City Press, 2016), p. 228.

Beyond the Dinosaur Park

Tianning Temple

The millenarian ancient Tianning Temple is located in the center of Changzhou, with the Grand Canal flowing gently not far away. Tianning Temple was originally built during the Zhenguan era of the Tang Dynasty. The Zen Master Farong, the first patriarch of the Niutou Sect, came to his hometown of Changzhou to raise funds for food when the monks in the mountains had nothing to eat. He built more than ten rooms to provide shelter for the monks, marking the beginning of the temple's establishment. During the Tianfu era of the Tang Dynasty, when Master Wei Kang passed through Changzhou and heard about Master Farong's past deeds, "he donated relics and chose a temple site" to officially build the temple named "Guangfu Temple." Since the Song Dynasty, the temple's dharma assemblies have been extremely prosperous, and the temple records state that "the prosperity of the dharma assemblies is well-known, with solemn and wonderful achievements, leading in the southeast." In the first year of the Zhenghe era (1111) of the Northern Song Dynasty, Emperor Huizong issued a decree to rename the temple as "Tianning Temple." After that, the temple's name was changed three times, and during the

Tianning Pagoda

Zhiyuan era of the Yuan Dynasty, it was renamed as Tianning Temple again, a name that has been used to this day. During the Qing Dynasty, Tianning Temple was thriving with incense and strict regulations, as well as solemn ceremonies, and Emperor Qianlong inscribed a plaque reading "Buddhism in Dragon City." The Pagoda of Tianning Temple, seen today, with its octagonal eaves and dignified appearance, towering into the clouds, was rebuilt in 2007. The temple is grand in scale, with towering ancient trees and winding paths, truly a rarely pure and joyful land in the bustling city.

Spring and Autumn Canal: The Grand Canal in Changzhou

The Changzhou section of the Grand Canal is 45.8 kilometers long, of which 23.4 kilometers run through the city. Throughout the ages, both sides of the canal have been the economically prosperous areas of Changzhou, leaving behind such historical names as Rice Market River, Bean Market River, Qingguo Lane, North Bank Fore and Aft the Canal, and so on. Today, the river in Changzhou City flows from Xishuiguan, along Xixiatang and Dongxiatang, across Xinfang Bridge and Yuanfeng Bridge to Dongshuiguan, and still retains the route of the canal during the Spring and Autumn Period, hence the name Spring and Autumn Canal. There are many cultural relics around the Grand Canal, such as the Mooring Pavilion, where Su Shi, the poet of the Song Dynasty, tied his boat, and the Imperial Dock, where Emperor Qianlong of the Qing Dynasty disembarked during his southern tour.

The Benniu Sluice is an ideal location for recounting the history of the canal. To the east of the Benniu Sluice, an ancient bridge known as Wanyuan spans the confluence of the Grand Canal and the old Meng River. Wanyuan Bridge is regarded as the most humane ancient bridge in Changzhou. From a distance, the bridge appears to be a busy thoroughfare, with people traversing it in both directions. Below the bridge, hundreds of barges navigate the waterway, creating a dynamic and impressive sight. The Grand Canal flows through the west gate of Changzhou, beneath a tall three-hole stone bridge which spans across the north and south sides of the canal. This bridge is known as Guangji Bridge, or alternatively as Xicang Bridge (literally West Warehouse Bridge). It is commonly referred to by this latter name derived from the fact that it is situated close to a warehouse.

Xicang Bridge End is the famous granary of Changzhou: Xicang Warehouse. This granary was built in the fifth year of the Zhengtong era (1440) of the Ming Dynasty, more than 60 years earlier than the Xicang Bridge. It is said that there was the Xicang Warehouse first, followed by the Xicang Bridge. At that time, Xicang Warehouse stored the grain of Wujin on a grand scale and was the largest official warehouse in Changzhou. Gradually, a famous rice market in the Jiangnan region formed around it, and this section of the river was thus named the Rice Market River. The commercial area near Lock Bridge Bay on the north bank of the canal was mainly composed of soybean businesses hence it was called Bean Market River. Speaking of Bean Market River, it is actually Bean Market Street, a famous bean market in the Jiangnan region. Changzhou's bean market started in the Xuande era of the Ming Dynasty. In the 28th year of the Guangxu era (1902) of the Qing Dynasty, with the successive excavation of Mengdu, Desheng, and Zaogang Rivers, Changzhou's water transportation was further improved, and the bean market also developed rapidly, reaching its peak in the early years of the Republic of China. By the 17th year of the Republic of China (1928), there were already ten bean firms in Changzhou, such as Tongfeng, Pan Tongchang, Baocheng, and so on.

Night view of the Grand Canal in Changzhou

Changzhou Bamboo Carving: A National Intangible Cultural Heritage

Changzhou bamboo carving is one of the traditional handicrafts of Changzhou and also has a place in the "garden" of Chinese arts and crafts. Changzhou bamboo carving is a technique that uses the thin layer of bamboo bark on the surface of the bamboo to carve patterns, removing the bamboo bark outside the pattern to reveal the texture below the bamboo bark. When carving, the author skillfully applies the skills of fully retaining, slightly retaining, not retaining, retaining more, and retaining less, making the work show layers, chiaroscuro, and shades, thereby presenting artistic expressiveness. Changzhou bamboo carving not only tests the author's carving skills and artistic expression ability but also reflects their attainments in carving, calligraphy, poetry, seal cutting, and modeling. It has high ornamental and collection value and has been loved and collected by celebrities and scholars of all ages.

Tianmu Lake Fish Head in Casserole

As one of the top ten famous dishes in Changzhou, Tianmu Lake Fish Head in Casserole is made from the fish head of the four-kilogram wild gray chub that is abundant in the Tianmu Lake, matched with the fresh and pure water of the Tianmu Lake and simmered over a long period of time over a mild fire. The salted vegetables are fresh but not fishy; the fish meat is fat but not greasy; and the soup is creamy and original. This dish is famous throughout the country.

Straw Duck

Straw duck is a specialty often found in the Changwu area. It is made with meticulous attention to ingredients and a complex process. The belly of the duck contains a variety of ingredients, such as honey dates, pine nuts, and ginkgo nuts. The duck is then wrapped in straw and deeply marinated, allowing the straw's aroma to penetrate the duck's flesh, creating a harmonious blend of fragrance and marinated flavor. The finished dish retains the shape of the duck, with tender meat and soft bones, and has a distinctive flavor.

Changzhou Vegetarian Ham

Changzhou vegetarian ham is made from tofu skin, and it takes several steps to make it right. First, make the brine, and soak the tofu skin in the brine; then roll up the tofu skin, tie it tightly with string, and put it in a steamer to steam; finally, take it out and let it cool. The finished vegetarian ham is soy-yellow in color, smells good, tastes slightly sweet, and has a texture that is both dry and fresh, tough and soft, with a smooth flavor and crunchy texture. Although it is not really meat, it tastes better than meat.

無錫
縣城
北門
東門
南門
西門
横浜
外吊橋
西吊橋
南吊橋
東吊橋
黄埝橋
高子橋
運河

Wuxi:

The Pearl of the Taihu Lake

A River-Encircled Ancient City

The Canal as a Moat

The Taibo River

There is a story about Taibo in the *Records of the Grand Historian · Annals of the Zhou Dynasty*. Gugong Danfu, also known as the King Tai of the Zhou Dynasty, had three sons: the eldest was Taibo, the second was Zhongyong, and the youngest was Jili whose son was later known as King Wen of the Zhou Dynasty. Taibo was aware that King Tai of Zhou wished to make his youngest son Jili to inherit the reins of power, so when King Tai of Zhou was sick, Taibo made excuses to venture deep into the mountains to gather medicinal herbs, and went to the "barbarian lands" of south China, present-day Wu region.[1] Regarding Taibo, Confucius extolled: "Surely we can say that Taibo possessed ultimate virtue! He declined rulership of the world three times ..." What is more, Taibo was capable, and he dug the earliest known artificial canal—the Taibo River. In 2019, unmistakable traces of human craftsmanship along the banks of the Bodu River (also known as the Taibo River in ancient literature) were uncovered during archaeological excavations at the Meili Site in Wuxi, confirming the

1 Jiang Boqian, *Four Books Reader* (Jiangxi Education Press, 2018), p. 147.

Map of Kangxi Emperor's Southern Tour, vol. 7 (partial, colored on silk)

authenticity of the Taibo River. This discovery simultaneously pushes forward the origin of Chinese canals by over a thousand years.

Water Alleyways of Jiangnan

The ancient canal within the urban area of Wuxi stretches approximately 11 kilometers from Wu Bridge in the north to Xiadian Bridge outside the South Gate. Despite its relatively short length, the scenery varies significantly between its upper and lower sections. In the wider stretches of the canal, it resembles the surface of a river; while in the narrower parts, residents on both banks can converse through the windows facing each other, akin to alleyways. Hence, the ancient canal of Wuxi is also hailed as the "water alleyways of Jiangnan."

Water alleyways of Jiangnan—the ancient canal of Wuxi

Huang Xie: The Lord of Chunshen

The significant contributions of Huang Xie, the Lord of Chunshen in Wuxi, where he constructed embankments and managed the lakes, resulted in the initial separation between the ancient waterways of Wu and the Furong Lake (now known as the Wuxi Lake). The *Annal of Piling During the Xianchun Period* of the Southern Song Dynasty states, "In the second year of King Zhuangxiang's reign (248 BC) of the Qin Dynasty, the Lord of Chunshen was enfeoffed to the east of the Yangtze River and established a city on the ruins of the State of Wu."

Huang Xie primarily focused on water management in Wuxi. At that time, the ancient waterways of Wu and the Furong Lake were intertwined, covering an area of 1,025 square kilometers, with a considerable water storage capacity. During the rainy season, floods were common. Consequently, Huang Xie constructed embankments along some sections of the waterways, separating the rivers from the lake. This not only facilitated navigation but also allowed the lake water to be used for irrigation, and flow into the Taihu Lake,[2] thereby making the rivers and the lake of Wuxi have functions of shipping, alleviating flooding and drought, and irrigation. After his efforts, the river in Wuxi began to be called a "pond." Hence, the name "Bei Pond" in the northwest of Wuxi, the "Nanmen Pond" in the south of the city, and even the Wuxi Canal was called the "Pond River." Many place names in Wuxi, such as "Huangbudun," "Dawangji," "Chunshenjian," "Huangtiangang,"

[2] *The Local History of Wu and Yue* states, "In Lishan of Wuxi, during the time of the Lord of Chunshen, cattles were used as sacrificial offerings in a grand ceremony. Additionally, a grand embankment was constructed along the southern shore of the Wuxi Lake." "Regarding the Wuxi Lake, the Lord of Chunshen oversaw the construction of embankments along its shores. Furthermore, he excavated the Yuzhao Canal, which extended eastward to the fields. These fields were named Xubei. Additionally, a large canal was dug from the fields of Xubei southward, leading to the Taihu Lake, to drain the accumulated water from the western outskirts of Wuxi County."

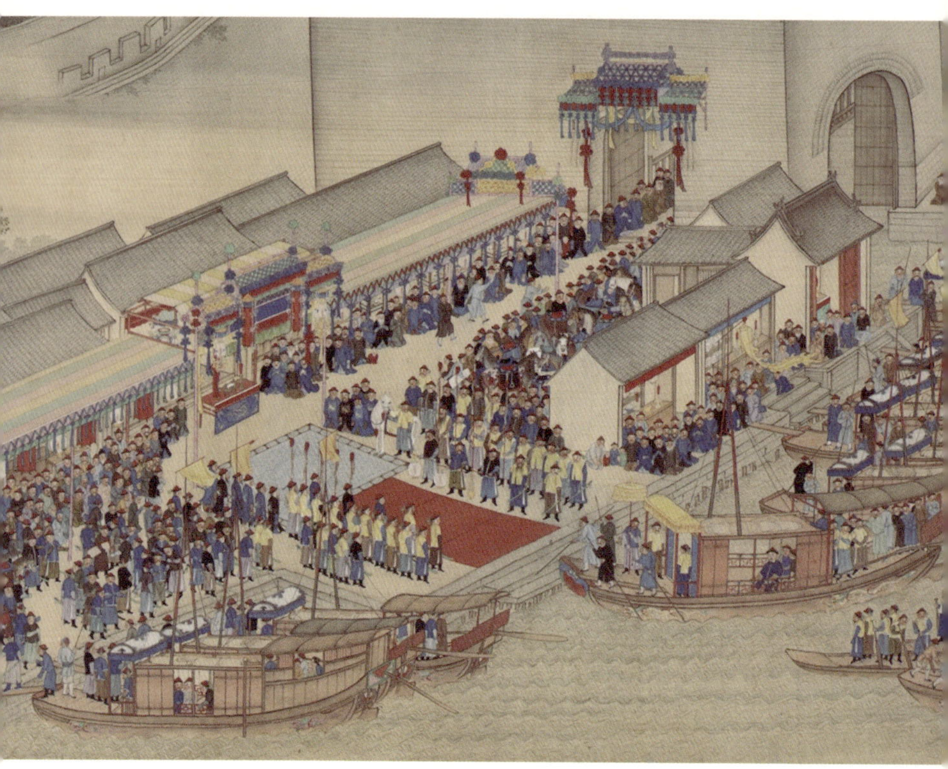

Map of Kangxi Emperor's Southern Tour (partial, from Wuxi to Suzhou, handscroll colored on silk)

"Chunshen Road," "Huangshan," etc., are all considered as public commemorations of Huang Xie, the Lord of Chunshen.

The Excavation of the Beijing-Hangzhou Grand Canal

During the Sui and Tang dynasties, the excavation of the Grand Canal had a significant impact on the canals of Wuxi. First, the canal in the south of Wuxi, originally flowing eastward from Bodu Port into Suzhou, was redirected southward through Wangting Town to enter Suzhou. Second, the canal in the northwest of Wuxi, which previously flowed northward from Yupu into the Yangtze River, was altered to bend northwest from the Yang Lake along the Tuyang Canal to cross the river in Zhenjiang. The width of the canals within Wuxi reached over 30 meters, meeting the requirement of Emperor Yang of the Sui Dynasty to accommodate dragon boats. Furthermore, in the ninth year of the Kaihuang era (589) of the Sui Dynasty, the first documented dam on the Wuxi Canal, the Wangting Dam, was constructed about 50 *li* southeast of Wuxi County. In the fourth year of the Daye era (608) of the Sui Dynasty, the Liangxi Bridge was completed to span the Liangxi River to the west of Wuxi. In the eighth year of the Daye era (612), the Lijin Bridge, the first bridge spanning the Wuxi Canal, was built. These developments greatly enhanced the transportation capacity of the Wuxi Canal, laying the foundation for its basic appearance since the Song Dynasty. Just as *The Chronicle of Wuxi County* states, "Since the Wude era of the Tang Dynasty, numerous dredging projects have been undertaken for the waterways in the southeast, resulting in most river branches within the postal city, all of which are tributaries of the canal."

Map of the Waterways Between Suzhou and Wuxi

The title of the map depends on its content; there are no legends or scales provided in the map, with directional annotations placed around its perimeter. The entire map is drawn in ink to depict city walls, lakes, marshes, and bridge piers, with textual annotations throughout the map. Wuxi belongs to Changzhou Prefecture, and the county's jurisdiction lies 49 *li* northwest outside the Chang Gate of Suzhou Prefecture (according to the "Territory" of *The Chronicle of Suzhou Prefecture*, vol. 2, during the Tongzhi period of the Qing Dynasty). The scope of the entire map covers the southern areas of Changshu County in Suzhou Prefecture, the vicinity of Changzhou County, and the jurisdictional boundaries of Wuxi County. Based on the information provided, it is difficult to determine the time frame of the map's creation, but as it is among the "Gordon Manuscripts," vol. 32, it can be inferred that the map was drawn approximately between the Xianfeng period and the beginning of the Tongzhi period in the Qing Dynasty.

The Premier of China's Four Great Rice Markets

"Springtime rice gleams bright as jade, / Drawing distant merchants by waterway trade."[3] These lines from the poet Gao Qi of the Ming Dynasty depict the rice produced in Wuxi, which is pure and tender, fragrant and smooth. Emperor Yang of the Sui Dynasty dredged the Grand Canal, connecting the northern water system with the canal system in the Jiangnan region. Wuxi, situated at the center of the canal system in the Jiangnan region, along with Suzhou, Changzhou, Jiangyin, and Changshu, enjoyed extremely convenient trade routes, leading to a thriving commercial hub.

By the Ming Dynasty, Wuxi rice had become the preferred rice for the imperial court, with a dedicated warehouse established to supply the palace. Wuxi was also recognized alongside Changsha, Wuhu, and Jiujiang as one of the "four great rice markets" in China. During the Qing Dynasty, the Grain Transportation Bureau of Shanghai was relocated to Wuxi, solidifying Wuxi's position as a major grain transportation hub in the Jiangsu-Zhejiang region. By the end of the Qing Dynasty, annual grain turnover in Wuxi had reached 450 million kilograms. In 1936, this figure soared to 900 million kilograms,[4] cementing Wuxi's reputation as the leading rice market among the "four great rice markets" in the country. Consequently, Wuxi earned the nickname "Rice Wharf."

Silk Wharf

Since ancient times, Wuxi has been renowned as the land of silk, with a history of over 3,000 years since the time of Taibo's cultivation of mulberry trees and silkworm rearing. In the 1860s, sericulture became a

---

[3] Pan Junming, annotated, *Selected Poems on Food of Suzhou Throughout the Ages* (Soochow University Press, 2013), p. 110.

[4] Zhuang Ruojiang, *A Thousand Years of Cultivation and Brilliant Chapters: A Humanities Reader of Wuxi* (Guangming Daily Press, 2019), pp. 143–144.

significant sideline for farmers in Wuxi, who spun raw silk for sale, gradually forming a sizable industry. Sericulturists from different regions would sell their silk near the city gates, with those from the southeast sold at the South Gate and those from the north at the North Gate, giving rise to several silk market centers in Wuxi. By 1929, Wuxi's silk exports had accounted for 28% of the national total, ranking first in the country.

The silk industry also spawned a new sector, the cocoon industry. In 1887, Sun Boyu and Gu Mianfu jointly established Renchang Cocoon House, the first cocoon house in Wuxi, gradually replacing the production model where sericulturists raised and spun raw silk themselves. Subsequently, numerous cocoon houses emerged in Wuxi, specializing in purchasing fresh cocoons and processing them. Among them, the largest was Xue Nanming's cocoon house. There was a saying circulating among sericulturists at that time, "You may walk until your shoes wear out, but you won't escape from Xue's house."

Jiangnan University

Wuxi was originally under the jurisdiction of Changzhou Prefecture, a small county in its own right. However, it now stands shoulder to shoulder with its neighboring cities, Suzhou and Changzhou, firmly holding a prominent position among Jiangsu's "thirteen prefecture-level cities." The rise of Wuxi during the late Qing Dynasty and the early period of the Republic of China cannot be ignored. In 1912, Wuxi was separated from Changzhou. During this period, due to its advantageous geographical proximity to Shanghai and Suzhou, Wuxi rapidly developed into one of China's six major industrial cities by the 1930s. Rong Desheng and Rong Zongjing were two prominent representatives of Wuxi's national industrialists at that time. Private Jiangnan University, the precursor of today's "Double First-Class" university, Jiangnan University, was established by the efforts of the

Rong brothers. It became one of the four most renowned universities in Jiangsu Province at that time, alongside National Central University, University of Nanking, and Soochow University.

Rong Zongjing and Rong Desheng (two brothers)

The Fuxin Flour Mill established by Rong Zongjing and Rong Desheng in Shanghai

The Yeqin Textile Factory

In 1895, Yang Zonglian and Yang Zonghan of Wuxi established the Yeqin Textile Factory at the Xinglong Bridge outside the East Gate. The name of the factory was inspired by the ancient adage: "Success lies in diligence, while failure in idleness." This marked the inception of Wuxi's first modern machine-operated factory and the nation's first commercial textile factory.

The Yeqin Textile Factory

Money Wharf

In addition to the industries developed in Wuxi due to the Grand Canal, there was also a significant presence of banking institutions. By the eighth year of the Tongzhi period (1869), Wuxi had already boasted seven money exchange shops engaged in currency exchange, issuing money notes, accepting deposits, and providing loans. In less than 30 years, the number of such establishments exceeded 20.[5] Without the influx of numerous foreign merchants brought by the Grand Canal, the prosperity of the silk industry, and the historical distribution of grains and rice, Wuxi might not have experienced such vibrant development, and its landscape could have been vastly different.

The Best Spot of the Taihu Lake and the Grand Canal

The Qingming Bridge: The Canal's Finest Spot

People often regard Wuxi as the supreme sight of Taihu Lake, but no one knows that the ancient bridge also collects the vivid memories of the Grand Canal. The ancient canal in Wuxi spans a total length of 40.8 kilometers, composed of "one loop and one alleyway." The term "loop" is used because the Grand Canal is typically straight, but in Wuxi, it seems to be reluctant to leave the local charm, taking a rare turn and winding around the city; the "alleyway" refers to the "water alleyway

[5] Lei Qunhu, ed., *Special Culture of Wuxi* (Suzhou University Press, 2006), pp. 85–86.

The ancient canal in Wuxi

of Jiangnan." The section from the Kuatang Bridge to the Qingming Bridge, about one kilometer of the ancient canal, is not only the oldest waterway of the Grand Canal but also the most quintessential part of Jiangnan Canal scenery, known as the "canal's finest spot."

The Qingming Bridge is the largest stone arch bridge in Wuxi and the entire bridge is meticulously crafted from granite. It was built during the period of Emperor Shenzong of the Ming Dynasty, with a history of more than 400 years. Every night, the Qingming Bridge is reflected into the shimmering ripples and its shadow connected to the bridge body, like an eye quietly observing the ancient canal and dwellings at the riverside. Hence, the old locals of Wuxi call it the "canal eye." East of the Qingming Bridge is the former residence of Zhu Dachun built in the late Qing Dynasty. Zhu Dachun, a businessman in China's modern history, was not only honored as the "king of the electrical industry," but also seen as a representative of carrying forward Wuxi's national industrial and commercial culture. South of the bridge is the Bodu River, just as Zhao Mengfu, a poet in the Yuan Dynasty, wrote in his poem "Mooring at Night by Bodu": "In the flat expanse, I seek tales of Wu, / By the Meili River, I load the boat with wine." About 1110 BC,

Taibo, the eldest son of King Tai of Zhou started to lead the villagers to dig the Bodu River. After that, when Helü attacked the State of Chu and Fuchai crusaded against the State of Qi, both of them passed the Bodu River. To the west of the Qingming Bridge are South Long Street, the square, and the Canal Museum. The Qingming Bridge Ancient Canal Scenic Area, acclaimed as the "open-air living museum" of canal culture, integrates temples, towers, rivers, streets, kilns, residences, workshops, lanes, and halls.

The Xihui Park

Mountain Hui was known in ancient times as Mountain Li and Xizhao Mountain. It was said that in the Tang Dynasty, Hui Zhao, a monk from the Western Regions, once lived here, so the mountain has been called Huishan since then. Mountain Xi, a bulge after the breakup of the Mountain Hui range, is only 75 meters high. The name comes from the fact that during the Zhou and Qin dynasties, the area was rich in tin ore. Following the excavation of the Yingshan Lake in 1958, Mountain Xi and Mountain Hui were united, and this area was inaugurated as the Xihui Park, featuring ancient landmarks such as Jichang Garden, the World's Second Best Spring, and Huishan Temple.

Jichang Garden, formerly known as Qin Garden, was originally a dormitory of monks in the Yuan Dynasty. It was turned into a private garden during the Zhengde period (1506–1521) of the Ming Dynasty. After Qin Yao was dismissed from his duty in the Ming Dynasty in 1591, the garden was renamed as Jichang (literally "Delight Finding") Garden as we know today. That was because Qin borrowed the meaning of a poem by Wang Xizhi in the Eastern Jin Dynasty: "Seek joy in kindness and wisdom, / Find delight in the shade of mountains and rivers." In the 11th year of the Qianlong period (1746), the garden was converted into an ancestral hall. Most of the buildings of Jichang Garden were destroyed in the Taiping Rebellion, and now there are only

Ni Zan, *Rongxi Studio*

Ni Zan was a painter from Wuxi during the late Yuan and early Ming dynasties. His early painting style was fresh and moist, while the later style was plain and simple, yet with profound implications with simple expressions. The painting was named after the Eastern Jin Dynasty poet Tao Yuanming's line: "Leaning by the south window to indulge in tranquility, / Finding ease in the simple comfort of a small dwelling" ("Returning Home"). Rongxi Studio was the residence of Pan Renzhong, a fellow townsman of Ni Zan, located at Mountain Xi. In the painting, "one lake and two banks" is depicted with a sparse and transparent composition, such as cold mountains and thin waters, withered trees and cold stones, and a painting style that is simple and elegant, which can be regarded as a "masterpiece."

some scenic spots, including Jinhui Rippling Pool, Seven Star Bridge, and Mountain and Stream Sceneries. The Xihui Park is home to a multitude of ancestral halls, among which are some celebrities' ancestral halls, such as the Hall of the Lord of Chunshen, the Hall of Fan Zhongyan, and the Hall of Gu Kejiu (a faithful official in the Ming Dynasty). This has led to the saying: "One water axis, two streets, and eight districts filled with clusters of ancestral halls."

The title "World's Second Best Spring" originated from Lu Yu, a sage of tea during the Tang Dynasty. After tasting springs in China, he ranked them into twenty categories, and the spring from Mountain Hui ranked second, hence the name.[6] The "World's Second Best Spring" now features attractions, such as the Upper Pool of the Second Spring, the Lower Pool of the Second Spring, the Wanjuan Tower, and the Lu Zi Temple.

Huishan Temple was originally established during the Northern and Southern Dynasties. It was originally the Lishan Thatched Cottage of Zhan Ting, minister of education during the Liu Song period (420–479) in Southern Dynasty. In the first year of the Jingping period (423) of the Liu Song Dynasty, the cottage was transformed into a monk's dwelling, known as Huashan Monastery. From the Dazhong to Xiantong period in the Tang Dynasty, the temple was reconstructed and renamed as Huishan Temple. The temple now preserves ancient relics, such as the Sutra Stele, the Vajra Hall, and the Yunqi Pavilion of the Tang and Song dynasties.

---

6 According to the evaluation of Lu Yu, the top five famous springs in the world are as follow: Gulian Spring in Lushan, Jiangxi; Huishan Stone Spring in Wuxi, Jiangsu; Lanxi Spring in Xishui County, Hubei; Luyu Spring in Guangjiao Temple in Shangrao, Jiangxi; and Daming Temple Spring in Yangzhou, Jiangsu.

Huangbudun: The Grand History on a Small Island

Not far from the ancient town of Huishan, south of Wu Bridge of Huishan, there is a floating island with ethereal buildings located in the center of the ancient canal at the mouth of Huishan Sitangjing, surrounded by water on all sides and called Huangbudun. It is only over 600 square meters, but it has witnessed the rise and fall of Wuxi for more than 2,000 years. *The Local History of Wu and Yue* in the Eastern Han Dynasty records, "During the time of the Lord of Chunshen … a dam was built in Wuxi … and the lake of Wuxi …," from which Huangbudun got its name. In the Tang Dynasty, this place was called the "Shegui Lake" (as seen in Lu Yu's work *The Record of Huishan Temple*), or the "Furong Lake." In the second year of the Deyou period (1276) of the Southern Song Dynasty, the famous general Wen Tianxiang wrote the verse, "Reading at night of Cheng Ying saving Zhao, / Each wave of sorrow brings tears to my brow," in his work "Passing Through Wuxi," directly expressing the pain of the broken country and the determination to endure hardships. According to *Brief Description of the Scenery of Xishan* by Wang Yongji in the Ming Dynasty, at that time, "there were Wenchang Pavilion, Huancui Tower, and Shuiyue Pavilion on the island, with weeping willows shading. Climbing the pavilion, you can see peaks of nine hills around you, and the fleeting sails passing through your desk from time to time." Its fairyland-like scenery was so enchanting that even Hai Rui, an honest and upright official of the Ming Dynasty, could not help but write words, "the finest tower to overlook the landscape," on the Huancui Tower. During their southern inspection tours, Emperor Kangxi and Qianlong of the Qing Dynasty stayed here many times and inscribed plaques or wrote poems to commemorate their visit. Even after returning to Beijing, Emperor Qianlong could not forget Huangbudun, so he built a Phoenix Mound at the south end of Kunming Lake in the Summer Palace, imitating Huangbudun. Huangbudun was originally a small island in the ancient lake of Furong. The Furong Lake has been continuously narrowed due to the land reclamation activities around the lake since the Ming Dynasty, gradually becoming a section of the Grand Canal. Huangbudun and "Xishuidun," another small island in the ancient canal, are listed as the "heavenly pass" and the "earth axis" in the Wuxi section of the ancient canal.

Yuantouzhu: The Best Spot of the Taihu Lake

The Taihu Lake was formerly known as "Juqu" in ancient China. It was also referred to as "Zhenze" and "Lize." It has gained a reputation for its breathtaking scenery. Guo Moruo, an eminent poet, lauded it in a poem, "The best spot of the Taihu Lake, / After all lies in Yuantouzhu." Yuantouzhu is a peninsula extending into the Taihu Lake. It is named after a giant stone that emerges from the lake and looks like a turtle with its head held high. There are more than ten tourist attractions in the area including Sunrise-Greeting Luding Hill, Spring Waves of Yuantouzhu Peninsula, Hengyun Mountain Resort, Spindrift-Rolling Waves, True Beauty of Lakes and Mountains, Cherry Valley, and Guangfu Temple. Yuantouzhu exhibits an abundance of natural splendor throughout the ever-changing four seasons. For example, at the place of turtle islet where one can observe the waves, the Taihu Lake microwave ripples when it is windy and warm, and the waves sound crisp and smooth; however, if fierce winds and pounding rain appear, monstrous waves will rise from the Taihu Lake, causing a thunder, just like ten thousand horses galloping ahead. The planting of cherry trees commenced in 1987 in Yuantouzhu, and it has now evolved into a picturesque landscape with a pavilion amid the thin red fog of spring. The falling cherry blossoms create an enchanting spectacle as they gracefully float upon the water, rendering it one of the distinctive features that define the allure of Yuantouzhu.

Huishan Clay Figurines: A National Intangible Cultural Heritage

Huishan clay figurines are traditional craftworks of Wuxi, Jiangsu Province. The raw material of Huishan clay figurines is black mud taken from the foothills about one meter below the ground on the northeast slope of Huishan Mountain. The black mud has excellent "molding" plasticity as it is delicate and soft for rubbing, consistent when bent, and does not crack when dry. Thus, it is quite suitable for kneading. Huishan clay figurines are renowned both at home and abroad for their full and concise shapes, smooth and lively lines, vivid and bright colors, and simple yet expressive forms. The exquisite craftsmanship and perfect artistic design reflect the wisdom and artistic achievements of working people in ancient times. The crafting technique of Huishan clay figurines comprises clay kneading and molding, color painting, and facial features carving. In terms of variety, it can mainly be categorized into "handmade opera clay figures" and "molded clay toys." Exquisite in workmanship, Huishan clay figurines boast beautiful shapes, vivid expressions, and vibrant colors. Craftsmen place great emphasis on portraying the personalities and expressions of Huishan clay figurines. Thus, these figurines have a strong local flavor and are deeply loved by people.

The "Three Whites" of the Taihu Lake

The "three whites" of Taihu Lake refer to the three kinds of freshwater fish in Taihu Lake—white fish, white shrimp, and white bait. All "three whites" are tender and delicious after cooking, making them unforgettable for people. When cooking these "three whites," you have to make sure that the ingredients are very fresh, and cooking methods, such as steaming and blanching, are often used to preserve the original flavor of the ingredients and make the freshness more prominent.

Wuxi Braised Spare Ribs

Wuxi braised spare ribs, known as "Wuxi meat bones," primarily use fresh piglet ribs. The dish features tender meat with a vibrant red and glossy appearance and is characterized with a sweet and sour flavor.

Magnolia Cake

Magnolia cakes, named after the blooming season of magnolia, are made with glutinous rice dough and various fillings, such as fresh meat, red bean paste, and rose flavor. After frying, they are golden and crispy outside while tender and delicious inside.

常州
金匱
無錫
昭文
常熟
新陽
崑山
鎮洋
蘇州
滸墅
吳江
震澤
宜興
荊溪
元墓
太湖
澱山湖
石湖
第九洞天
長興界

Suzhou:
The Paradise of Wu and Yue

The Land of Fish and Rice in Jiangnan Region

A Paramount Heaven of Luxury and Romance on the Canal

The Jiangnan Canal

In 514 BC, under the orders of King Helü of Wu State, Wu Zixu presided over the construction of Helü City, which featured eight water gates and eight land gates. The city was interconnected with inner and outer waterways, and protected by a moat. On this basis, to advance the northern conquest, Wu Zixu was ordered to dig an artificial canal connecting the Suzhou, Wuxi, and Changzhou regions in 495 BC. He also excavated the Xu River, which extended from present-day Suzhou to Liyang and Gaochun, finally emptying into the Yangtze River at Wuhu. This formed the original waterways of the Jiangnan Canal. Over a thousand years later, Emperor Yang of the Sui Dynasty ordered the excavation of the Jiangnan Canal based on this groundwork. Since then, despite continuous repairs and renovations through successive dynasties, the Suzhou section of the canal has basically maintained the appearance of the Grand Canal established during Emperor Yang's reign of the Sui Dynasty.

Water Town

The Grand Canal flows from the northwest to the southeast, merging into the water system of Suzhou City. Upon exiting Suzhou, it splits

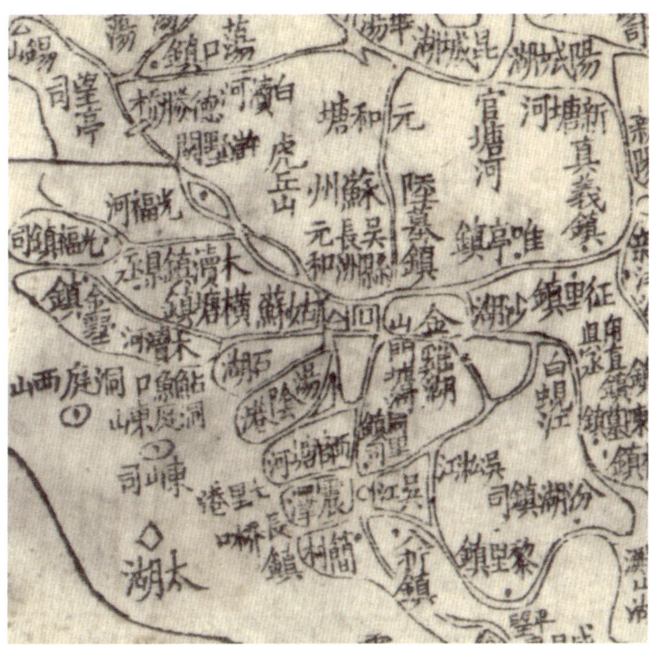

Complete Map of Jiangsu (section of Suzhou)

into three branches, namely the Shantang River, the Shangtang River, and the Xu River. It can be said that Suzhou City itself is an integral part of the Grand Canal. Wu Zixu built Helü City at the intersection of water and land years ago, which laid the foundation for the scenery of Suzhou's look of a water town in the Jiangnan region. Walking along Shantang Street, one can have a panoramic view of the ancient landscapes of Suzhou along the canal.

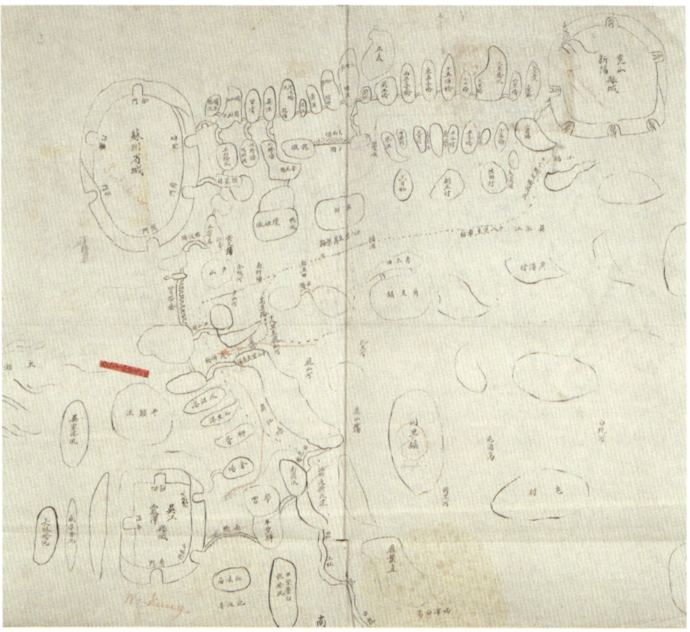

The Topographical Map of Suzhou Prefecture

This map was drawn between Xianfeng and the early Tongzhi period of the Qing Dynasty. The title of the map was devised based on its content. It depicts the boundaries of Suzhou, including Kunshan and Wujiang counties. A red label is attached at the edge of the Taihu Lake, with the inscription: "There are river piles at the crossroads bridge."

The Topographical Map of the Area Outside the Chang and Xu Gates of Suzhou Prefecture

This map was drawn during the Tongzhi period of the Qing Dynasty. The title of the map was formulated based on its content. The entire map meticulously depicts the western part of Suzhou City, including the Chang and Xu gates, as well as the topography outside the city walls, showing the terrain and features of the mountains and the Taihu Lake.

Suzhou's Tribute of Unpolished Rice

In 1971, eight inscribed bricks from the Empress Wu Zetian period were unearthed at the Hanjia Granary[1] site in Luoyang. One of these bricks was engraved with the inscription "Suzhou's Tribute of Unpolished Rice," which is tangible evidence that Suzhou rice was presented as a tribute to the capital of the Tang Dynasty.

It can also be seen from these words that Suzhou was not the fertile land of a "water town." At that time, the region of Wu was covered with wild vegetation and abundant in rivers and lakes, making it unsuitable for cultivation. *The History of the Han Dynasty · Geography Section* describes the Wu and Yue regions as having "muddy and marshy land, inferior for farming." In the 13th year of the Zhenguan period (639) of the Tang Dynasty, the population of Suzhou was the smallest in the Suzhou-Wuxi-Changzhou-Hangzhou region and even only half of the population of nearby Changzhou.[2]

Inscribed bricks unearthed from Hanjia Granary

1 Hanjia Granary was a transshipment station for grain from the Guandong and Jianghuai regions during the early Tang Dynasty, which was the largest grain storage facility of its time.

2 Liang Fangzhong, *Statistics of Population, Land, and Taxes in Chinese History* (Shanghai People's Publishing House, 1980), p. 82.

Transporting Grain from Wu

Lü Wen, a scholar of the Tang Dynasty, once remarked, "After the period of Tianbao of the Tang Dynasty, the people of Central Plains abandoned their plows, and they wore clothes transported from Yue and ate food transported from Wu." The Central Plains were in turmoil after the An Lushan Rebellion, and the Tang Court lost strong control over major grain-producing regions like Hebei, Longyou, Lianghuai, and Bashu. In the meantime, the continuous wars triggered the second large-scale population migration from north to south after the southward exodus during the period of Yongjia in the Western Jin Dynasty. Consequently, the Tang Court intensified the maintenance of the Jianghan transport line and the development of agriculture in the

Shen Zhou, *Dongzhuang Album (Volume 10)* (rice field)

Eastern Yangtze River. During his tenure as the governor of Suzhou, Han Huang, a famous minister of the Tang Dynasty, shouldered the responsibility of supporting the Tang Court. Han Huang's Zhenhai Army was responsible for transporting grain from the Wu region to the imperial court, saving the Tang Court in Luoyang multiple times. Afterward, Suzhou, as a significant transportation area for grain, gradually developed. "Throughout the mid-to-late Tang Dynasty, thirty-five out of sixty-four Suzhou governors had biographies, far exceeding that of the glorious age of Tang Dynasty, and the vast majority of those who had biographies had made achievements in the field of agricultural water conservancy."[3] During the Ming and Qing dynasties, Suzhou's grain production was extremely high, allowing for "five years of cultivation enough surplus to provide food for an additional two years." Suzhou Taicang is also known as the nation's granary for its vast grain reserves. Therefore, it is directly named "Taicang"[4] and continues to be used until now.

The Taicang Shipyard

Besides the Longjiang Shipyard in Nanjing, Zhu Di, Emperor Yongle of the Ming Dynasty, also established a shipyard in Taicang, Suzhou. These two shipyards were jointly responsible for constructing the ships used in Zheng He's voyages to the West. In addition, Taicang served as the anchor and home port of Zheng He's fleet. All the materials for the

---

3 Ma Xiangyu, "Transporting Grain from Wu Through the Sea: Recalling the Era of Suzhou as the Nation's Granary," WeChat Official Accounts of Museum of Wu Culture, https://mp.weixin.qq.com/s/FvoI-7obxoJ2lqyqoKHIpw.

4 In *Records of the Grand Historian · Pinghuai Book*, it is recorded: "The grain in Taicang piled up year after year, overflowing because there was no more space, to the extent that some of it had rotted and become inedible." Here, "Taicang" refers to the grain storage warehouse of the capital during the Han Dynasty. In later dynasties, such as Sui, Tang, and Song, the system of the Ever-Normal Granary was established, so the meaning of Taicang expanded to refer to grain storage warehouses in the capital and its surrounding areas.

voyages were gathered in Nanjing and transported by treasure ships built at the Longjiang Shipyard down the river to assemble in Liujiagang, Taicang. With flags flying high, the ships created a magnificent and awe-inspiring spectacle.

Taicang Wharf

Taicang became the departure point for treasure ships mainly because of its significant role. According to the *Chronicle of Taicang Prefecture* compiled by Sang Yue, a scholar of the Ming Dynasty, "In the 19th year of the Zhiyuan period (1282) of the Yuan Dynasty, pacification commissioners Zhu Qing and Zhang Xuan moved from Chongming to Taicang, creating a maritime route for grain transportation. As a result, various foreign merchants could engage in trade here. The surrounding residents gathered, and the markets

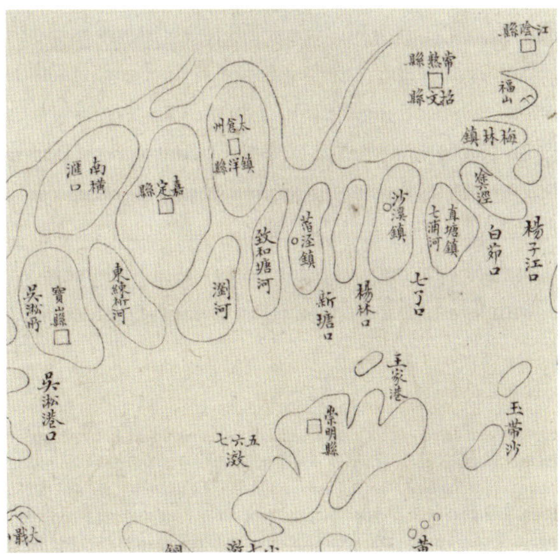

Map of the Coastal Regions of Seven Provinces (partial)

and shops connected seamlessly. Grain boats, sea vessels, foreign merchants, and traders flocked together." The wharf of sea transport is referred to as Liujiagang. At that time, Liujiagang was located at the mouth of the Yangtze River, with an embankment dock nearly 30 *li* long, just one day's journey from the capital, Nanjing at that time. Therefore, it was selected not only as the starting point for voyages to the West but also as a port for diplomatic exchanges with various nations.

The Suzhou Weaving Bureau

Whether it is Suzhou Song brocade or Nanjing brocade, their production techniques actually matured during the Ming Dynasty after the development in the Song and Yuan dynasties. Additionally, as canal transportation gradually recovered in the Ming Dynasty, the transportation of fabrics became more convenient in both Nanjing and Beijing compared to earlier times. The Suzhou Weaving Bureau, along with the Jiangning and Hangzhou Weaving Bureaus, developed during this period. Suzhou silk earned the reputation of "producing ten thousand pieces of silk daily, clothing the world." In the Qing Dynasty, the Suzhou Weaving Bureau became the largest silk weaving workshop at the time.[5] According to *The Records of the Suzhou Weaving Bureau* compiled by Sun Pei, a scholar of the Qing Dynasty, it was not until the Ming Dynasty that Jiangnan weaving was regarded as a significant source of fiscal revenue, with its establishment and development recorded in historical annals.[6]

---

5 Compiled by the *Land of Fish and Rice: Jiangsu* Compiling Group, *Land of Fish and Rice: Jiangsu*, vol. 1 (China Travel & Tourism Press, 2015), p. 195.

6 *The Records of the Suzhou Weaving Bureau* states: "The history of weaving in Suzhou has seen many changes and is difficult to fully trace back. The activities during the Song and Yuan dynasties are ancient and remote. From the Hongwu period of the Ming Dynasty to the reign of Emperor Chongzhen, the establishment and cessation of weaving are frequently recorded in historical documents and can be examined accordingly."

Golden Bricks

The construction of the Forbidden City brought together skilled craftsmen and materials from all over the country. Among them, the "golden bricks" in the Forbidden City were produced in Taihu Lake. The "golden bricks" (*jin zhuan*, 金砖 in Chinese) were originally called "Beijing bricks" (*jing zhuan*, 京砖 in Chinese), which were used exclusively for the royal family to build palaces. Due to a phonetic similarity, they came to be known among the people as "golden bricks." Another explanation is that these bricks, being fine and dense in texture, produced a metallic sound when struck, so they had the name "golden bricks."

The saying "a piece of gold for a brick" was not an exaggeration. These "golden bricks" laid on the ground were smooth and mirror-like with a faint light. It was also necessary to have a decree from the emperor to produce, and it was said that the process from clay extraction to kiln firing took 720 days.[7] In the Ming Dynasty, Song Yingxing mentioned in his book *Tiangong Kaiwu* that the quality of southern mud was excellent, which was "sticky without scattering, powdery without becoming sandy." The mud of the Taihu Lake possessed these qualities, so it could be an excellent raw material for brick production. Lumu in Suzhou, a major producing area of Beijing bricks, was named as "imperial kiln" by Zhu Di, Emperor Yongle of the Ming Dynasty. These bricks, intended for the royal family, traveled along the Grand Canal with grain ships and reached Beijing directly.

These golden bricks were also favored by scholars and literati. Today, both the Jiashi Pavilion in Suzhou's Humble Administrator's Garden and the Lion Grove have a golden brick. It is said that the golden brick in the Lion Grove was used to practice calligraphy.

---

7 Shan Jixiang, *The Grand Canal Drifting to the Forbidden City* (Encyclopedia of China Publishing House, 2020), p. 9.

A Paradise Blessed by the Grand Canal

Pingjiang Road: An Ancient City Under the Monumental Topography

Inside the Confucian Temple in Suzhou (present-day Suzhou Museum of Monuments and Inscriptions) stands a stone monument erected in the second year of the Shaoding era (1229) of the Southern Song Dynasty. It was carved by the Governor Li Shoupeng at that time on the basis of the entire city of Suzhou in the Southern Song Dynasty, using the traditional Chinese painting technique of combining architectural planes and simple perspective to perpetuate the memory of the former Pingjiang City on the rock.

The site of Pingjiang City[8] has remained unchanged since it was inherited from the ruins of Helü City in the Spring and Autumn Period and extended down to Suzhou today. It is a rectangle with a length of

[8] In the 8th year of the Kaibao era (975) of the Song Dynasty, the Zhongwu Army was transformed into the Pingjiang Army; in the third year of Zhenghe (1113) of the Song Dynasty, it was promoted to the Pingjiang Prefecture. In the 13th year of Zhiyuan (1276) of the Yuan Dynasty, it was changed to Pingjiang Road; in the 16th year of Zhizheng (1356) of the Yuan Dynasty, Zhang Shicheng set his capital at Pingjiang and changed it to Longping Prefecture; in the 17th year of Zhizheng (1357), it was changed to Pingjiang Road again; in the 27th year of Zhizheng (1367), Zhu Yuanzhang's army conquered Suzhou, and changed Pingjiang Road to Suzhou Prefecture.

more than four kilometers from north to south and a width of more than three kilometers from east to west. The central part of the *Layout of Pingjiang City* is the sub-city, divided into six districts, which includes temples, courtyards, government warehouses, government residences, gardens, city walls, city gates, mountains, rivers, bridges, etc. There are 305 bridges, the largest of which is the stacked bridge over the canal outside the Panmen Gate, which is still in existence today. There are ten kinds of water bodies, including canals, city rivers, lakes, swings, rivers, ponds, bays, pools, etc., of which the city rivers are the most numerous. The *Layout of Pingjiang City* is the largest surviving map tablet in China, and as a map of the city, its size is rare in the world, leaving valuable physical data for the study of city construction, administrative system, culture and art of the Song Dynasty. The tablet is an unparalleled treasure with fine inscriptions and artistic value.

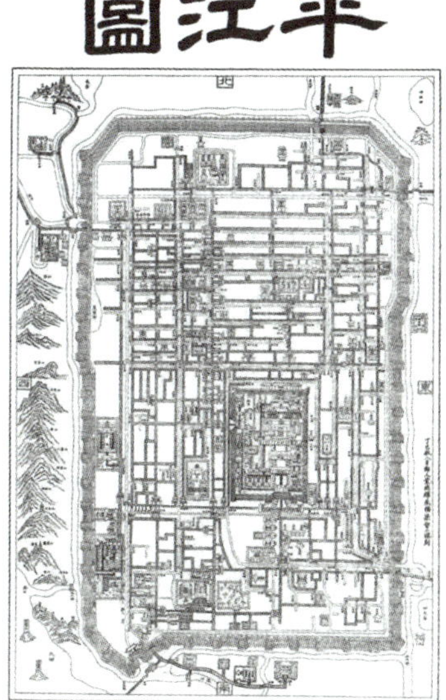

The *Layout of Pingjiang City*

If people today want to find the charm of the ancient Pingjiang City, they should prefer Pingjiang Road in Suzhou. Pingjiang Road starts from the Yuan Bridge in the east section of Ganjiang Road in the south, and connects to the Huayang Bridge in the north, crossing Northeast Street and Bajia Lane, with a total length of about 1,600 meters. It preserves the city's layout dating back to the Tang and Song dynasties, renowned for its parallel land and waterways, where streets and rivers run side by side. Pingjiang River on the west side of the road is the third straight river in Suzhou,[9] with green willows and black tiles on the banks of the river, permeated with the Jiangnan atmosphere of "small bridges and flowing rivers." On Pingjiang Road, the Tongli Bridge, the Huxiangshi Bridge, and the Ice-Cream Bridge are engraved on the *Layout of Pingjiang City*, which profoundly shows the history of Pingjiang City across the millennium.

The gates of the ancient Pingjiang City were different from those of the ancient cities in the north, which were orientated in a correct and symmetrical way, whereas the gates location of the city of Pingjiang were mainly determined according to the topography and the direction of the inlet and outlet of the river. The city of Suzhou was first built by Wu Zixu, named the city of Helü, with eight gates, which were reduced to five in the Song Dynasty: Pan Gate in the south; Qi Gate in the north; two gates in the east, with the Feng Gate in the south and the Lou Gate in the north; and one gate in the west, Chang Gate. These gates can be found today. When the Grand Canal reached outside the city, it was divided into two branches at the Chang Gate and Pan Gate: One branch passed around the west and south of the city

[9] There are seven main rivers running through the city of Suzhou. They are connected to the canal and called the "three horizontal and four straight lines." "Three horizontal lines" refer to the three main rivers running from west to east in the ancient city, called the horizontal rivers; "four straight lines" refer to the four main rivers running from north to south in the city, called the straight rivers.

outline; the other entered the city from the Chang Gate and Pan Gate, connected with the river in the city, and passed through the city after the first straight river and the first horizontal river. The first straight river was close to the Pan Gate in the south, and the northern end of it was connected with the Chang Gate, and it was in fact the hub of the city's external traffic and transportation. "Voices chatter and laugh in the cool evening breeze, / Ten thousand windows glow as lights reflect on the pond" ("Entering the Pan Gate in the Evening" by Fan Chengda, a poet of the Southern Song Dynasty). Businessmen from all over the country gathered here, and large and small examination halls, post stations, and commercial shops were built along the river, which contributed to the prosperity and development of the city of Pingjiang.

The Most Famous "Sorrow" on the Canal

> The moon has set, crows cry, and frost fills the sky,
> Maple trees by the river and fishing lights flicker nearby.
> Sleepless, I lie, burdened with sorrow and care,
> As midnight bells from Hanshan Temple fill the air.

The world knows that there is the Maple Bridge and Hanshan Temple outside Suzhou City because of this poem. The Maple Bridge was built in the early Tang Dynasty and is a single-arch stone bridge over the Wu River, a tributary of the Grand Canal. In fact, the Maple Bridge (*Feng Qiao*, 枫桥 in Chinese) was not originally called the bridge of "枫" (*feng*, maple) but the bridge of "封" (*feng*, block), because it was located at the junction of the river and the city wall. "*Feng Qiao*" (封桥, Block Bridge) and the adjacent Tielingguan Pass were both the main wharves crossing of the canal and the necessary crossing of the ancient stagecoach route. Whenever the grain was transported, the river and the city gates were blocked tightly, hence the word "block" (封). The

Picture of Hanshan and Shide (Song Dynasty)

change of name began with Zhang Ji's poem mentioned above. Before the Northern Song Dynasty, it was common to mix the two names, and it was not until the chancellor of the Northern Song Dynasty, Wang Gui, handwrote the poem "Mooring at Night by the Maple Bridge" and engraved a stele that the name "Maple Bridge" was established.

During the Northern and Southern Dynasties, Hanshan Temple was a small Zen temple with only a few rooms, built by Zen Master Puming of the Tiantai Sect during the Liang Dynasty of Southern Dynasties. After his death, his disciples changed the name of the temple to "Miaoli Puming Pagoda." The name "Hanshan Temple" comes from the monk Hanshan in the Tang Dynasty. Yao Guangxiao of the Ming Dynasty wrote in his *Record of the Re-Emergence of Hanshan Temple* as follows:

Wen Zhengming, *The Picture of Hengtang*

> Less than ten *li* west of the Chang Gate, you'll come to the Maple Bridge, and very close to the south of the bridge is Hanshan Temple. Near the Grand Canal, there is an embankment, which is an important place … During the years of Yuanhe of the Tang Dynasty, there was a man called Hanshanzi who wore wooden shoes and blue wisp clothes, laughing and singing freely, and he came here to bind the straw to live in … He traveled to the Cold Rock of Tiantai, where he became friends with Shide and Fenggan, and finally retreated into the rock. Zen Master Xiqian built a temple here, hence the name of Hanshan Temple …

Hanshan and Shide were famous poet monks in the Tang Dynasty. Legend goes that the two monks acted strangely and talked oddly. Today, there is a Hall of Hanshi in Hanshan Temple as a memorial, which enshrines the statues of Hanshan and Shide.

By mistake, certain misunderstandings would lead to a classic. "Midnight bells from Hanshan Temple" by Zhang Ji, in fact, was the toll from Huqiu Temple, which was not far from the Maple Bridge. At midnight, perhaps to inform the monks of the time of the "evening class," Huqiu Temple would toll to indicate that the first half of the night had passed and the second half of the night was coming, known as the "midnight bell." Hanshan Temple became famous for Zhang Ji's poem, and later, a bell tower was built in the temple, and the "midnight bell" started to ring. Now visitors can only hear the distant sound of the bell on New Year's Eve every year.

Nearly nine *li* downstream from Fengqiao to the Grand Canal was the Hengtang Post, one of the few amphibious posts along the Jiangnan section of the Grand Canal and the only remaining structure of the ancient post. The Hengtang Post was located at the westernmost tip of the small island of the Xujiang River, where the Grand Canal and the

Xujiang River converged. The former is connected to the ancient city of Suzhou by its bloodline, while the latter is the mother river of Suzhou, designed by Wu Zixu when he built the city, and is also the lifeline of the ancient city of Suzhou. In ancient times, the post station was a place for official documents to be delivered and for officials to rest during their journeys. In the Hengtang Post, the existing couplet on the stone pillars of the Post Pavilion reads, "The guest arrives and cooks tea in the hostel as a host" (to the left), and "the lamps are hung to wait for the moon, and the Post Pavilion reflects the Xujiang River from afar" (to the right). According to records, Suzhou used to have a number of large famous posts, such as Gusu Post, Wangting Post, Hengtang Post, Songling Post, etc. Nowadays, only the Hengtang Post remains.

Suzhou *Pingtan*: A National Intangible Cultural Heritage

Suzhou *pingtan* (评弹) is the general term for Suzhou *pinghua* (评话, a popular form of oral literature in ancient Chinese folklore) and Suzhou *tanci*, which is a traditional form of storytelling and theatrical performance in the Wu dialect. It originated in Suzhou and is popular in the Jiangsu, Zhejiang, and Shanghai regions, sung in the Suzhou dialect. Suzhou *pingtan* can be roughly divided into three major schools, namely, Chen (Chen Yuqian) Tune, Ma (Ma Rufei) Tune, and Yu (Yu Xiushan) Tune. After more than a hundred years of development, there are new schools that inherit the styles of these three famous artists as well as create and develop their own styles, which have developed and multiplied, forming a prosperous scene of various styles of singing in Suzhou *pingtan*, and enabling the art of Suzhou *pingtan* to endure for more than 200 years without decline.

Suzhou *pingtan* contains speaking and singing. It can be roughly divided into three forms, solo, duet, and trio. Notably, the solos usually focus on performing stories of historical events and the mighty chivalrous heroes. And the duets display those romantic novels and folk tales. Player A carries a *sanxian* (三弦, a three-stringed traditional Chinese lute) and Player B plays *pipa* (琵琶, a traditional Chinese plucked string instrument) or Chinese lute. For the trio, the players all play and sing their own accompaniment instruments, including the small *sanxian* and *pipa*. Suzhou *pingtan* originated from *pinghua* and *tanci*, both of which are famous for their exquisite singing. The soft Wu dialect is very appealing. The performance is often interspersed with some jokes, full of wit and fun. *Tanci* is sung in Wu tone, with soft, clear and slow cadence. The strings are very pleasant to the ears.

Hairy Crabs of the Yangcheng Lake

When the "autumn wind picks up and the crabs' feet itch," it is also the time when the hairy crabs of Yangcheng Lake are plump and full of fat. Hairy crabs of the Yangcheng Lake are at their best when the female crabs are in September and the male crabs are in October of the lunar calendar. When cooked, the female crabs are golden and the male crabs are like white jade, a unique and delicious dish that is popular throughout the country.

Suzhou-Style Mooncake

Originating in the Tang Dynasty and flourishing in the Song Dynasty, the Suzhou-style mooncake is the traditional food for the Mid-Autumn Festival. Suzhou-style mooncakes are made through the process of making dough, filling, wrapping, shaping, and baking. It has a crispy skin, beautiful and shine color, fat but not greasy filling, sweet and salty, and crunchy texture.

Fengzhen Noodles

Fengzhen noodles are made of fresh broth with a refreshingly elegant tone. The noodles are made of good pork and stewed for at least four hours, which makes the meat tender and melts in your mouth. The noodles are thin, long, tough, and refreshing, and do not go off after long cooking. The noodles are sharp and clean. No wonder there are so many different kinds of noodles in Suzhou, and Fengzhen noodles are at the top of the list.

Qian Weicheng, *Lion Grove Scroll*

ABOUT THE CONTRIBUTORS

On the tenth anniversary of the Grand Canal's successful inscription as a UNESCO World Heritage Site, the Yangzhou Municipal Government has carefully planned and organized the compilation of the book *Exploring China Along the Grand Canal: A Journey Through Jiangsu*, published by Hohai University Press.

The series' chief editor, Professor He Yun'ao, is a doctoral advisor at the School of History at Nanjing University, Director of the Institute of Cultural and Natural Heritage, a member of the National Expert Advisory Committee on the Construction of Cultural Parks, and the head of the Archaeology and Cultural Heritage Branch of the Grand Canal Cultural Belt Research Institute. He has published millions of words in papers and monographs covering history, archaeology, and cultural heritage studies.

The volume editor, Professor Zhang Bing, is the chief expert at the Research Institute of Ecological Civilization and Watershed Protection at Hohai University and the Jiangsu Yangtze River Protection and High-Quality Development Research Base.

The English translation was completed by a team led by Professor Zhang Hairong, Dean of the School of Foreign Languages at Hohai University.